SAGE was founded in 1965 by Sara Miller McCune to support the dissemination of usable knowledge by publishing innovative and high-quality research and teaching content. Today, we publish over 900 journals, including those of more than 400 learned societies, more than 800 new books per year, and a growing range of library products including archives, data, case studies, reports, and video. SAGE remains majority-owned by our founder, and after Sara's lifetime will become owned by a charitable trust that secures our continued independence.

Los Angeles | London | New Delhi | Singapore | Washington DC | Melbourne

E-COMMERCE
in India

E-COMMERCE
in India

ECONOMIC AND
LEGAL PERSPECTIVES

Edited by

PRALOK GUPTA

SSAGE

Los Angeles | London | New Delhi
Singapore | Washington DC | Melbourne

First published in 2020 by

SAGE Publications India Pvt Ltd
B1/I-1 Mohan Cooperative Industrial Area
Mathura Road, New Delhi 110 044, India
www.sagepub.in

SAGE Publications Inc
2455 Teller Road
Thousand Oaks, California 91320, USA

SAGE Publications Ltd
1 Oliver's Yard, 55 City Road
London EC1Y 1SP, United Kingdom

SAGE Publications Asia-Pacific Pte Ltd
18 Cross Street #10-10/11/12
China Square Central
Singapore 048423

Published by Vivek Mehra for SAGE Publications India Pvt Ltd. Typeset in 10.5/13 pt Adobe Caslon Pro by Zaza Eunice, Hosur, Tamil Nadu, India.

Library of Congress Control Number: 2020937344

ISBN: 978-93-5388-356-0 (HB)

SAGE Team: Rajesh Dey, Neena Ganjoo and Rajinder Kaur

To

my children

Aarohi
and
Arshabh

Thank you for choosing a SAGE product!
If you have any comment, observation or feedback,
I would like to personally hear from you.

Please write to me at **contactceo@sagepub.in**

Vivek Mehra, Managing Director and CEO, SAGE India.

Bulk Sales

SAGE India offers special discounts
for purchase of books in bulk.
We also make available special imprints
and excerpts from our books on demand.

For orders and enquiries, write to us at

Marketing Department
SAGE Publications India Pvt Ltd
B1/I-1, Mohan Cooperative Industrial Area
Mathura Road, Post Bag 7
New Delhi 110044, India

E-mail us at **marketing@sagepub.in**

Subscribe to our mailing list
Write to **marketing@sagepub.in**

This book is also available as an e-book.

Contents

List of Illustrations

Figures

Tables

Foreword

A defining feature of the last decade of the 20th century was technical change, particularly in the means of communication. The growth of the Internet, and in particular of the Internet of things (IoT), has implied that the nature of transactions between groups of individuals has undergone a sea change. Today, this has led to large number of debates around e-commerce. In its simplest form, e-commerce, implying transactions between two or more individuals, involves issues such as data secrecy, control of data, etc. Most companies now are gauging their strength in market arrangements through their control of personal and other databases of consumers.

This implies that a large part of the debates of the previous century will now be re-cast in the context of e-commerce. For example, how does the regulatory framework change to accommodate non-physical transactions? What about issues of taxation of e-commerce transactions and logistics? What is the role of new technologies like blockchain used to conduct e-commerce? How to define a country's jurisdiction for invisible transactions that transcend national borders?

This edited book by Dr Pralok Gupta is a timely publication, as it presents views by various authors on many of the issues listed above. I feel it is also a useful primer to research students who will study still very contentious issues of how transactions are conducted in the 21st century. I recommend the book to both practitioners and students.

Manoj Pant
Director
Indian Institute of Foreign Trade
(Deemed to be University)
New Delhi

Acknowledgements

At the outset, I would like to thank Professor Abhijit Das, Head of the Centre for WTO Studies, IIFT, New Delhi, for his guidance and constant support during the writing of this manuscript. I would also like to express my gratitude towards all the faculty members and staff of the Centre for WTO Studies for their invaluable help. Last but not least, I thank my family members for their unending love and support and for bearing with me while I devoted my time to working on this manuscript at home.

CHAPTER 1

Introduction

Pralok Gupta

1.1. Broader Context

E-commerce is growing at an exponential rate in India. Although estimates of growth and size of e-commerce market in India differ across various sources, one common finding across these estimates is that e-commerce is witnessing high growth rate which is expected to continue in future. According to the Deloitte and Retail Association of India 2019 report, the e-commerce market in India is expected to touch $84 billion in 2021 as against $24 billion in 2017.[1] Another estimate by the India Brand Equity Foundation (IBEF) expected Indian e-commerce market to grow to $200 billion by 2026 from $38.5 billion as of 2017.[2] This high growth rate could be attributed to the increasing Internet and smartphone penetration in India during the last ten years. In spite of this exponential growth, e-commerce in India is still in an evolving stage as economic and regulatory frameworks pertaining to various segments of e-commerce are being put into place

---

[1] https://www.business-standard.com/article/pti-stories/indian-e-commerce-market-to-touch-usd-84-billion-in-2021-report-119022600459_1.html
[2] https://www.ibef.org/industry/ecommerce.aspx

by the government. In India, most of the large e-commerce companies operate through marketplace model as foreign direct investment is not permitted for inventory-based model of e-commerce.

The strong emergence of e-commerce has placed pressure on its various segments, such as payment systems, logistics, consumer retention, etc. These companies constantly review their business model to suit the changes made in the regulatory environment as well as to lure the customers. The segment has innovated and adjusted to the Indian market by bringing new practices. For instance, 'cash on delivery' model was introduced by e-commerce companies in India to allay consumers' fears pertaining to shopping from a distance. While these companies have made suitable changes in their models according to Indian regulatory requirements, various stakeholders have raised concerns about frequent violations of such regulations by e-commerce companies.

Against this backdrop, this book is an attempt to delve into various regulatory and economic issues pertaining to the growing e-commerce in India. These issues include FDI regulations, e-commerce taxation, valuation of e-commerce companies, e-commerce market structure and competition, payment mechanism, blockchain technology and cryptocurrencies, e-commerce logistics, etc.

Most of the chapters of this book were presented during the International Conference on E-Commerce and Its Linkages with Services and Investment, held on 7–8 March 2019 at New Delhi, organized by the Centre for WTO Studies, Indian Institute of Foreign Trade, New Delhi.

1.2. Outline of the Book

Each chapter of the book is devoted to understand and analyse specific e-commerce issues in greater detail so as to make the reader familiarize not only with the issue at hand but also the technicalities involved thereof. After the Introduction (Chapter 1), the second chapter of the book explains the ecosystem of e-commerce and various types of e-commerce transactions. It analyses the regulatory framework for e-commerce and brings out emerging issues pertaining to this segment in India. The issues highlighted include FDI regulations, draft e-commerce policy, privacy issues, consumer protection issues, competition issues, participation of small and medium enterprises (SMEs), taxation and international jurisdiction to assess whether the existing regulations are sufficient to address the challenges emanating from new technology, abuse of dominant power and monopoly of big giants.

The rapid developments in Internet technologies have unveiled greater economic growth through a newly emerging e-commerce sector in the modern world. In the context of India, Chapter 3 tries to establish a relationship between the factors of e-commerce growth and economic progress. The chapter also tries to analyse the role of Internet and technological developments in promoting e-commerce growth to its impact on GDP. In the previous decade, India witnessed a surge in these developments along with its GDP. However, the results of the analysis manifest that despite having a significantly positive correlation between them, the e-commerce growth factors were not able to influence the increasing trend of GDP. The correlation matrix proves that e-commerce is a vibrant industry for economic boost in the globalized world; hence, the authors tried to identify the gaps that are responsible for the negligible impact in the regression analysis. Based on the challenges identified and inter-country comparison between India and top e-commerce performing markets, the authors conclude that India still needs to undertake relevant steps to unfold the benefits of the emerging sector and propose approaches that would serve as a guide for the headway of e-commerce industry towards economic growth and development in India.

Chapter 4 is exploratory in nature as it attempts to unveil the nature of market structure followed by majority of dominant e-commerce platforms and the concerns associated with them. It also throws some light on the implications of changing market share and the existing barriers to entry on the fair and healthy competition in the economy. The chapter eventually tries to raise concerns with respect to the possible gap between developed and developing nations owing to the unbalanced growth of the Internet-based economy as the e-platform players around the globe have immense potential either to reduce or widen the gap of economic equality.

Chapter 5 attempts to explore factors that contributed to the unprecedented growth of e-commerce in India and attracted the sizable volume of foreign investment in a very short period. In this connection, the chapter adopted two distinct methodologies. First, it conducted a primary survey in various Indian cities covering a sample size of 1,000 to understand the reason and pattern of online purchases. Second, it modelled the empirical analysis by treating the equity inflows of foreign players in e-commerce as amounts dependent on the variation in the number of mobile and Internet subscribers and purchasing power at the aggregate level. The chapter uses the ordinary least squares (OLS) regression model with the time series data for the period 2000–2017.

Chapter 6 analyses the pattern of funding of e-commerce companies and concludes that investors are now shifting their focus on sustainability, profitability and scalability. The infusion funding has skewed as investors are now cautious of the 'Valuation methodologies' being employed by these companies which do not include customer acquisition cost, cash burns, excessive discounts and cashbacks resulting in flawed valuations. This chapter focuses upon different models deployed for the valuation of e-commerce companies in India. It further compares the fundamentals of unlisted and listed companies. The chapter suggests investment and profitability metrics for e-commerce companies at different time horizon that depicts the shift in investor's focus towards profitable business model.

Taxation of digital economy, and related transactions, is an emerging issue that has remained unsettled for both developed and developing countries. The growing e-commerce in India has led the government to start taxing such transactions. While the Goods and Services Tax (GST) is applicable on purchases made on online platforms, there exist a regulatory void with regard to taxation of online entities and their activities. Chapter 7 covers important taxation issues pertaining to e-commerce. These include applicability of GST for e-commerce transactions and equalization levy imposed by the

Government of India, WTO custom moratorium on electronic transmissions, taxing online advertisement revenue, the OECD approach for taxation of digital economy, etc. While the discussion focuses on India, the chapter also draws upon taxation practices for e-commerce in other jurisdictions.

Chapter 8 analyses different models of e-commerce and their logistics implications. The models for analysis include the fulfilment model—Business-to-Business-to-Consumer (B2B2C) and the direct selling model (B2B) that is courier mode for small shipments and postal mode for small shipments. The chapter discusses how to regulate the cross-border movement of Business-to-Consumer (B2C) small shipments and the implications of the discussions in World Customs Organization (WCO) working group and Universal Postal Union (UPU). The chapter also discusses facilitating e-commerce exports from India from logistics perspective. It highlights logistics issues in domestic e-commerce and brings out how logistics for e-commerce is different from that related to traditional trade.

Chapter 9 deals with the transformation of the payment domain in India and its impact on the various e-commerce domains such as multi-brand retail, hotel and travel booking, over-the-top (OTT) services' subscriptions. The authors also analyse in this chapter the level of sensitivity among the millennials about the data privacy and its utilization by the applications they use in their daily lives. The data used in this chapter was procured from diverse section of the society, but major contributors or respondents were millennials aging between 18 and 25 years.

Today, markets have changed their faces. Physical markets are now becoming obsolete as the consumers are shifted to the digital screen market place. Initially, Internet was used as a tool for communication between people. With the passage of time, people realized the remarkable capacity of the Internet to interact and create unlimited new opportunities. E-commerce is now being used in all types of business, including manufacturing, retail and services. E-commerce has made business processes more reliable and efficient. Consequently, e-commerce is now essential for businesses to be able to compete in the global marketplace. E-commerce has made an incredible journey from the financial industry to the dot.com 'bomb'. But, as nothing comes without drawbacks, cybercrime is one of biggest problem for the e-commerce trade which includes millions of rupees frauds, personal data theft, etc. Cybercrimes are the hurdles in the road to success for online businesses. Against this backdrop, Chapter 10 examines the origin of e-commerce and describes retail trade on the Internet, process of e-commerce, legal position of e-contracting, e-payment systems in India, the role and liability of intermediaries in e-commerce, the legal issues that relate to e-commerce and the legal safeguards that are available in India.

Chapter 11 is devoted to understand the competition issues with respect to e-commerce platforms. In this chapter, the author has taken the 'search engine cases' decided by the European Commission and the Competition Commission of India to compare their stands on the relevance of network effect in determining dominance. Network effect is a phenomenon widely popular in e-commerce platforms. It is a phenomenon wherein the increase in the use of any good or service increases the value of that good or service for other users. Since the business model of search engines are generally supported by advertising revenue and no fee is charged from the users for the information provided, the whole business runs on the 'traffic'. The author deals with three important questions in the process: Whether network effect ensures market power in e-commerce? Whether market power so acquired is illegal? And when is network effect an anticompetitive concern?

Understanding the e-commerce scene with the emerging trends of blockchain is very important in the era of IoTs. Chapter 12 covers the concept of blockchain and its intermediaries, cryptocurrency as well as smart contracts. It discusses the need for the blockchain technology to be part and parcel of the financial market and how it would radically bring changes in the use of e-commerce as a platform for its necessary interplay. It further deliberates on the issue of legality and future of cryptocurrencies and smart contracts in the evolving digital world. The chapter aims at making the reader aware of the major reasons for blockchain acceptance and how it will revolutionize e-commerce. It also provides necessary suggestions and recommendations for the legal incorporation of blockchain into e-commerce.

The last chapter, Conclusion, discusses various approaches for regulating e-commerce and the literature on such regulations. It provides strategic directions and policy suggestions to deal with the regulatory and economic challenges associated with the growing e-commerce in India.

The issues selected for inclusion in this book appear as discussion points in policy debates, research forums and popular media on a regular basis. However, the information on these issues are scant and often scattered. This book fulfils such gaps in the available literature on e-commerce. It is a collection of regulatory and economic issues that are important for all stakeholders of e-commerce, be it e-commerce companies, policymakers, think tanks, researchers, lawyers or other readers.

CHAPTER 2

E-Commerce in India
Regulatory Framework and
Emerging Issues

Pralok Gupta and Vaishali Gupta

2.1. Introduction and Context

Although there is no unanimously accepted definition of e-commerce, the term 'electronic commerce' is generally understood to mean the distribution, purchase, sale, marketing and service of products or services using technology media such as the Internet and computer networks. Although it involves online transactions between the supplier and the buyer, it involves a range of activities such as payments and electronic funds transfer, logistics and supply chain management, online advertising, online marketing, online transaction processing, automated inventory management systems, data collection systems and consumer grievance redressal mechanism.

The last decade has seen exponential growth in e-commerce activities not only in India but also across the globe. The surge in electronic commerce activities has been triggered by lower cost communications and growing penetration of smartphones. These smartphones with high-speed Internet facilities allow online transactions through mobile apps of the e-commerce vendors. Therefore, most of the businesses not only maintain websites but also allow the purchase and/or delivery of their products through apps installed on the mobile phones of the consumers. Although such penetration is more in developed countries, developing countries are also showing an increasing trend and, in some cases, developing countries are even among the first to adopt the new technologies.

Keeping in pace with other countries of the world, e-commerce business is rapidly spreading its wings into Indian consumer market space. An important emerging trend in this regard is that e-commerce revolution is not limited to the metro or big cities. As Internet penetration is increasing throughout the length and breadth of the country, a significant part of e-commerce transactions is coming from Tier II cities of India. Another important trend is the increasing feminization of e-commerce industry happening in India, as women are increasing their participation in online shopping.

Thus, the e-commerce market has huge growth potential in India. On these lines, a number of big names, such as, Amazon, Flipkart, Reliance, etc., are getting aggressive on the digital platform and e-commerce market segment in India. The emergence of big brands in Indian e-commerce arena could kick-start a new phase in the burgeoning digital commerce industry in India. It also brings challenges for policymakers and regulators to ensure that the gains of the growing e-commerce activities are distributed to all stakeholders.

Against this backdrop, this chapter discusses e-commerce and related regulatory challenges in detail. The next section provides conceptual understanding of e-commerce by explaining the e-commerce ecosystem and various categories of e-commerce transactions. Section 2.3 discusses the regulatory framework for e-commerce in India. Section 2.4 highlights emerging issues pertaining to growing e-commerce, including the ongoing discussions at the World Trade Organization (WTO) on e-commerce, privacy issues, FDI regulations, consumer protection issues, etc. Section 2.5 concludes the chapter and suggests steps to regulate and facilitate e-commerce in India.

2.2. Conceptual Understanding of E-Commerce

2.2.1. Ecosystem of E-Commerce[1]

E-commerce transactions involve a number of actors, each having a significant role in the growth of e-commerce business. Some of these work at the backend to provide supporting facilities, whereas some work at the frontend and are directly involved in online transaction and associated delivery of goods and services. Figure 2.1 shows the major or key actors involved in any e-commerce business.

The Internet service provider (ISP) purchases a set amount of bandwidth from a network provider and provides access to the Internet users. E-commerce business owners run their business through

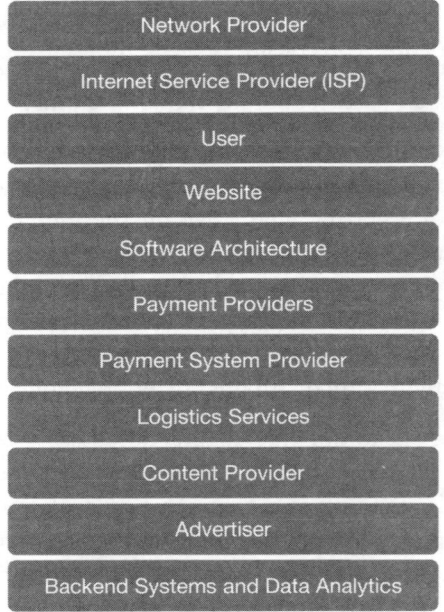

Figure 2.1 *E-Commerce Ecosystem*

Source: http://www.indiaitlaw.com/ecomm.htm

---

[1] The discussion in this subsection is based on http://www.indiaitlaw.com/ecomm.htm

websites. These are computer programmes existing on computers (known as servers) which are connected to the Internet. Software architects or browsers (such as Internet Explorer, Mozilla Firefox) provide the software that enables the websites to be connected to an ISP and allows users to browse the site. Users pay to e-commerce business through payment mechanism (net banking, credit card, debit card, e-wallet, etc.) through payment systems providers who supply the technology and expertise to effect financial transaction during an e-commerce activity. Logistics services provider delivers the online purchased material at the doorstep of the consumer and also helps in return pick-ups in case of defected or exchanged products.

The website used for e-commerce purpose purchases goods/services from a content provider. The content provider may also own the website and may offer the goods/services from more than one website.

Apart from their core business of online delivery of goods and services, e-commerce websites also generate revenue through online advertising of others' goods and services. For this purpose, the advertisers purchase space on websites. The fees for advertising are fixed or charged on 'per click basis'.

The backend system, although not involved directly in e-commerce transactions, is very important for the success of an e-commerce business. It ensures adequate inventory, accounting, data analysis of consumers and their purchasing behaviour, etc. It also helps in targeted advertising for retaining existing customers and attracting new customers to the e-commerce platform.

2.2.2. Categories of E-Commerce Transactions

The e-commerce transactions or online business between buyers and suppliers of goods or services can be classified into various categories, depending upon the nature of the suppliers and buyers. These categories are pictorially shown in Figure 2.2.

There are some other categories of e-commerce that one comes across, particularly with respect to transactions with the government. These are Government-to-Government (G2G), Government-to-Employee (G2E), Government-to-Business (B2B),

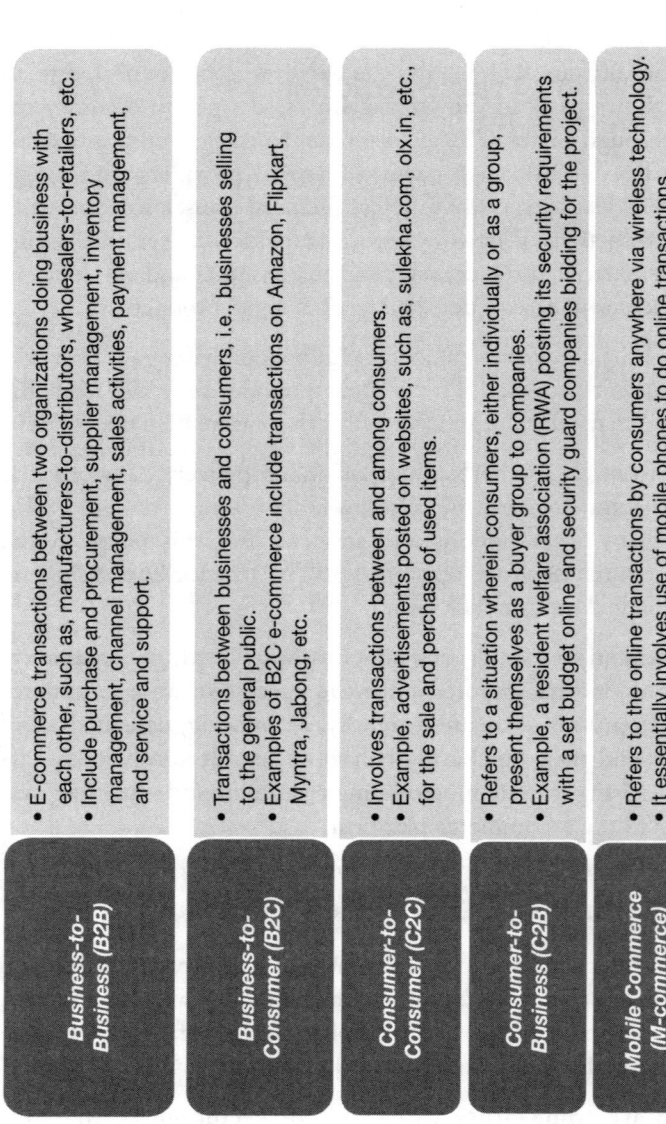

Business-to-Business (B2B)
- E-commerce transactions between two organizations doing business with each other, such as, manufacturers-to-distributors, wholesalers-to-retailers, etc.
- Include purchase and procurement, supplier management, inventory management, channel management, sales activities, payment management, and service and support.

Business-to-Consumer (B2C)
- Transactions between businesses and consumers, i.e., businesses selling to the general public.
- Examples of B2C e-commerce include transactions on Amazon, Flipkart, Myntra, Jabong, etc.

Consumer-to-Consumer (C2C)
- Involves transactions between and among consumers.
- Example, advertisements posted on websites, such as, sulekha.com, olx.in, etc., for the sale and perchase of used items.

Consumer-to-Business (C2B)
- Refers to a situation wherein consumers, either individually or as a group, present themselves as a buyer group to companies.
- Example, a resident welfare association (RWA) posting its security requirements with a set budget online and security guard companies bidding for the project.

Mobile Commerce (M-commerce)
- Refers to the online transactions by consumers anywhere via wireless technology.
- It essentially involves use of mobile phones to do online transactions.

Figure 2.2 Categories of E-Commerce Transactions

Business-to-Government (B2G), Government-to-Citizen (G2C) and Citizen-to-Government (C2G).

2.3. Regulatory Framework for E-Commerce in India

As far as regulatory framework governing e-commerce activities is concerned, there are no dedicated e-commerce laws in India. Various ministries and departments of the Government of India deal with different aspects of e-commerce. For instance, the Ministry of Electronics and Information Technology looks after the technical aspects of e-commerce through the Information Technology Act, data privacy issues, etc. The Department of Consumer Affairs takes care of the consumer protection issues. The Department for Promotion of Industry and Internal Trade deals with the foreign investment-related matters on e-commerce. The Department of Commerce deals with the WTO discussions on e-commerce.

Although there is no dedicated law governing e-commerce, such activities are governed by a number of laws and regulations applicable to various segments of the e-commerce value chain. Some of these laws come under the purview of central government whereas others fall within the jurisdiction of state governments. These are discussed in the next subsections.

2.3.1. Registration Regulations[2]

Registration as an E-Commerce Company (Companies Act, 2013):

- Registering an e-commerce business either as a company or a firm or a limited liability partnership (LLP) or sole proprietorship. At least two people are needed to register as a private limited company.
- A memorandum with the objective, liability of member, capital clause of the company and article defines powers of the management.
- A clear objective of the company.

[2] Based on https://www.business-standard.com/article/companies/an-idea-is-not-enough-to-start-an-e-commerce-business-114012801057_1.html

Tax Registration:

- Registration for Goods and Services Tax (GST) if the sales or turnover crosses more than ₹20 lakh annually or ₹10 lakh in case the establishment is in the northeast states.

Other Registration:

- If there are 20 or more workers in a firm, registration with the Employees' State Insurance is necessary (Section 1(5) of the Employees' State Insurance Act, 1948).
- If customer care services are not outsourced, other service provider (OSP) registration with the Department of Telecommunication is needed for bandwidth and phone.
- If labourers on contract are more than 20, registration with the contract labour department and compliance with labour rules are needed (Contract Labour (Regulation & Abolition) Central Rules, 1971).
- Trademark registration for securing brand name of the business is also required in some cases.

2.3.2. Information Technology Regulations

Information Technology Act, 2000 (IT Act 2000):

- The IT Act 2000 is the sole cyber law in India which also governs, to some extent, the online issues of e-commerce in India.
- Although the IT Act focuses mainly on digital signature and related aspects, it mandates that the e-commerce entrepreneurs and owners must ensure cyber law due diligence in India.

Data Protection Regulatory Framework (IT Amendment Act, 2008):

- Section 79 sets out conditions under which an intermediary will not be liable for any third-party information, data or communication link made available or hosted by him.

- Data protection has been made more explicit through the insertion of Clause 43A that provides for compensation to a person whose personal data may have been compromised by a company.
- Under Section 72A, punishment for the disclosure of information in breach of a lawful contract is prescribed. Any person including an intermediary who has access to any material containing personal information about another person, as part of a lawful contract, discloses it without the consent of the person will attract punishment with imprisonment of up to three years and/or a fine of ₹5 lakh.
- Section 69 on crimes against national security has been made stronger for interception and monitoring.
- Sections 66 and 67 on hacking and obscene material have been updated by dividing them into more crime-specific subsections, thereby making cybercrimes punishable.

2.3.3. Financial Regulations

Payment and Settlement Regulations[3]:

- To allow online payments receipt and disbursements for e-commerce activities, one has to take a license from the Reserve Bank of India (RBI).
- Payment and settlement systems are regulated by the Payment and Settlement Systems Act, 2007 (PSS Act) and Settlement System Regulations, 2008.
- As per Section 4 of the PSS Act, no person other than the RBI can commence or operate a payment system in India unless authorized by the RBI.
- The RBI has since authorized payment system operators of prepaid payment instruments, card schemes, cross-border in-bound money transfers, automated teller machine (ATM) networks and centralized clearing arrangements.

[3] https://www.rbi.org.in/scripts/PaymentSystems_UM.aspx

Prepaid Payment Regulations[4]:

- Prepaid instruments are payment instruments that facilitate purchase of goods and services against the value stored on these instruments.
- These instruments can be issued in the form of smart cards, magnetic stripe cards, Internet accounts, Internet wallets, mobile accounts, mobile wallets, paper vouchers, etc.
- Subsequent to the notification of the PSS Act, policy guidelines for the issuance and operation of prepaid instruments in India were issued to regulate the issue of prepaid payment instruments in the country.
- The use of prepaid payment instruments for cross-border transactions has not been permitted, except for the payment instruments approved under Foreign Exchange Management Act (FEMA), 1999.

Online Payment Regulations[5]:

- Online payments are enabled through own payment gateways or third-party service providers called intermediaries.
- In payment transactions involving intermediaries, these intermediaries act as the initial recipient of payments and distribute the payment to merchants. In such transactions, the customers are exposed to the uncertainty of payment as most merchants treat the payments as final on receipt from the intermediaries.
- To safeguard the interests of customers and to ensure that the payments made by them using electronic/online payment modes are duly accounted for by intermediaries receiving such payments, directions were issued in November 2009.
- Directions require that the funds received from customers for such transactions need to be maintained in an internal account of a bank and the intermediary should not have access to the same.
- Further, to reduce the risks arising out of the use of credit/debit cards over Internet/IVR (technically referred to as card not present

---

[4] Ibid.
[5] Ibid.

or CNP transactions), the RBI mandated that all CNP transactions should be additionally authenticated based on information not available on the card and an online alert should be sent to the cardholders for such transactions.

Mobile Payment Regulations[6]:

- Enabling mobile payments services to banking customers involve the collaboration of banks, mobile payments service providers and mobile network operators (MNOs).
- Services can also be provided as a proximity payment system, where the transactions are independent of the MNOs.
- In mobile payment systems, banks provide the basic service framework, ensure compliance to KYC/AML norms, create a risk management and mitigation framework and ensure settlement of funds.
- Mobile payments service providers are intermediaries for providing the technology framework for the implementation of the mobile payment services.
- MNOs provide the telecom infrastructure and connectivity to the customer, their role limited to providing the SMS/WAP/GPRS/USSD/NFC, GSM or CDMA voice and data services connectivity and in hosting the certain technology solutions like USSD.
- In a non-MNO-based system, proximity or contactless channels such as Infrared Data Association (IrDA), radio-frequency identification (RFID), optical and near field communication (NFC), are used for communication between point of sale (POS) and the mobile phone of the customer.

Storage of Payment System Data[7]:

- All system providers shall ensure that the entire data relating to payment systems operated by them are stored in a system only in India.

---

[6] https://www.rbi.org.in/Scripts/bs_viewcontent.aspx?Id=1365
[7] https://www.rbi.org.in/scripts/NotificationUser.aspx?Id=11244

- This data should include the full end-to-end transaction details/information collected/carried/processed as part of the message/payment instruction.
- For the foreign leg of the transaction, if any, the data can also be stored in the foreign country, if required.
- For cross-border transaction data, consisting of a foreign component and a domestic component, a copy of the domestic component may also be stored abroad, if required.

2.3.4. Consumer Protection Regulations

Consumer Protection Act (CPA), 1986:

- There seems to be some vagueness regarding the coverage of e-commerce under the CPA 1986. On one hand, the Minister of State for Food and Consumer Affairs said in a written reply to the Lok Sabha that 'E-commerce operations are already covered under the Consumer Protection Act, 1986',[8] on the other hand, Union Minister for Consumer Affairs, Food and Public Distribution said that the Centre has decided to amend the CPA 1986, to strengthen the three-tier grievance redressal system stipulated under it and include e-commerce, product liability, misleading advertisements within its purview.[9]
- No special condition is laid down in most of the consumer laws regarding the applicability or non-applicability of electronic transactions.
- Rights of a consumer as provided by domestic legislations like Section 6 of CPA 1986 are also available to electronic consumers.

CPA 2019:

- The new Act brought e-commerce transactions under its ambit by widening the definition of 'consumer' to include any person who

---

[8] http://timesofindia.indiatimes.com/tech/tech-news/E-commerce-now-covered-under-Consumer-Protection-Act/articleshow/45349457.cms

[9] http://timesofindia.indiatimes.com/india/Centre-to-amend-Consumer-Protection-Act/articleshow/45326493.cms

buys any goods, whether through offline or online transactions, electronic means, teleshopping, direct selling or multi-level marketing.

- It provides flexibility to the consumer to file complaints with the jurisdictional consumer forum located at the place of residence or work of the consumer.
- Facility for consumers to file complaints electronically and for hearing and/or examining parties through video conferencing has been included.
- The concept of product liability applicable to the product manufacturer, product service provider and product seller, for any claim for compensation has been included. The term 'product seller' would also include e-commerce platforms.

2.3.5. FDI Regulations[10]

- 100 per cent FDI is allowed through automatic route in B2B e-commerce and not in B2C e-commerce.
- 100 per cent FDI under automatic route is permitted in marketplace model of e-commerce.
- FDI is not permitted in inventory-based model of e-commerce.

---

[10] For the purpose of FDI regulations, e-commerce entity means a company incorporated under the Companies Act 1956 or the Companies Act 2013 or a foreign company covered under Section 2(42) of the Companies Act, 2013 or an office, branch or agency in India as provided in Section 2(v)(iii) of FEMA 1999, owned or controlled by a person resident outside India and conducting the e-commerce business. Inventory-based model of e-commerce means an e-commerce activity where inventory of goods and services is owned by e-commerce entity and is sold to the consumers directly. Marketplace-based model of e-commerce means providing of an IT platform by an e-commerce entity on a digital and electronic network to act as a facilitator between buyer and seller (Press Information Bureau, 2018).

2.3.6. Miscellaneous Regulations

Apart from the above-mentioned laws and regulations, e-commerce companies are also subject to various laws which are applicable to ordinary companies. These include, for instance, anti-competitive practices (Competition Act, 2002), advertising guidelines, criminal frauds, FEMA, etc.

It is also worth noting that legal and regulatory issues of e-commerce in India are not same for different categories of e-commerce. For instance, electronic trading of medical drugs in India requires more stringent e-commerce and legal compliances as compared to other e-commerce activities.

2.4. Emerging Issues Pertaining to Growing E-Commerce in India

2.4.1. FDI Policy for E-Commerce[11]

FDI policy pertaining to e-commerce in India has seen significant changes over the years. In 2012, the Department for Industrial Policy and Promotion (DIPP) permitted 100 per cent FDI through automatic route in B2B e-commerce. However, there were allegations that many e-commerce companies selling products directly to consumers on their platforms have foreign funding. In 2016, DIPP allowed 100 per cent FDI in e-commerce activities under the 'marketplace model' to legitimize the existing e-commerce companies operating in India. FDI in 'inventory-based model' of e-commerce was not allowed. DIPP has issued Press Note No 2 (2018 Series) on 26 December 2018 which amends the applicable provisions of the earlier FDI policy. These provisions have taken place with effect from 1 February 2019.

The marketplace e-commerce companies in India are having a troubled time as the FDI policy changes announced in December 2018 took effect from 1 February 2019. Although the government considers these changes as a mere reiteration of earlier policy, the

---

[11] This section is based on Gupta (2019).

market reaction and analysis of these changes reveal that the new obligations on marketplace companies go much beyond reiteration and create new obligations for marketplace model of e-commerce in India.

The applicability of the 'group companies' concept has been turned on its head. Earlier, the group companies' obligation was applied on vendors, but now it is applicable to marketplace entities. Accordingly, the inventory of a vendor will be deemed to be controlled by e-commerce marketplace entity if more than 25 per cent of the purchases of such vendor are from the marketplace entity or its group companies. This new criteria for considering vendors' inventory as the inventory of marketplace entity has resulted into substantial change in the business model of the marketplace entities.

The onus of conforming to this provision is on marketplace entity through statutory audit to be submitted to the RBI. It seems that the problems of implementation are not taken into consideration while devising this new criterion. First, how does a marketplace entity will assess whether more than 25 per cent of purchases of a vendor are from the marketplace entity or its group companies as the marketplace entity will not have access to books of accounts of thousands of its vendors? Even if this is included as a contract condition by the marketplace entity with its vendors, what if the vendor changes name and purchases the same goods from the marketplace entity with different name? Who will audit the vendors? The statutory audit seems to be only for marketplace entities and not for vendors.

The earlier policy required that an e-commerce entity would not permit more than 25 per cent of the sales affected through its marketplace from one vendor or their group companies. The new policy does not have any such provision included. It is not sure whether this condition is now withdrawn or still be applicable to marketplace entities.

Other new obligations for marketplace entities include, first, e-commerce marketplace entity or other entities in which e-commerce marketplace entity has direct or indirect equity participation or common control should provide fulfilment, logistics, warehousing, advertisement/marketing, payments, financing etc., to vendors on the platform at arm's length and in a fair and non-discriminatory manner; second, cashback provided by group companies of marketplace entity to buyers shall be fair and non-discriminatory; third, e-commerce marketplace entity will not mandate any seller to sell any product exclusively on its platform only; fourth, e-commerce marketplace entity will be required to furnish a certificate along with a report of statutory auditor to RBI by 30 September of every year for the preceding financial year.

Through these policy changes, government intended to prevent violation of the earlier FDI policy on e-commerce and circumvention of restrictions on multi-brand retail trading. But instead of plugging the gaps remained in the earlier policy, it created new grey areas. First, it created an ambiguity with regard to ownership or control of inventory. On one hand, it prevents e-commerce entities providing a marketplace from exercising ownership or control over the inventory. On the other, it specifies that the present policy does not impose any restriction on the nature of products which can be sold on the marketplace. This would imply that the present policy does not prevent selling of private labels. By their nature, private labels are owned by the entities creating them. Thus, it could mean that inventory ownership in the form of private labels is allowed.

Second ambiguity is with respect to cashback provided on e-commerce platforms. The policy requires that cashback provided by group companies of marketplace entity to buyers shall be fair and non-discriminatory. What about cashback provided by marketplace entity itself and not by its group companies? Is fair and non-discriminatory clause not applicable to cashbacks provided by marketplace entity itself?

Third, it specifies that in marketplace model, goods/services made available for sale electronically on the website should clearly provide name, address and other contact details of the seller. Post sale, delivery of goods to the customers and customer satisfaction will be the sole responsibility of the seller. What about services? Since this specifies satisfaction only with respect to goods, does that mean any dissatisfaction with regard to post-sale delivery of services will not be a responsibility of the seller?

Given substantial changes in the FDI policy on e-commerce, it would have been better if the government consulted various stakeholders, including foreign players, before changing the policy and deciding the timelines for the changes to take place. Since these players are allowed to do business in India by the government itself, they should have been given an opportunity to be heard. It is a different matter what policy options government would have chosen after consultations, considering the overall benefits to the economy, as the government has full right to change its policy stance given the evolving e-commerce in India.

2.4.2. Draft E-Commerce Policy

The government has recently come out with a draft of much-needed policy on e-commerce. Both domestic and international concerns must have guided the framing of such policy. At the international front, e-commerce is actively discussed in the WTO, and many member countries are demanding to start negotiations and to frame multilateral rules on e-commerce, although the existing mandate is only for discussion and not any rule-making. India has so far resisted the proposals to start negotiations on e-commerce in the WTO, but any future intervention by India in the WTO will require a clear understanding of what is good and what are the red lines for the country in the e-commerce space. This would not be possible without having a comprehensive policy on e-commerce. So, this draft policy is a step in the right direction.

On the domestic front, the lack of regulations or perceived lack of understanding of regulations for different segments of e-commerce is resulting into unfair and unethical practices by various players. Huge growth and investment prospects in e-commerce should not be an excuse to allow or to continue with such practices. This policy intends to curb these practices. For instance, there is no denial of the fact that a significant capital dumping is happening in the Indian e-commerce space by those having money powers to grab the market. Significant losses are being incurred to offer deep discounts in the market. Even the sellers listed on the platforms are compelled to offer massive discounts, failing which they are delisted from the platforms or their products are not shown properly. Therefore, it is important to put a check on capital dumping and such unfair practices. There are valid questions such as how to determine the threshold for allowing discounts, whether alternate models can be used to prevent foreign capital dumping, etc. These are the next steps in the process, but we should first understand and acknowledge that this is a problem area.

The draft policy has a number of facilitative elements for e-commerce players. For instance, the recommendation to establish a central registry for KYC will reduce the cost and burden of KYC compliance by the payment systems. Similarly, the provision to have controlling stake in spite of minority share by the promoters will allow the young entrepreneurs to grow and seek funding support without giving up control in their entity.

There were criticisms of the draft e-commerce policy as it was considered as a regressive step by many. However, one must see this policy from developments at the international arena pertaining to e-commerce. The proposals submitted in the WTO on e-commerce tend to include almost everything under the sun, including physical trade, online trade, payment systems, consumer protection, telecommunication networks, spam mail and source code, to name a few. If all these things are being discussed in the WTO, and may be negotiated in future, the government must know its landing zone in all these spheres. The draft policy intended to find such landing zones in international negotiations on various elements of e-commerce

The critics of the policy have probably misunderstood the context in which this policy has been framed. While overemphasizing on a few specific elements, the critics erred in understanding 'trees' as the 'jungle'. Basic economics teaches us that market forces do not always produce optimum results; rather, there are market failures too. This is particularly true for the markets that are monopoly or oligopoly. The e-commerce market in India is no different. Therefore, some government intervention is required for the benefit of all.

2.4.3. Privacy Issues[12]

The Supreme Court of India in a landmark judgement in August 2017 said that right to privacy is a fundamental right. The right to privacy includes an individual's right to make personal choices. The judgement also covered privacy issues in the context of technological development and use of data by private players generated by individuals actively or passively on Internet.

In the present age, almost each action of individuals and businesses—a simple online search, a social media activity or an online transaction—generates data. This data contains important information about human behaviour and customer choices, tastes and preferences. If one searches flight options for a destination on Google, s/he gets promotional messages advertising flight options for the same destination on his Facebook and on other webpages. It implies that the data about a person's choices, taste and preferences is shared by one online entity with another entity without explicit consent of the consumer. Could it be termed as the violation of an individual's right to privacy?

In this context, it is important to note the relevant excerpts of the judgement delivered by Justice Sanjay Kishan Kaul in the 'Right to Privacy' case. He wrote that one aspect of the right to privacy is an individual's right to control the dissemination of his personal information, and this aspect has gained special significance in view of technological improvements. The right of an individual to exercise control over his personal data and to be able to control his/her own life would also include his right to control his existence in the virtual world. The right to privacy could be endangered both by the State and non-State actors. Social network providers, search engines, e-mail service providers and messaging applications are examples of non-State actors. Due to technological developments, not only the State but also big corporations and private entities can behave like the 'big brother'. There is an urgent need for regulations pertaining to storing, processing and use of information by non-State actors,

---

[12] This section is based on Gupta (2017).

and State intervention may be required for enforcing claims against them. Therefore, it could be inferred from the judgement that there is a need for regulatory intervention by the government for protecting data privacy of its citizens.

Another pertinent question would be whether a company can force individuals to agree to its terms and conditions of sharing personal information with other entities as part of its service agreement. Would such forced consent also constitute the violation of the right to privacy? One may like to recall the terms and conditions of WhatsApp's new privacy policy a few years back that forced users to give consent to share their data including phone numbers with its parent company Facebook. The matter is sub judice, and the Supreme Court has set-up five-judge bench in April 2017 to decide on the petition challenging the privacy policy of WhatsApp.

The Supreme Court decision indicates active role of the government in protecting the right to privacy through regulations in the context of the dissemination of personal information by private entities. The Government of India had set up a Committee of Experts under the Chairmanship of Justice B. N. Srikrishna in July 2017 to examine various issues related to data protection in India and recommend methods to address them.

A Draft Personal Data Protection Bill, 2018 has been prepared by the Ministry of Electronics and Information Technology. The Bill regulates the processing of personal data of individuals (data principals) by government and private entities (data fiduciaries) incorporated in India and abroad. According to this Bill, processing of data is allowed if the individual gives consent, or in a medical emergency, or by the State for providing benefits. The data principal has been provided with several rights with respect to their data, such as seeking correction or seeking access to their data, which is stored with the fiduciary. On the other hand, the fiduciary has certain obligations towards the individual while processing their data, such as notifying them of the nature and purposes of data processing. The Bill allows exemptions for certain kinds of data processing, such as processing in the interest of national security, for legal proceedings, or for journalistic purposes. The Bill also requires that a serving copy of personal data be stored within the territory of India. Certain critical personal data must be stored solely within the country. A national-level Data Protection Authority is to be set up under the Bill to supervise and regulate data fiduciaries.[13]

2.4.4. Consumer Protection Issues

Despite rapid growth in e-commerce transactions in India, such transactions are prone to information asymmetry between the sellers and buyers. It creates uncertainty in online purchases as consumers cannot physically test or experience the products prior to purchase. Consumers face a number of service issues while making e-commerce transactions. These include the non-delivery of items to consumers at the time of his/her choice, return pick-up of items delivered but not acceptable to consumer, ease of payment and credit back in case of return of items, post-delivery warranty commitments, consumer grievance redressal in case of defective products, etc. Such issues not only have consequences for consumers but also for e-commerce companies and the sector as a whole. Figure 2.3 highlights the nature of consumer grievances pertaining to e-commerce transactions in India.

As per the National Consumer Helpline (NCH, 2018) *Annual Report 2017–18*, the booming sector of e-commerce has registered the highest number of grievances at NCH, totalling 76,615 dockets for the fiscal year 2017–2018. According to this report, consumers have a number of concerns pertaining to online purchases, such as delivery of wrong products, deficiency in data privacy and identity theft. Numerous grievances are filed for receiving a wrong product which can be the result of a shipping mix up, courier agency or customer malpractices. Grievances are also registered which do not meet the return policy of the e-commerce portal. At times, the product is returned successfully but the process of refund takes a long time. Grievances regarding fake, spurious, counterfeit, poor quality products are more common with electronic gadgets and sports shoes.

---

[13] https://www.prsindia.org/billtrack/draft-personal-data-protection-bill-2018

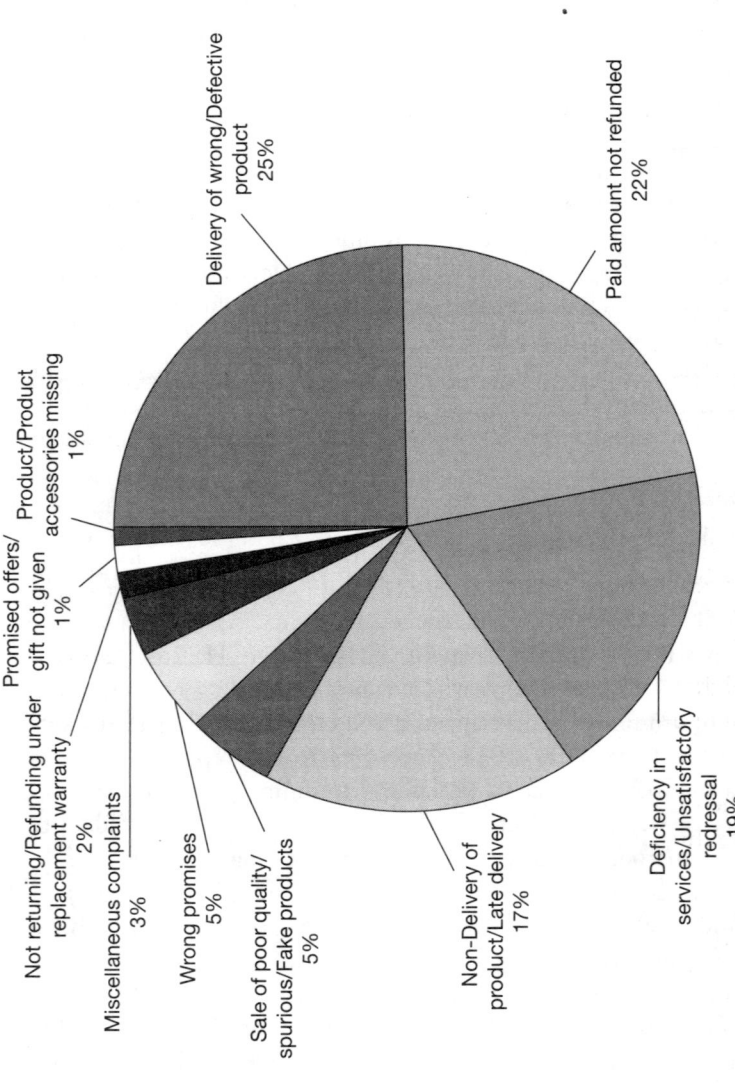

Figure 2.3 *Nature of Grievances in E-Commerce Sector, 2017–2018*
Source: Reproduced from NCH (2018, 15).

Consumers have also complained of receiving inferior commodities, products nearing expiry and incomplete packages. The report stated that misleading or lack of information on the quality of products sold on e-commerce websites suggests for amendments to the existing laws.

Therefore, consumer protection issues are growing alongside the growth of e-commerce in India which require remedial actions for healthy growth of this sector. The newly enacted CPA 2019 is a step in the right direction on this matter. The new Act tightens the existing rules to safeguard consumer rights and proposes to introduce a central regulator, the Central Consumer Protection Authority (CCPA). It also proposes imposing strict penalties for misleading advertisements and redressing complaints related with defects in goods and deficiency in services purchased online, and outlines a framework for e-commerce and electronic service providers. The Act allows consumers to file their complaint with the court from anywhere.

2.4.5. Competition Issues

Economists believe that free market forces bring optimum benefits to the economy as they result into competition and efficiency among the producers. This may hold true for traditional markets but may not for digital markets. The competitive forces of market are failing in the digital world, and those who have technology and money power take all the gains. This is happening all over the world, and India is no exception.

The online market in India is getting consolidated to have only two or three big players, and the start-ups are either getting acquired by the giants or closing down owing to the deep pockets and capital dumping by the tech giants. The big players of e-commerce receive huge funding from the investors which further fortifies their position in the market and enables them to come up with irrational offers that small competitors find difficult to match. Therefore, only the giants with immense financial backing end up being in the market by driving out the small players. This consolidation is very well visible across various sectors of e-commerce, be it grocery, travel, food delivery or any other.

The four big giants of the digital space, commonly described as GAFA (Google, Apple, Facebook and Amazon), enjoy significant market power in their respective digital space. These companies are facing lawsuits in many geographies for their abuse of dominant power. For instance, Google was recently fined by the Competition Commission of India (2018) for abusing its dominant position in online general web search and web search advertising services. In 2017, it was also fined by the European Commission (2017a) for abusing its market dominance as a search engine by promoting its own comparison shopping service in its search results. Apple is facing investigation in the USA and a criminal probe in France for software updates that compelled its consumers to shift to new phones as these updates slowed down their iPhones (BBC, 2018). Facebook was found guilty by the German Antitrust Body, the Bundeskartellamt, which stated that the extent to which Facebook collects, merges and uses data in user accounts constitutes an abuse of a dominant position (Bundeskartellamt, 2019).

Tech giants could also abuse their dominant position and arm-twist small players by including arbitrary clauses in their agreements to dictate their preferred terms and conditions. A case in point is the European Commission investigation initiated against Amazon, dominant player in e-book distribution in the European Union. The Commission was concerned about certain clauses in the e-book distribution agreement of Amazon with the publishers. These clauses mandated the publishers to offer Amazon similar or better condition as to its competitors by the publishers. Also, if any alternate or favourable terms were provided to other competitors, then the same has to be brought to Amazon (European Commission, 2017b). Amazon agreed to remove these clauses to end the investigation.

Therefore, anticompetitive behaviour and abuse of dominant power in digital markets is frequent and not an exception. Nobel laureate Joseph Stiglitz once mentioned that firms compete not only for price but also for products and innovation. This is exactly what is happening in India's digital space. Tech giants not only indulge in price wars but also monopolize products and innovation. This has grave implications for start-ups and employment creation and hence should not be overlooked by the government given the employment creation as the top priority.

2.4.6. Participation of Small and Medium Enterprises

A significant aspect related to E-commerce is that of the increasing participation by small and medium enterprises (SMEs) either as service suppliers or consumers. The Internet has opened many business opportunities to small- and medium-sized suppliers in many countries. It has also helped in stimulating entrepreneurial activities across the globe. In India also, as the availability and penetration of Internet has increased over the years, many e-commerce companies came into existence and engaged with the SMEs sector. It is often argued that e-commerce has opened up new opportunities for SMEs so that they can engage in international trade and become a part of the global economy. Although this is true to some extent, there are a number of barriers and challenges that have reduced or eliminated the commercial value of such opportunities. Highly concentrated nature of e-commerce across the globe also puts the SMEs at the receiving end with no or very less bargaining power.

E-commerce players often misuse their dominant power to oust well-performing SMEs from the market. SMEs made huge efforts to make their brand and products successful at e-commerce platforms. However, when a particular product becomes highly demanded on these websites, these e-commerce players start purchasing these products in bulk directly through the manufacturers and start supplying at low rates through dummy companies, thereby eliminating SMEs from the market.

SMEs also have a shortage of trained staff that keeps track of their receivables, payables, inventories, shipment, etc. This results into their over dependence on the e-commerce service providers. Many times, these SMEs continue to sell their products offering heavy discount without having proper accounting of their net receipts and later realize that they have occurred a heavy loss and hence need to stop their participation on such e-commerce platforms.

Availability and quality of Internet is also an issue that affects SMEs participation in e-commerce. While SMEs working from metro cities may have access to high-speed Internet, the same may not be the case with enterprises operating from Tier II and Tier III cities. Another similar issue is the lack of Internet security that does not only affect SMEs participation in e-commerce but also makes them more vulnerable to online frauds and cheating. Unlike big companies, these enterprises neither have awareness about Internet threats nor have resources to install state-of-the-art mechanism to counter online attacks.

Thus, there are a number of challenges that SMEs face while participating in the growing e-commerce market in India. It needs to be analysed in greater detail how much benefit is accruing to SMEs out of such participation, as mere participation is not enough for their sustained benefits.

2.4.7. E-commerce Taxation Issues

The applicability of taxation for online transactions happening within countries and also cross-border is also an important issue for policy-makers. As the sector is growing at an exponential rate, it should also contribute to government's tax kitty. However, there are practical difficulties in applying taxes on various kinds of online transactions. The Government of India has levied GST for e-commerce. This creates non-level playing fields for domestic producers vis-à-vis foreign suppliers, as foreign suppliers are not subject to GST. Apart from these, taxation of online revenues of various platforms is also emerging as a significant discussion point not only in India but also in other countries.

2.4.8. E-Commerce and Jurisdiction Issues

Cross-border trade in services is significantly affected by the increased feasibility and reduced costs of electronic delivery of goods and services. The Internet and e-commerce have enabled and aided cross-border trade in many services which earlier required physical proximity between the consumer and the supplier. Whereas financial services, tourism and computer services are early adopters of online means of supply, more recently, professional services, education and healthcare have also benefited.

A significant aspect with regard to international trade perspective of e-commerce business is the jurisdiction issue. The e-commerce companies may have their offices in one country, server in another country and consumers in some other country. The fact that parties to an e-commerce contract are located in different jurisdictions may have implications for the interpretation and enforcement of the contract. In such situation, it is not very clear whose jurisdiction will be applicable, if a problem arises between the online service provider and the consumers.

2.5. Conclusion and Policy Suggestions

In India, e-commerce is rapidly growing and is likely to change the way business is performed. Many online companies are venturing into Indian e-commerce market space to take the first mover advantage. However, it is observed that many e-commerce companies are not adequately following the rules and regulations pertaining to the e-commerce business. This is partly due to the fact that e-commerce laws in India are in an evolving stage.

India does not have dedicated laws for various types of e-commerce activities. Some of the e-commerce activities are very important from a public policy perspective and hence require specialized rules and regulations to safeguard the consumers against any wrongdoing. For instance, online sales of prescribed medicines in India. The government needs to have specialized laws on these issues as applicable in other countries. For instance, in the USA, the Health Insurance Portability and Accountability Act of 1996 (HIPAA) and Health Information Technology for Economic and Clinical Health Act (HITECH Act) are some of the laws that take care of medico-legal and techno-legal issues of e-health and telemedicine.

There are many areas that require focused attention, discussion with stakeholders and concrete policies in order to facilitate e-commerce business in India. These include, for instance, establishment of independent regulator, such as TRAI for telecom services. It will not only help an orderly growth of e-commerce business in India but also protect consumers from being exploited. The regulator should have effective grievance system and legal remedies if anything goes wrong with respect to the online transactions.

India also needs an alternative dispute resolution (ADR) mechanism to resolve e-commerce disputes. E-commerce regulations and laws in India are limited in nature, and this does not allow the use of ADR mechanisms and technology-driven solutions. For instance, while European Union and other nations are increasingly using online dispute resolution for resolving many aspects of e-commerce disputes, it is still unknown in India.

Therefore, it can be said that the growth of e-commerce activities has given birth to new challenges that need to be taken care of in order to facilitate and support e-commerce business in India. As most of these challenges relate to the lack of appropriate regulatory infrastructure, the government needs to come forward to initiate various legislations related to the online transactions.

References

BBC. (2018). Apple investigated by France for 'planned obsolescence'. https://www.bbc.com/news/world-europe-42615378

Bundeskartellamt. (2019). Administrative proceedings: Decision under Section 32(1) German Competition Act (GWB). https://www.bundeskartellamt.de/DE/Missbrauchsaufsicht/missbrauchsaufsicht_node.html

Competition Commission of India. (2018). Case Nos. 07 and 30 of 2012. https://www.cci.gov.in/sites/default/files/07%20&%20%2030%20of%202012.pdf

European Commission. (2017a). Antitrust: Commission fines Google €2.42 billion for abusing dominance as search engine by giving illegal advantage to own comparison shopping service. https://ec.europa.eu/commission/presscorner/detail/en/IP_17_1784

European Commission. (2017b). CASE AT.40153 E-book MFNs and related matters (Amazon). https://ec.europa.eu/competition/elojade/isef/case_details.cfm?proc_code=1_40153

Gupta, P. (2017). Privacy right's bearing on e-commerce. *The Financial Express*, 31 August.

Gupta, P. (2019). Smoothen out the e-Dges. *The Economic Times*, 12 February.

NCH. (2018). *Annual Report (2017–18)*. New Delhi: Department of Consumer Affairs, Government of India.

Press Information Bureau. (2018). Review of policy on Foreign Direct Investment (FDI) in e-commerce. Government of India. https://pib.gov.in/newsite/PrintRelease.aspx?relid=186804

CHAPTER 3

E-Commerce in India
An Economic Boon, Yet to Be Realized

Himani Aggarwal and Samridhi Jain

3.1. Introduction

E-commerce has become not just a growing area for exploration but also an integral part of a country's competitive strategy. Past two decades have observed huge developments in the field of information and communications technology (ICT) and a revolution in the business strategies, which earlier was beyond imagination. Connected strictly with these rapid technological developments, e-commerce is a new-reality in the globalized world. It involves buying and selling of information, goods and services online through Internet. This can include e-tailing (business-to-consumer or B2C) and business-to-business (B2B) transactions, intranets and extranets, online advertising, e-banking, online stock trading, online education and consultation services or simply an online presence of any form used for some type of communication and transaction. The anytime and anywhere access facility provided by e-commerce platforms, characterized by asynchronous communication between firms and potential consumers, allows considerable flexibility in making transactions with greater interactivity. Costs involved in to say establishing a brand name, marketing channels, accumulating information on sources for demand, obtaining detailed content regarding consumer preferences, etc., in a brick-and-mortar business are reduced in an e-commerce setting. Online platforms can help firm in reducing the sunk costs involved in physical setups by opening up newer avenues and allowing firms to operate with minimal costs which helps in increasing economies of scale in the business strategies with a ready platform.

In order to become e-commerce friendly and penetrate the global market space, countries should facilitate higher Internet penetration, high-class logistics and infrastructure, and suitable regulatory framework (Department of Industrial Policy and Promotion [DIPP], n.d.). As a part of the revolution in information technology, e-commerce has been widely used in the world trade in general and Indian economy in particular. There have been various factors— commercial, demographic and technical—responsible for the growth of Indian e-commerce sector. With the growing technology, the logistics solutions have become more advanced which has helped making the delivery system easier and faster. Not just that, with Internet becoming common among the masses, there has been supportive environment for the penetration of e-commerce sector, and digital penetration has been accommodated. The increasing mobility with the advent of smartphones and increase in network towers and declining Internet tariffs, e-commerce sector has become popular among the masses.

The trending growth and increase in online customers in India have led to an increase in overall growth of this sector, making the markets more competitive. From online shoppers to Internet penetration, the world has seen an instantaneous growth and so has Indian markets. The Indian e-commerce sector reported almost 35 per cent compound annual growth rate (CAGR) from 2009 to 2013, and, since then, there have been significant improvements in the sector (Sharma, 2014). Indian e-commerce sector is growing exponentially and is projected to acquire 6.5 per cent of the total retail market by 2023.[1] It has helped

---

[1] Stats, figures & facts: Learn about glorious Indian ecommerce growth. https://www.fatbit.com/fab/stats-figures-facts-learn-glorious-indian-ecommerce-growth/

the country in generating employment opportunities and increasing the competitive pricing for consumers along with a reduction in the cost of inventory, distribution and delivery. The open and inclusive e-commerce business strategies have extended opportunities for small manufacturers and merchant partners by offering them access to a large audience. The advent of e-commerce in the trading sector has not only made the world a smaller place but has also opened the markets in a broader sense. Therefore, the boost in the sector is directed towards a positive impact on the economic growth and development of the country.

With the rapid adoption and development of Internet technology in the globalized society, accompanied by e-commerce as an emerging industry, a country's overall development is a natural consequence. Henceforth, it is necessary to study the degree of impact of the e-commerce sector on the economy and examine the challenges faced by the sector in making greater contribution to the development of a country. Based on the economic theory, we developed a model to analyse the impact of the development of ICT factors responsible for the growth of e-commerce sector on economic development. The results indicate that despite having a positive correlation, e-commerce sector in India had a non-appreciable effect on economic growth. Therefore, we tried to explore the possible gaps in the current structure and compared the performance of the sector in India to the top e-commerce markets, namely China, the USA, the United Kingdom, Japan, Australia, Singapore and Brazil, to suggest some policy measures that can be effective in realizing the full potential of the industry.

The chapter is outlined as follows: Section 3.2 describes the mechanism of the model adopted to study the relation between e-commerce and economic growth, followed by the empirical analysis and results discussed in Section 3.3. Section 3.4 discusses various challenges faced by Indian e-commerce sector with respect to the framework developed. Section 3.5 lays out a comparison between the top e-commerce performing markets in the world and the Indian e-commerce market. Section 3.6 suggests various policy measures concerning the challenges listed in the previous sections, and the final section concludes the chapter.

3.2. Effect of E-Commerce on Economic Growth: Mechanism

Internet is a major medium of communication and a source of information, which has realized the most important and exponential growth in the history. One of the most important facilities offered by Internet network in the modern world is e-commerce, providing the capacity to access information and make transactions, eliminating all geographical barriers and time constraints (Albastroiu, 2007). The anytime, anywhere and flexible access offered by the electronic networks helps in strengthening the foundation of e-commerce over traditional commerce which has further added new dimensions to economic growth and is a driving force for economic development. In view of the fact that digital revolution involving the use of Internet has set the stage for e-commerce, this chapter examines the impact of e-commerce sector as a driving force for economic growth and the challenges faced by this sector in India.

In order to explore the potential of the e-commerce in realizing economic growth, we would study the impact of the ICT developments (the major force responsible for driving progress in e-commerce in the last two decades) on gross domestic product (GDP). GDP is one of the most widely used measures of economic development. According to the expenditure approach, GDP combines consumption, investment, government expenditure and net exports.

First, e-commerce has enabled increase in consumer spending as a result of wider product range and facilities that satisfy not only the material but also basic and cultural needs of the consumers. Also, growing consumer confidence in the prospects of e-commerce encourages increased consumer spending on digital gadgets and Internet networks. Along with the rapid development in e-commerce, there is an expansion in logistics and ICT infrastructure industry, providing more employment opportunities in computer and Internet technology industry and thus stimulating consumption.

Second, as an emerging sector, e-commerce attracts investments from businesses and companies to increase their productivity and thus income in the competitive era. From providing consumer-specific demands to promoting themselves online, they require funds to invest in areas such as ICT infrastructure, digital advertising, development of online platform or cost of registration on an existing platform, etc., leading to an increase in the fixed capital investment.

Third, there is not only an increase in the requirement for appropriate transportation and logistics with the expansion of e-commerce industry but infrastructural developments, such as increased Internet and communication networks, power generation, etc., are also in demand. Therefore, related government procurement expenditures would entail higher value added to the sector. In addition to this, to ensure confidence of businesses and consumers and smooth functioning in the e-commerce sector, government expenditure is a necessity in areas such as secure network, data security and corporate business and personal credit.

Finally, since time and place are no longer the constraints with Internet, cross-border trade has seen profound transformation. With the immense growth in ICT industry and technological advances, obvious potential of e-commerce through international trade can be realized. E-commerce enables the enterprises to gain from participation in the international market in terms of expanded reach and increased efficiency from exposure to competition. Therefore, with healthy development of the economy, e-commerce is bound to become a mainstream in international trade.

3.3. Empirical Analysis and Results

Based on the mechanism described above, GDP as dependent variable representing economic development and four factors as independent variables representing consumer spending, business investment, government expenditure and international trade in digital revolution (or Internet and technology adoption) to reflect e-commerce development are selected for the empirical analysis. The four factors include percentage of population using the Internet (X1), scale of online advertising (X2), number of domain registrations in .in zone (X3) and number of worldwide domain registrations by registrants from India (X4). The data is collected for the years 2004–2017 from the World Bank Open

Table 3.1 *Correlation Coefficient Matrix between GDP and E-Commerce Development Factors*

		GDP	X1	X2	X4	X5
GDP	Pearson Correlation	1.000	0.902***	0.855***	0.904***	0.909***
	Significance		0.000	0.000	0.000	0.000
X1	Pearson Correlation	0.902***	1.000	0.984***	0.997***	0.996***
	Significance	0.000		0.000	0.000	0.000
X2	Pearson Correlation	0.855***	0.984***	1.000	0.988***	0.987***
	Significance	0.000	0.000		0.000	0.000
X4	Pearson Correlation	0.904***	0.997***	0.988***	1.000	0.999***
	Significance	0.000	0.00	0.000		0.003
X5	Pearson Correlation	0.909***	0.996***	0.987***	0.999***	1.000
	Significance	0.000	0.000	0.000	0.003	

Notes: *** $p < 0.01$, ** $p < 0.05$ and * $p < 0.1$.

Data,[2] Domain Name Stat website and an info graphic by Acodez: digital advertising in India-statistics and trends.[3] GDP is evaluated at current US dollar in trillions, and the scale of online advertising is accounted in million US dollars.

In order to assess the association and test the statistical strength of the relationship between GDP and the selected indicators, first we used Pearson correlation coefficient method, the results for which are shown in Table 3.1. The correlation analysis is done based on the following hypothesis:

H_0: There is no significant linear correlation between GDP and the four indicators respectively.

H_1: There is a significant linear correlation between GDP and at least one of the four factors.

[2] https://data.worldbank.org/
[3] https://acodez.in/digital-advertising-india/

Table 3.1 shows that the correlation coefficients between GDP and the four indicators—percentage of population using the Internet, scale of online advertising, secure servers available per one million people, number of domain registrations in .in zone, and number of worldwide domain registrations by registrants from India—are 0.902, 0.855, 0.894, 0.904 and 0.909, respectively. All the coefficients are statistically significant at 1 per cent level of significance. Therefore, the null hypothesis is rejected.

To further study the impact of the e-commerce development indicators, the chapter uses multiple linear regression model, given as follows:

$$\text{GDP}_t = \beta_1 + \beta_2 X1_t + \beta_3 X2_t + \beta X3_t + \beta_5 X4_t + \varepsilon_t$$

where GDP_t is the GDP of the country in year t, from $X1_t$ to $X4_t$ represent the respective factors in year t, β_1 is the constant, from β_2 to β_5 are the respective parameters of interest for each factor and ε_t is the error term. The results for the analysis are shown in Table 3.2.

As shown in Table 3.2, there is a significant impact of the parameters on GDP; however, the impact is negligible. The results of correlation matrix in Table 3.1 indicate that there is a positive and significant relationship between the four indicators and GDP, which further explains that the development of e-commerce factors would lead to economic growth of the country. However, according to the regression model analysis, although the indicators had a significant impact on GDP, it was negligible. Moreover, the coefficients for the two parameters—Internet advertising spending in US million dollars and number of domain registrations in .in zone—are negative.

Over the years, the four indicators have shown a positive growth trend in India, as shown in Figure 3.1. Following the results of Table 3.1, the rapid increase in Internet technology demographics should account for a significant contribution towards the growth of GDP; however, as exhibited by Table 3.2, the results are contradictory. This implies that the use of these ICT developments is not focused towards increasing the productivity which would further benefit the economic growth.

Table 3.2 *Multiple Linear Regression Analysis for GDP and E-Commerce Development Factors*

	Coefficient
Percentage of population using the Internet	0.1519***
	(0.0351)
Internet advertising spending in USD million	−0.0015*
	(0.0007)
Number of domain registrations in .in zone	−0.00004***
	(0.0000)
Number of worldwide domain registrations by registrants from India	0.00002***
	(0.0000)
R-squared	0.9794
(Adjusted *R*-squared)	(0.9656)
Number of observations	14

Notes: The table shows multiple linear regression analysis on the impact of the e-commerce development factors on GDP. Standard errors are in parentheses. *** $p < 0.01$, ** $p < 0.05$ and * $p < 0.1$.

3.4. Discussion

Although there is a considerable upswing in the driving forces of e-commerce industry over the years, yet their minute contribution in impacting GDP positively demonstrates that the contribution of Internet technology through consumer spending, business investment, government expenditure and net exports has been inadequate. The results from the analysis present an important implication that the potential of the Internet-related factors in affecting e-commerce industry is not yet realized; therefore, there is a gap in the current structure that needs to be identified.

For Indian consumers, preference is majorly skewed towards in-store personalized experience instead of online. Despite the fact that by the end of 2014, according to the data analysed by e-Marketer, India accounted for the third largest Internet user base in the world with 200 million users, only 20 per cent of them conducted an online

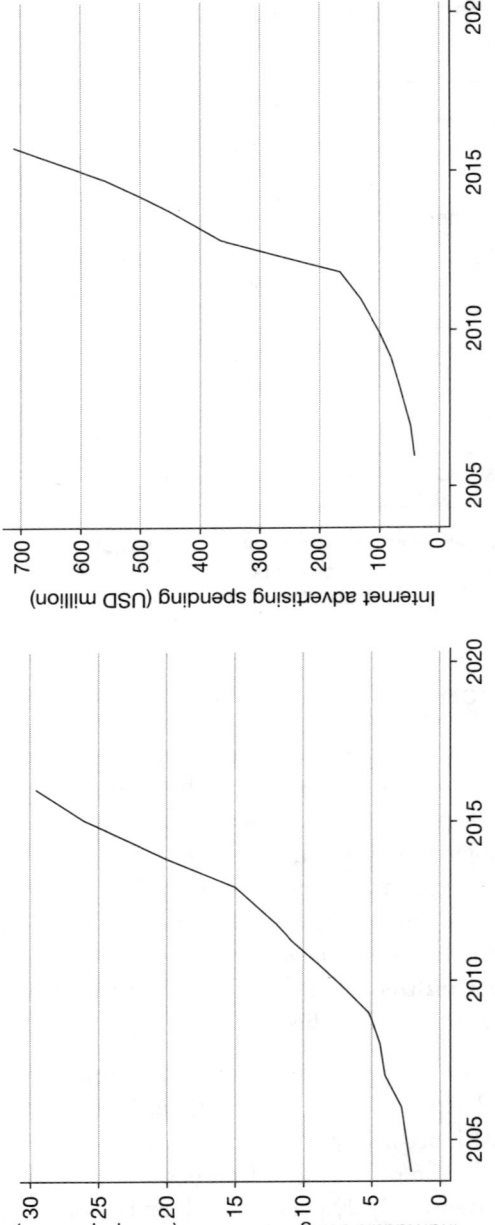

Figure 3.1 *Graphs Showing a Positive Growth Trend in the Selected E-Commerce Growth Factors*
Source: World Bank Open Data.

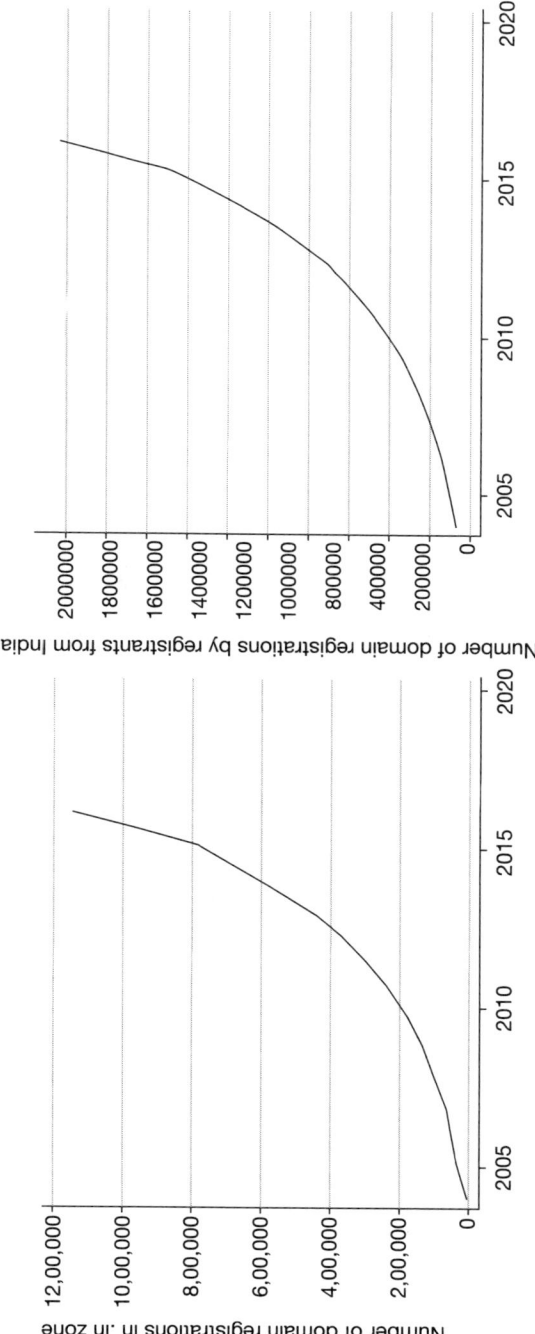

Figure 3.1 Continued

transaction (Saha, 2015). A study by Bain & Company, Google and Omidyar Network (2017) revealed, 'Only 40 per cent of India's 390 million Internet users transact online. The remaining 60 per cent do their research online but complete the undertaking offline'. The study disclosed that in 2017 there was a significant variation in the Internet penetration across regions such that the user base graph was biased in the favour of urban penetration with 55 per cent as compared to only 15 per cent penetration in rural areas. Also, there is a high gender disparity, where male penetration accounted for 33 per cent as compared to only 22 per cent penetration among females. The vast Internet base in Digital India is therefore characterized by large disparities across the demographics and low proportion of the population actually transacting online (Bain & Company et al., 2017).

The per-capita GDP of India is at a considerable low as compared to other countries in the world. A considerable part of the population lives below the poverty line and is unable to afford the odds and ends required to step in the world of e-commerce. Also, a large number of people in rural and urban areas lack knowledge about the emerging digital technologies, which further descends consumer participation (Wu, 2016). However, there is an increase in awareness about the emerging sector, and a majority of the population is added to the world of online services. For them, cyber-security issues are among the prime concerns, affecting their participation rates in the e-commerce industry. The facts in support of the issue are also outrageous. During 2013–2015, there has been an increase of up to 30 per cent in the number of complaints against online fraud (Mehra, 2015). Fear of disclosure and modification of data, fraud and denial of service or abuse of network issues hamper the trust of the consumers and thus affect e-commerce negatively (Singh, 2014). Therefore, due to the low proportion of population with adequate availability of facilities for the adoption of new technology, undesirability to pay online via digital payment systems, lack of digital literacy and lack of trust in the new systems, the e-commerce sector is struggling to create a nationwide enabling environment for consumers.

One of the biggest challenges to dynamically changing Indian retail sector is the abundance of manpower with low levels of skills. From the point of view of business, with capital goods investment in ICT, the labour can benefit from overall capital deepening. Thus, e-commerce investment does not only provide efficiency to the business processes but also helps in raising the multifactor productivity. While the Indian retail sector is highly unorganized, it is also characterized by a majority of workforce with low level of literacy and non-existent levels of digital literacy. The statistics reveal that only 2 per cent of the total workforce in India was skilled, much lower in comparison to other developing countries (Economic Survey 2014–15). E-commerce does create employment opportunities for masses; however, since it is majorly dependent on cutting-edge technology, skilled workforce with specialized knowledge in tech areas is demanded. With few skilled workers and decades of neglect in training the individuals specifically for the assigned job, the retailers find it hard to construct new business strategies and establish themselves in e-commerce industry.

Cash is the most commonly accepted payment mechanism in India. In 2015, while 15 per cent of the online consumer transactions were conducted using debit cards, 11 per cent using credit cards and 8 per cent and 9 per cent respectively via mobile wallets and online banking, almost 57 per cent of the transactions were through cash on delivery (CoD). According to a study conducted by Internet and Mobile Association of India (IMAI) and KPMG, almost 60 per cent of the transactions in 2015 still involved CoD as payment mechanism (Mehra, 2015). India is a cash-obsessed economy to an extent that major platforms such as Amazon and Flipkart had the obligation to assimilate CoD as a payment option in their business structure to tap a large consumer base. Additional 3 per cent costs associated with it in the form of additional verification calls for CoD orders, collection charges by courier companies raises the delivery costs for the firms (Mehra, 2015). Thus, apart from capital investment in e-commerce, the transaction costs involved in making the product or service available to consumer borne by the firms are sometimes high.

Moreover, inefficient supply chain and logistic system further increases the cost of trade for the firms involved. Most of the goods are transported via air which increases the delivery costs for the companies. Indian e-commerce sector is still emerging with new customers on regular basis. First-time users are mostly inexperienced in shopping online which often leads to dissatisfaction and thus return of the product purchased. The lack of infrastructure facilities further aggravates the problems associated with reverse logistics and raises the costs for e-retailers. As a result, e-retailers who were dependent on the third-party service providers earlier have now started establishing their own captive logistics counterparts such as regional warehouses which has further pushed up the delivery costs (Sharma, 2014).

As the firms try to cover up for the increase in delivery costs, it ultimately leads to an increase in the buying costs for consumers in the form of shipping charges. The SAP Consumer Propensity Study found that along with the issues of out-of-stock items, higher shipping charges are among the major reasons for the consumers to ditch their online shopping carts and switch to an offline store (ETtech, 2018). While 42 per cent of the consumers discontinue shopping online when faced with out-of-stock issues, higher shipping charges diverts the purchase decision of more than 50 per cent of the consumers from online shopping. Long delivery periods or delays in the delivery of product because of poor last-mile connectivity and supply-chain infrastructure also affect the consumer's decision of buying online. The perplexed system associated with the return policies further hampers the e-commerce growth (Saha, 2015).

The hole in the e-commerce industry is the result of not only an unfit trend being followed in terms of consumer spending and business investment but also an out-turn of the incomprehension from the government perspective. To be a part of the e-commerce industry, the basic infrastructure requirement is access to Internet. As a result of meagre amount of government expenditure on e-commerce-specific development projects, the ICT infrastructure such as routers, fibre optic links and servers to provide Internet access to the public are scarce in India (Wu, 2016). India is a country with more than 650,000 villages of which majority are off the map, isolated and remote, providing habitation to more than half of the population. According to the India Brand Equity Foundation (IBEF) e-commerce report 2017, out of 100,000 pin codes in India, the online retailers could manage to deliver goods and services to about only 15 per cent of them (IBEF,

2017). Poor last-mile connectivity as a result of lack of proper links in the supply chain infrastructure and low ICT infrastructure access limits the access of the benefits to a significant portion of the population (DIPP, n.d.).

E-commerce industry in India also struggles with some gaps in the regulations and policies. The existing e-commerce policy of the government does not allow foreign direct investment in the B2C e-commerce transactions and foreign companies are not able to sell their products online directly to the consumers in India. This has compelled the global e-commerce platforms such as Amazon, Alibaba and eBay, which are Internet-based hosts for the third-party sellers to restructure their business model according to the rules and regulations in India. Therefore, liberalization laws are yet to be defined for the sector in India, and, hence, it is majorly a domestically owned sector (Horowitz & Phelan, 2015). Further, there is no clear policy to define the tax systems on e-commerce transactions in India. The current foreign trade policy in India does not account for clear taxation and customs for e-commerce exports.

Additionally, the rules of e-commerce sector are not governed by a specialized section in the department, rather by various agencies of the government. Issues related to the intellectual property rights (IPRs) are faced by e-commerce platforms, as they patent business models both domestically as well as internationally. IPR violations are difficult to monitor globally and therefore are a major concern for the e-commerce traders. There is a cyber cell under the police department of India to tackle cyber security issues, but these matters need focused law to be implemented with a special emphasis on e-commerce sector. Online transactions involve exchange of personal data from a consumer to the seller and therefore strong data privacy and protection laws are a necessity. The Information Technology Act, 2000 governs the use of personal information over the Internet, and other aspects related to consumer protection in online transactions are covered under laws such as Payment and Settlement Systems Act, 2007 and the Consumer Protection Act, 1986. Thus, there is a clear absence of e-commerce-specific framework that brings clarity on the key issues, such as national security and data protection regulations, IPRs and consumer privacy policies, and gears the country to engage globally in the sector.

3.5. Challenges Compared to Top E-Commerce Countries

India and China are at the top of the list for having large and growing population with an exponential increase in the percentage of Internet users, but India still stands much behind China in terms of e-retail users and in other ICT demographics. Although, India was exposed to Internet technology during the same time as China, the approach to a tech-friendly environment was completely different in the two countries. Chinese government developed Internet in three phases, beginning 1987, and, by 2002, almost every citizen had access to e-commerce services. Whereas in India, by 2002, only 15 million lines were added with considerable disparity between the states (E-commerce Digest, n.d.). In 2016, India topped the list of countries with largest offline population, with 864.7 million people without access to Internet as compared to the American countries Brazil and the USA with 70.5 and 37.2 million unconnected people, respectively. Therefore, India is still in the early stages of e-commerce industry, where even the basic knowledge of digital economy and its benefits is yet unrevealed to a major proportion of the population.

As per 2017 data, the top 3 e-commerce markets ruling the world are China, the USA and Japan with online retail sales amounting to $499.15 billion, $446.8 billion and $111.33 billion respectively, followed by the United Kingdom amounting to $90.71 billion. In terms of Internet users per 100 inhabitants, Japan and the United Kingdom topped the list with 93.3 and 92.0 users per 100 inhabitants respectively, followed by Australia and Singapore at 84.6 and 82.1, respectively, whereas in India, there were only 26 users for every 100 people in 2015. In the new era with the rapid adoption of smartphones and next-generation networks, e-commerce industry is believed to see a spurt in its growth. India is among the top countries in the world with respect to the number of smartphone users, accounting for 199.08 million smartphone as per 2015 data. In corollary to this, in terms of smartphone penetration as a share of total population and active mobile broadband subscriptions per 100 inhabitants among the countries, India falls much below in the graph (as shown in Figure 3.2). Additionally, in terms of secure servers, India ranks much below to other countries with only 11.69 secure servers per one million people as compared to 6,352.91 secure servers available per one million people in the USA. Since access to Internet and modern technology devices and availability of secure servers are among the major concerns for consumers, the digital buyer penetration stood at 24.4 per cent in India in 2015, far below the global average of 41.6 per cent (Jain, 2016).

In the USA, the United Kingdom and China, people started exploring the e-commerce industry by 2002 and therefore got an early mover advantage. Today, these countries are among the biggest e-commerce markets, experiencing a boom of more than 40 per cent of the total markets share. They are not just expanding domestically but also serving as big cross-border markets for each other (Suominen, 2017). In comparison to them, Indian e-commerce platforms are majorly the replications of the models developed by these countries and therefore are not modified specific to the needs of public (Jain, 2016). Therefore, global multinationals such as Amazon, Alibaba, Walmart, Google, Airbnb, etc., enjoy a major share in the India's e-commerce industry (Sethi, 2018). E-commerce market in India is dominated by Flipkart and Amazon. Since 2013, Flipkart, India's most successful e-commerce start-up is facing a tough competition from the US-based e-commerce global behemoth Amazon, and now, Walmart, an American multinational is stepping into the country's e-commerce market by acquiring a major stake in Flipkart (Sridharan, 2018). Alibaba, Chinese e-commerce giant took control of one of the most popular digital payment systems in India, that is, Paytm, and is therefore getting access to a major part of the population in both rural and urban areas (Mundy & Lucas, 2018). Hence, one of the major hurdles in e-commerce growth is that the Indian companies are not competitive enough to compete with the global giants in the market.

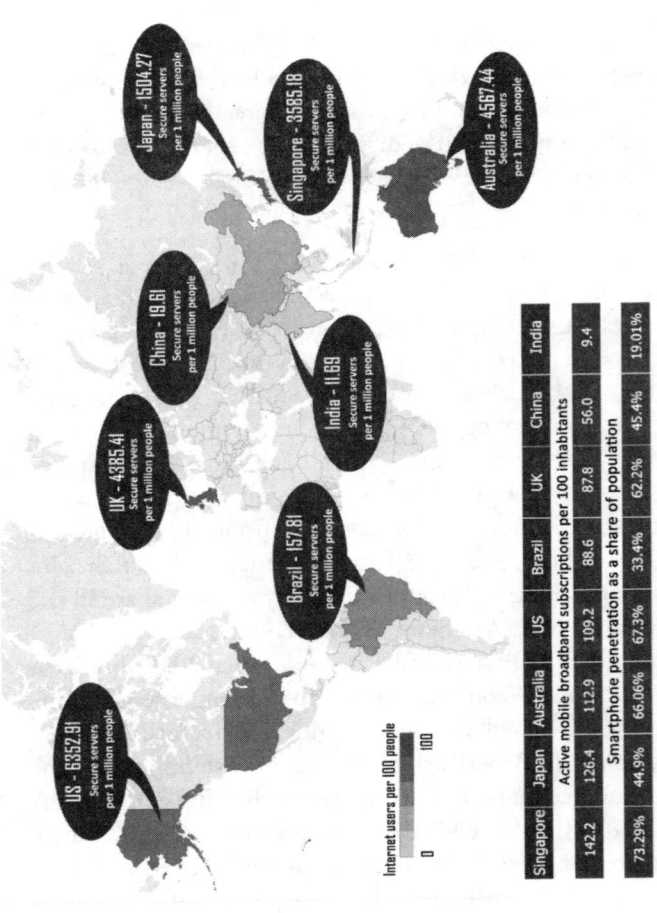

Figure 3.2 *ICT Demographics of India in Comparison to Selected Countries for Year 2015*

Source: World Bank Open Data, World Integrated Trade Solutions and Statista.

Disclaimer: This figure is not to scale. It does not represent any authentic national or international boundaries and is used for illustrative purposes only.

	Singapore	Japan	Australia	US	Brazil	UK	China	India
Active mobile broadband subscriptions per 100 inhabitants	142.2	126.4	112.9	109.2	88.6	87.8	56.0	9.4
Smartphone penetration as a share of population	73.29%	44.9%	66.06%	67.3%	33.4%	62.2%	45.4%	19.01%

The statistics suggest that in 2018, India stood at a total transaction value of $50,215 million in e-commerce via digital payments, of which $2,131.3 million accounted for mobile POS payments and the rest $38,512.6 million accounted for online payment methods. In addition, there has been a significant increase in the number of users using virtual mobile wallets, from 240.46 million users in 2017 to 318.54 million users in 2018. However, compared globally, India does not even account for one-third of the transaction value by the top four countries in terms of digital payments; rather, it is the top fourth economy with largest number of cash users (Oliveboard, n.d.). As shown in Figure 3.3, the debit and credit card penetration—primary digital payment system—was low in India in comparison to other countries. In 2018, China recorded the highest e-commerce digital payment transaction value of $1,269,792 million and the USA, Japan and the United Kingdom followed with transaction value at $884,506 million, $151,036 million and $14,911 million respectively. While the statistics for Australia and Singapore are much below that of India at $37,916 million and $9,161 million, the two countries majorly rely on digital payment systems for online transactions. Credit and debit cards are among the most popular payment options as preferred by the Australians and Singaporeans. In Australia, approximately 70 per cent of all online payments are processed using credit and debit cards and remaining 30 per cent are processed via PayPal. Similarly, Singapore has the most well-defined payment mechanism in Southeast Asia, where the overall credit or debit card penetration is very high.

While the e-commerce industry in India still struggles with some gaps in the regulations and policies with strict rules for foreign investments, Chinese government had recently opened the doors for foreign investors through free-trade zones (Horowitz & Phelan, 2015). According to the United Nations Conference on Trade and Development (UNCTAD) E-commerce Readiness Index, 2014, the United Kingdom and Australia have been ranked in top 10 countries worldwide, but, among the developing countries, Singapore and Brazil are part of the top 10 (UNCTAD, 2015). Singapore is the only Asian country to have a firm regulation system for e-commerce development in the country. It realized the importance of liberalization in providing an open-market access to e-commerce providers and took a lead in

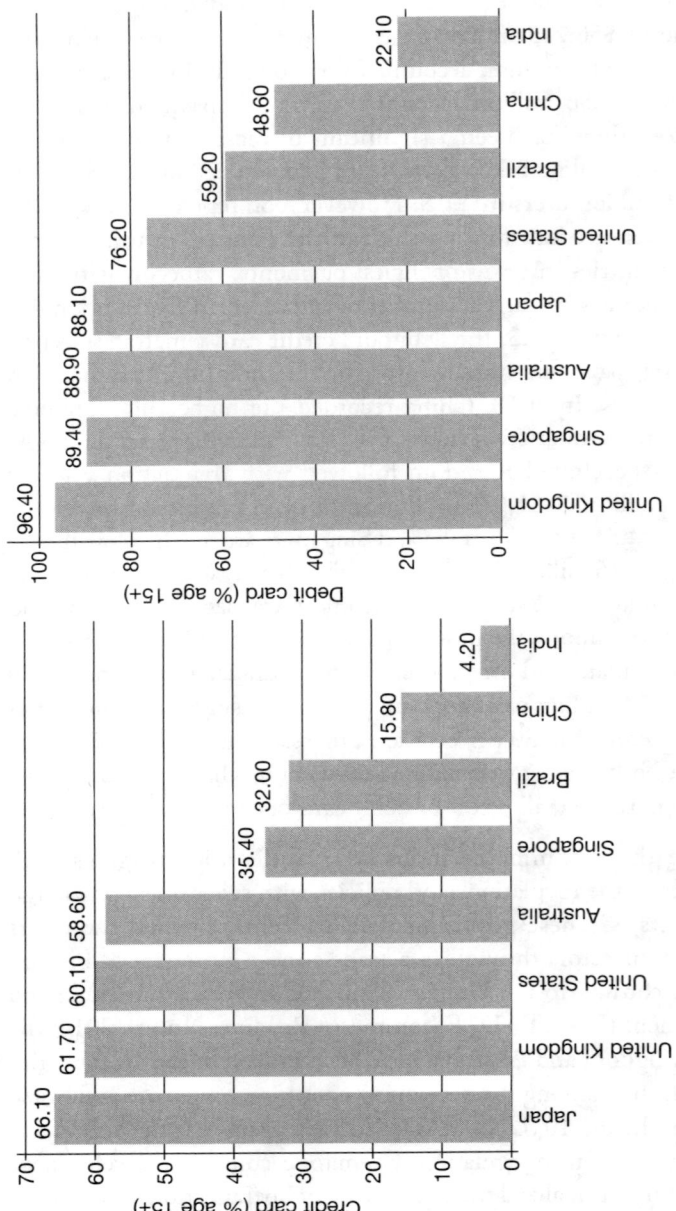

Figure 3.3 Credit and Debit Card Penetration in the Selected Countries in 2014

Source: World Integrated Trade Solution.

lowering the trade barriers and adopting many dynamic regulations to facilitate an enabling environment for growth in cross-border e-commerce. Singaporean e-commerce market is also governed by sophisticated and strengthened policies that are implemented from time-to-time since 1998 to boost consumer confidence in the industry. In Brazil too, the Brazilian Chamber of Electronic Commerce was founded by the government in May 2001 to be a representative of the digital economy. The role of the department has been fundamental for the formulation of public policies, promotion of security in electronic transactions and for the improvement of sectoral regulatory frameworks that provide legal support to the e-commerce industry. In comparison to these, India, until date does not have specific rules and regulations that govern the activities of e-commerce sector; rather, the sector faces multiple regulations from various departments on different aspects.

3.6. Policy Suggestions

In the chapter, we discussed the scenarios and issues that exist in the Indian economy concerning e-commerce, and, in addition to that, we presented a comparative study of Indian e-commerce market with the top e-commerce performing markets to highlight the gaps in India. In this section, we try to suggest some key policy changes that can be adopted by the Indian government to provide an interactive environment for the growing market.

First, there is a need for a set of rules and regulations for the e-commerce industry in India, governed by a specific department under the Ministry of Commerce and Industry, with a special focus on enhancing international trade to boost economic growth. From consumer's point of view, proper cyber-security cell should be established to protect the interests of the consumers and strengthen digital buyer penetration in the country. There is a need for discrete laws to be formulated as this sector is growing exponentially, but better policies can be formulated only with the backing of proper data. A huge lag of database for e-commerce-specific sales or exports in India makes it tough for the analysts and policymakers to track the performance and make recommendations. Therefore, e-commerce companies should start capturing the consumer database, and it should be made mandatory under the specified rules and regulations that the private companies dealing with online selling of products domestically or internationally should record it and share it with the respective Ministry to attain a better picture of digital commerce in the country.

For Indian rural areas, Internet technologies and e-commerce are still naive. Although the government has been trying to work on the digitalization of the economy since last 4–5 years and there are huge developments in the urban areas, the pace has not reached the rural masses yet. There is an urgent need to build an appropriate infrastructure and provide access to Internet and modern technological devices to these deprived regions. One of the strategies adopted by China was to cover the rural masses with smartphones instead of focusing on computers or laptops to unroll digital economy. Since smartphones are affordable, handy and easily adaptable, these can help to trap a larger population effectively and efficiently. Also, for the promotion of digital literacy and providing training for online dealings to the masses, special skill development centres should be encouraged by the government nationwide, especially in rural areas, with the help of non-governmental organizations, private companies and corporate unions, educational institutions, etc.

Another major challenge faced by Indian e-commerce sector is that although some major e-commerce platforms are domestically owned (such as Flipkart and Paytm), most of the stakes of the companies are vested in the hands of foreign investors. Huge foreign investments in Indian companies reward them with a major share in the profits and the decision-making power as well. In order to alter the situations and empower Indian investors, a law should be devised to make them preference shareholders rather than equity shareholders or, at least, to reduce the ratio of power that foreign investors can hold. Moreover, there should be a track of mergers to define and enforce the limits in power-sharing process. The government can also seek to give more control and power to the founders of Indian businesses rather than the investors. This would not only enable a shift in Indian e-commerce sector to more domestically-dominated sector but will also be a step ahead towards establishing a giant Indian e-commerce company globally.

E-commerce provides a promising platform to the micro, small and medium enterprises (MSMEs) to reach global markets and flourish their businesses. However, registering and running a business over private platforms is costly and hence not affordable by MSMEs. In such a case, a government-operated platform can be instrumental. Hence, government must aim to embark an official e-commerce platform which would provide enrolment services at subsidized rates with complete guidance for allowing ease in access to online presence for MSMEs. With the increasing universal acceptance for Indian handicrafts and handlooms, an online platform operated by the government can help in facilitating higher cross-border trading of the goods and therefore will add up to the export revenue with higher value addition to the economy. The government can start digitalization of the agricultural industry by promoting selling and buying of crops through an online platform. Although there have been certain efforts like eNAM, but those platforms are domestically operated and need to be provided with an international base. Such e-commerce platforms can also help Indian producers (especially, artisans and farmers) to buy tools and fertilizers online at cheaper rates. Thus, it can establish a link between different markets and solve the problem of price distortion.

In addition, major international giants such as Amazon, Alibaba or eBay are capturing huge market share by encouraging sale of international products in India. They are earning huge profits on Indian land, which are ultimately adding profits to the foreign markets. Thus, there is a need for realizing the share of earned profits domestically, and, for that, what can be suggested is the promotion of domestic production whereby the e-tailer advertises and sells 100 per cent 'made-in-India' products online that helps in keeping the control of firms operating in Indian mainland in the hands of domestic leaders. This will further enhance employment opportunities in India, encourage higher value additions in the economy realized at different stages of the supply chain and stimulate a regressive shift towards the growth of domestically owned e-commerce platforms.

3.7. Conclusion

In this chapter, we tried to evaluate the impact of e-commerce growth factors on economic development in the Indian context. The main purpose of the analysis was to investigate whether the rapid expansion in Internet and technological factors affecting e-commerce sector have contributed to the growth in GDP over the years. While there is a significant positive correlation between them, the regression results show a negligible effect of these developments in directing economic growth. This indicates that the current structure of Indian e-commerce sector comprises of significant gaps. As the e-commerce sector is swelling at a much faster rate than anticipated, it has become one of the key development areas in a country like India. It has helped in capitalizing the economy and creating a tech-savvy environment. It bestows a readymade platform for the businesses to break into the markets domestically as well as internationally and facilitates global trade at much lower costs. Measured in terms of social factors, e-commerce can be beneficial in skill enhancement for the population and in creation of more employment opportunities.

We further identify the key challenges faced by Indian e-commerce sector and conduct a country-wise comparative study to stress on the fact that India is still at an embryonic stage in this industry. Based on the discussion in the last two sections, we recommended a few policy suggestions that can be executed to realize the potential of e-commerce as a stepping stone towards achieving development goals. The inability to assess the direct impact of e-commerce sector on GDP mainly because of the lack of requisite data obstructs core regressions. However, since there is a necessity for formulating specifically designed policies for the development of the sector, further empirical research into the potential reasons for the inconsiderable amount of contribution of technological developments in actualizing the effect of e-commerce on economic growth, is encouraged.

References

Albastroiu, I. (2007). Contribution of the e-commerce to the economic development. *Review of Management and Economical Engineering, 6*, 3–8.

Bain & Company, Google, & Omidyar Network. (2017). Unlocking digital for Bharat: $50 billion opportunity. https://www.omidyar.com/sites/default/files/Unlocking%20Digital%20For%20Bharat_Final.pdf

DIPP. (n.d.). Discussion paper on e-commerce in India – 2013–14. Department of Industrial Policy & Promotion. https://acorninternational.org/wp-content/uploads/attachments/discussionpaper.pdf

E-commerce Digest. (n.d.). Differences: India and China. http://www.ecommerce-digest.com/regional-differences-india-and-china.html

ETtech. (2018). More than 50% of Indian consumers don't buy online after browsing: Report. *Economic Times*. https://tech.economictimes.indiatimes.com/news/internet/more-than-50-of-indian-consumers-dont-buy-online-after-browsing-report/65591418

Horowitz, J., & Phelan, A. (2015). China and India: The growing arenas for e-commerce. *USITC Executive Briefings on Trade*. https://www.usitc.gov/publications/332/executive_briefings/chinaindia_e-commerce-commissionreview.pdf

IBEF. (2017). *E-Commerce*. https://www.ibef.org/download/Ecommerce-July-2017.pdf

Jain, N. (2016). Why Indian e-commerce needs to be 'made in India'. *YourStory*. https://yourstory.com/2016/09/indian-e-commerce-made-in-india

Mehra, A. (2015). E-commerce industry in India. https://www.coursehero.com/file/20072007/Atin-Mehra-IMT-E-Retail-Final-6/

Ministry of Finance. (2015). *Economic Survey of India 2014–15*. Economics Division, Ministry of Finance, Government of India.

Mundy, S., & Lucas, L. (2018). Alibaba targets India as key ecommerce battleground. *Financial Times*.

Oliveboard. (n.d.). India's movement towards a cashless economy: An Analysis. https://www.oliveboard.in/blog/cash-to-cashless-digital-india-economy-analysis-upsc-ias-current-affairs-gk-exam-study/

Saha, D. (2015). E-commerce market: India way behind China. *The Hans India*. https://www.thehansindia.com/posts/index/Hans/2015-06-18/E-Commerce-market-India-way-behind-China/157804

Sethi, S. (2018). Why India's ecommerce policies have missed their mark. *Economic Times*. https://economictimes.indiatimes.com/small-biz/startups/newsbuzz/why-indias-ecommerce-policies-have-missed-their-mark/articleshow/64072169.cms?from=mdr

Sharma, M. R. (2014). Evolution of e-commerce in India: Creating the bricks behind the clicks. PwC India and ASSOCHAM. https://www.pwc.in/assets/pdfs/publications/2014/evolution-of-e-commerce-in-india.pdf

Singh, J. (2014). Review of e-commerce security challenges. *International Journal of Innovative Research in Computer and Communication Engineering*, *2* (2), 2850–2858.

Suominen, K. (2017). Fueling the e-commerce boom in U.S.-UK Trade. Centre for Strategic and International Studies.

Sridharan, V. 2018. Flipkart vs. Amazon—the online retail battleground heating up in India. DW Akademie. https://www.csis.org/blogs/future-digital-trade-policy-and-role-us-and-uk/fueling-ecommerce-boom-us-uk-trade

Statista. Statistics and market data about e-commerce. https://www.statista.com/

UNCTAD. (2015). *Information economy report 2015: Unlocking the potential of e-commerce for developing countries.* New York and Geneva: United Nations.

World Integrated Trade Solution. https://wits.worldbank.org/

Wu, H. (2016). 900 million Indians can't get online: Here's why. *CNN Tech.* https://money.cnn.com/2016/03/09/technology/india-internet-access/.

CHAPTER 4

The E-Platform Economy
A Study of Market Structure and Implications

Zaki Hussain and Parkhi Vats

4.1. Introduction

E-commerce platforms (e-platforms) around the world are comforting day-to-day life of humans, be it ordering our food, hailing a cab, paying online, befriending an old lost friend or sharing your thoughts on social media. It is an easy, fast and convenient medium. With each step, we are becoming an integral part of the digital economy. With the creation of digital economy, it is pertinent that there will be change of rules in the existent traditional market structures. The change of rules in market structure of e-platforms mainly occurs because of its typical features such as first-mover advantage, network effects, type of business model (multi/two-sided), role of data, etc. It has been estimated that the value of cross-border data flow could reach up to $20 trillion by 2025, which shows the enormous potential that e-platforms can have on any economy. Owing to this enormous potential, it becomes imperative to study their market structure and the implication on the economy.

This chapter is exploratory in nature, as it attempts to unveil the nature of market structure followed by the majority of dominant e-platforms and the concerns associated with them. It also throws some light on the implication of the changing market share and the existing barriers to entry in the fair and healthy competition in the economy. The chapter eventually tries to raise concerns with respect to the possible gaps between developed and developing nations because of the unbalanced growth of the Internet-based economy, as e-platform players around the globe have immense potential either to reduce or widen the gap of economic equality.

The chapter has been broadly divided into six sections. Section 4.2 attempts to decipher the business model of e-platforms and tries to raise some concerns associated with them. Section 4.3 talks about the concept of the relevant market of e-platforms, followed by the analysis of some judgements with respect to the relevant market of e-platforms. Section 4.4 discusses the basic fundamentals of the market structure and their different forms, followed by a literature review with respect to the similarities between the oligopoly and the e-platform. Section 4.5 talks about the key characteristics of market structure with the focus on market share and barriers to entry to e-platforms. Section 4.6 analyses the implication of the growing market share of few dominant players on fair competition in the economy. This section also tries to raise concerns regarding the barriers to entry faced by new e-commerce entrants. Last section, that is, Section 4.7, concludes the entire study.

4.2. Business Model of E-Platforms: Functioning and Emerging Concerns

The marketplace of e-platforms can be broadly categorized into two forms: (a) two-sided market and (b) multi-sided market. Two-sided markets genarally have two communities of users such that a viable economic model ensures that both these communities have incentive to participate (Tirole, 2017). For example, payment systems, like American Express, have to ensure that they attract consumers who can readily use them and, at the same time, make sure that the merchants accept the same. Therefore, Tirole (2017) in his book, *Economics for the Common Good*, states that 'every two-sided platform faces the chicken–egg problem' as they do not know which side of the market will grow first. He further adds that in such markets, the pricing is based on the elasticity of demand of the respective community of users. Such that,

> If one side of the market benefits a lot from the interactions with the other side, then the platform can charge more to the former and in a 'seesaw' pattern, will want to charge less to the later side to make it attractive to join. (Tirole, 2017)

Under certain cases, it might happen that one section is enjoying the services for free while the other pays for both.

A multi-sided platform (MSP), on the other hand, 'provides a support that facilitates interactions (or transactions) among the two or more constituents (sides) that it serves, such that members of one side are more likely to get on board the MSP when more members of another side do so' (Hagiu, 2009). Alphabet Inc.-owned Google. com is a classic example of MSP (see Figure 4.1), as it has affiliation with many sides, including customers of its multiple products, software and application developers, advertisers, and the companies that are manufacturing hardware products like Nexus smartphones and tablets, Chromecast and Chrome OS notebooks, etc., for them.

The e-platforms globally have been found to have two peculiar attributes: The first is the network externality. 'Network effect/

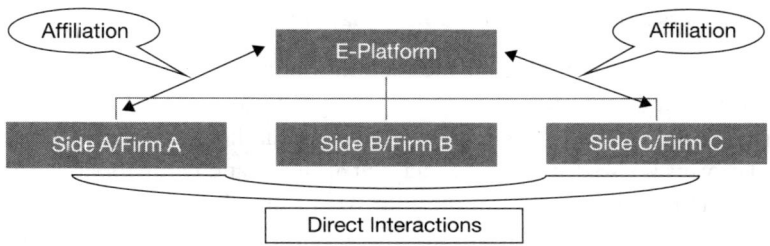

Figure 4.1 *E-Platforms/Multi-Sided Platforms*

externality has been defined as a change in the benefit, or surplus, that an agent derives from a good when the number of other agents consuming the same kind of good changes' (Margolis & Liebowitz, 1998). The most common example is that of a fax machine: An increase in the popularity of a fax machine will lead to its increasing value since it will have greater use. Similarly, if our friends are on Facebook, we have an urge to be there too. Network effects have direct impact (e.g., the increase in fax machines sold or more users joining Facebook) and indirect impact (e.g., an increase in the demand of toners, cartridges and an increase in the popularity of social networking sites). The second is the unique pricing strategy followed by e-platforms. E-platforms pricing technique usually involves charging low prices on one side of the market, which in most of the cases creates a scenario of predatory pricing in order to drive out competition, and charging higher prices on the other side of the market, which creates the scenario of 'monopoly pricing' (Tirole, 2017).

We have often witnessed that due to its peculiar attributes, e-platform markets are highly concentrated and are often dominated by one or few companies, for example, Google in the search engine market, Facebook in the social networking market and Amazon in the Internet retail market. This dominance of a few companies in the area of e-platforms creates a significant impact on the competition and market structure. A study conducted by Lina M. Khan (2016) argues, 'real competition in the twenty-first century marketplace—especially in the case of online platforms—requires analyzing the underlying structure and dynamics of markets'. The study further argues that 'a company's power and the potential anticompetitive nature of that power cannot be fully understood without looking at the structure of a business and the structural role it plays in markets'.

Due to the complex business models and their potential impact on the competition, it becomes imperative to look into their market structure in detail. The need to study the market structure of these platforms is also driven by the fact that antitrust and regulatory policies affecting business that compete in MSPs should also consider the implication for the small and medium enterprises (SMEs), specifically in the developing world. Hence, it is important that we analyse what kind of market structure the online platforms are trying to create and whether the benefits are passed on to the producers, consumers and the market at large.

4.3. Theoretical Framework for Establishing E-Platforms as Relevant Markets

To discuss any form of market structure, it is a prerequisite to define a specific market or a sector for which the analysis is required to be done. Under the traditional market structure, relevant markets have been broadly divided into product market, geographic market and temporal market (Slot & Farley, 2017). Table 4.1 shows some of the categories for establishing relevant markets under the traditional market structure. However, in most of the cases, all the three concepts are taken into consideration simultaneously, subject to the characteristics of the product.

So, based on the categorization as depicted in Table 4.1, is there any possibility of juxtaposing relevant market categories of the traditional markets over the e-platforms? Now, at the product level, e-platforms deal in both homogenous and heterogeneous products and services. With respect to the geographical markets, any person who has access to Internet comes under the relevant market for a particular set of product or services provided at the e-platforms. As no clear winner emerges under these specific scenarios, we need to analyse other attempts made in order to establish e-platforms as relevant markets.

A study by the Belousova (2010) focused on 'whether e-commerce forms a new relevant market, or whether e-commerce shapes a new retail channel, which competes with traditional retail channel, and lies within the same market'. The study in its conclusion stated that e-commerce creates a new channel to trade a physical product and

> the competition authorities could identify the relevant product market for the physical product traded online as: 1) a distinct relevant product market and 2) a part of the relevant product market consisting of two retail channels: in-store and the Internet,

Table 4.1 Categories of Relevant Markets under Traditional Market Structure

Category	Definition	Measures/Cases
Product market	Products which are adequately substitutable for the product under investigation fall under the category of product market. In other words, say for product A, firms manufacturing that product will constitute the relevant market	1. Cross elasticity $$\text{Cross Elasticity of Demand} CED_{X,Y} = \frac{\%\text{ increase in quantity demanded of A}}{\%\text{ increase in price of product B}}$$ If cross-price elasticity is positive and significant then it can be concluded that the products are indeed substitutes for one another. Any product that has significant cross-price elasticity with say product A should belong to the appropriate market for that product. 2. Small but significant and non-transitory increase in price (SSNIP) test The basic purpose of the test is to check whether the consumer will switch from one product to another if the price of all supply were increased by small amount, and, if the consumer switch, the products can be constituted as substitute and subsequently the relevant market could be defined. 3. Elzinga-Hogarty Test This involves two major steps. For instance, if one is interested in finding the relevant market for hospital X, then (Step 1) the focus will be to figure out geographical spread of a significant fraction of the existing hospital patients (usually, 90%) and (Step 2) will be to identify all hospitals that a significant number of patients in this region (usually, 90%) visit for their medical needs. In this case, the market for hospital X encompasses all those hospitals identified in the later step (see a Boshoff, 2006)
Geographical market	The firms that are located very far from each other do not pose competitive threat to each other.	
Temporal market	In such cases, supply or the demand becomes heavily dependent on the time. For example, during the time of Christmas one could easily see the surge in the supply of Christmas gifts or related items	For example, in a case related to OPEC, the relevant market for oil was limited to a specific period of time.

the current case law states that a physical product traded over the Internet constitutes a separate relevant product market.

4.3.1 Analysis of Some Judgements with Respect to the Relevant Market of E-Commerce Platforms

While exploring the legal text and the judgements with respect to the relevant market in case of the e-commerce platforms, it was seen that the judgements have taken into consideration both quantitative and qualitative dimensions. However, they vary on case-to-case basis, with more emphasis on quantitative proxies. An example is the Otto/ Grattan case[1] from the early 1990s of separate markets for products sold on Internet. Here, catalogue mail ordering was considered as a separate relevant product market for non-food products; the reason given was the different shopping experience than that of product differentiation. Another case (of merger) was that of Bertelsmann/ HAVAS,[2] where the commission distinguished separate product markets for the books traded in store and for the books sold by the distance selling including the Internet. However, both these cases were developed in the late 20th century. Since it was a time when selling thing over Internet was considered an emerging activity and the e-selling was expanding rapidly, more recent judgements on the issue are required to be explored.

In India, recent and prominent cases regarding this issue include the Mohit Manglani vs Flipkart case[3] and Ashish Ahuja vs Snapdeal case[4] where, in the former, Competition Commission of India (CCI)

---

[1] See Case No IV/M.070 - OTTO/GRATTAN of Commission of the European Communities, 1991. https://ec.europa.eu/competition/mergers/cases/decisions/m70_en.pdf

[2] See Case No IV/M.1459-BERTELSMANN/HAVAS/BOL of Commission of the European Communities, 1999. https://ec.europa.eu/competition/mergers/cases/decisions/m1459_en.pdf

[3] CCI Case No. 80 of 2014. https://www.cci.gov.in/sites/default/files/802014.pdf

[4] CCI Case No. 17 of 2014. https://www.cci.gov.in/sites/default/files/172014.pdf

left open the definition of relevant market for e-portals as a separate market or as a sub-segment of the market for distribution. In the latter case, the CCI explained that both offline and online markets differ in terms of discounts and shopping experience. However, in a case against Flipkart, Amazon, Jabong Snapdeal and Myntra with respect to the predatory pricing, the CCI refused to demarcate online market as a distinct market of goods/service transactions, and have recognized it only as a distribution channel rather than a separate market. Moreover, in the Fast Track Call Cabs and Meru vs Ola case,[5] the CCI defined separate relevant market for radio taxi services, distinguishing it from other modes of transport such as auto-rickshaws, buses and other private taxis in the country. The commission stated that radio taxi services are similar to the services given by e-platform for taxi services (e.g., Ola, Uber, etc.).

Some jurisprudence with respect to the definition of relevant markets for digital products includes a European Commission case in which a conclusion was made that 'digital product shapes a distinctive relevant product market on basis of immediate access and content consumption in comparison with acquiring a physical CD'. In another case related to print media industry, it was concluded that, 'the digital versions (including the CD-ROM and online download) and paper versions belong to different relevant product markets due to special marketing reasons, high price and without possibility to substitute a digital version from supply side' (Belousova, 2010)

In conclusion, based on different judgements, it can be said that the concept of relevant markets, especially with respect to e-platforms/e-commerce, is very fluid in nature such that it varies on a case-to-case basis, considering the situation and maturity of the e-commerce indus-try/sector of a country. However, to implement the concept of relevant market for e-platforms, a harmonized set of rules can be prepared with the help of past judgements of the competition authorities of different countries around the world.

---

[5] CCI Case No. 6 & 74 of 2015. https://www.cci.gov.in/sites/default/files/6%20%26%2074%20of%202015.pdf

4.4. Fundamentals of Market Structure and Its Linkage with E-Commerce Platforms: Exploration of Existing Literature

Traditionally, market structures are divided into two forms: the perfect competition and the imperfect competition. The perfect competition market structure is based on a simple fundament: There are many firms such that an individual firm has no power to influence the market, and, consequently, each firm must accept the price set by the forces of demand and supply. This form of market structure is generally associated with classical economist theorists see perfect competition as a prerequisite for market clearance (Marshall, 2009; Robinson, 1969). Classical economic theorists believed that markets generally regulate themselves, when free of coercion. Adam Smith (1937) referred to this concept as 'invisible hand'.

On the other hand, the imperfect competition market structure is considered identical to the realistic market conditions where different markets such as monopoly, oligopoly and duopoly exist and dominate the market conditions. The elements of these market structures include the number and size of firms/sellers, entry barriers/conditions, pricing, profit margins, information about other firms and standardization of product/product differentiation (Nguyen & Kira, 2001). For different forms of market structure and their characteristics, see Table 4.2.

Based on the broad characteristics of e-commerce markets in different countries, there is a general perception that they represent oligopoly form of market. This perception is generally made because of three reasons: the dominance of a few firms in this market, presence of high entry barriers for new firms and tough price competition among the dominant firms. However, just on the basis of perception, one cannot generalize that e-platforms have oligopoly structure. To find whether there is any link between the two, it become imperative to understand the oligopoly market. In broad terms, oligopoly is a market structure in which there are a few rival sellers and many buyers; every firm (seller) deals in specific sets of products or services; there are high barriers to entry for other firms that want to enter into the same business and compete; however, these characteristics are best defined by the actual behaviour of the rival firms.

Table 4.2 Major Characteristics Different Market Structure

Characteristics	Perfect Competition	Oligopoly	Monopoly	Monopolistic Competition
Sellers	Numerous	Few sellers	Only one seller	Many suppliers of same product
Market share	Low	High	Very high	Low
Price	Price taker	Price maker	Price maker	Price maker
Product	Homogeneous products	Homogeneous/ slightly differentiated	Differentiated products	Differentiated product
Barriers to entry and exit	Free entry and exit	Low percentage of entry	Entry is blocked	Low barriers to entry
Profitability	Low	High	Very high	High
Interdependence on firms	No dependency	High rate of dependency	No dependency	No dependency
Information	Full information	Low information	Low information to buyers	Low information

Source: Authors compilation based on the studies by Koutsoyiannis (1975) and Nguyen and Kira (2001).

In addition, an important element of this structure is the interdependence of these rival firms. If these firms realize their mutual interdependence, they collude maximizing their industry's profits. Whereas, whenever they fail to realize this interdependence, they fail to maximize industry's profits and often cause price wars and market failures. In the former case, they are called collusive oligopolies and, in the latter, non-collusive oligopolies. The presence of these oligopolies in any product or service market significantly affects the level of competition faced by the existing firms and potential entrants in the market.

Goods and services under e-commerce platforms are mainly bought and sold through six modes or market segments involving businesses, consumers and administration which are Business-to-Business (B2B), Business-to-Consumer (B2C), Consumer-to-Consumer (C2C), Consumer-to-Business (C2B), Business-to-Administration (B2A) and Consumer-to-Administration (C2A). A study conducted by Zhang and Wang (2018) on C2C and B2C e-commerce market in China has found that these marketplaces have a counterintuitive structure of outer market resembling oligopoly and inner markets resembling effective competition. They distinguished the two by defining inner markets as the virtual markets facilitated by marketplace platforms and outer markets as the market for platform providers. Table 3 depicts the characteristics of B2C and C2C retail markets in China as per the study conducted on three Alibaba-owned companies Taobao, Tmall and JD.com (Zhang & Wang, 2018).

The outer market (platform providers) shares many characteristics of the oligopoly market structure, including limited competition, domination of a few firms, high entry barriers, asymmetric cost and firm's taking into consideration their rival's reaction. While the inner market, which constitute numerous third party sellers with large consumer base (example: buyers and sellers of products in Amazon and Flipkart) which are price takers with low market concentration demonstrates the characteristics of perfect competition market structure.

A similar analysis, as discussed above, can be done for this chapter, but, due to lack of data availability, such analysis was not feasible. However, the chapter will attempt to find similarities between the

Table 4.3 *Assessment of Market Structure and Outcomes of B2C and C2C Markets in China*

	Outer Market (Platform Provider)	*Inner Markets Other Sides/Buyers/Sellers*
No. of sellers and buyers	Few/mainly 3	Many/numerous
Market concentration	High (~83%)	Low
Price	Price-maker	Price-taker
Cost	Asymmetric	Asymmetric
Information transparency	High	High
Barriers to entry and exit	High	Low-medium
Profitability	High	Majority low
Model of market structure	Oligopoly	Effective competition

Source: Compiled by authors based on the study by Zhang and Wang (2018).

Note: The assessment is based on three firms: Taobao, Tmall, JD.com

e-platforms globally and the oligopoly market structure by focusing on the key characteristics of the latter.

4.5. Key Characteristics of the Market Structure with Respect to E-Platforms

4.5.1 Market Share (Dominance) and Market Concentration

The economic analysis with respect to the market share and concentration of the undertakings is of great importance in the application of the competition law, specifically with respect to mergers around the world. This is because it helps competition authorities to know the presence of dominant position and the abuse of dominance by the undertakings. 'A large combined market share among a few undertakings may indicate that they form a dominant group and that a situation exists which poses a danger to competition' (OECD, 1999). Analysis of market share helps competition authorities to control the emergence of oligopoly in the market (e.g., if a dominant oligopoly already exists in a particular relevant market, then a merger between two of its undertakings will lead to the oligopoly becoming even stronger).

Many countries have tried to define their criteria for determining the presence of dominant position and the abuse in their antitrust/competition law. This also includes market share of undertakings as a criterion. For instance, in German law, within the framework of merger control, Section 19 of the Act against Restraints of Competition says that 'an oligopoly is presumed to be dominant if it:—consists of three or fewer undertakings reaching a combined market share of 50 percent, or—consists of five or fewer undertakings reaching a combined market share of two thirds' (OECD, 1999). The European Commission, while defining oligopoly under Article 2(3) of the EC Merger Regulation states,

> [T]he Commission will look at the market shares of the suppliers in the market. If a few companies have very large market shares, say three companies have 25 percent each, and the rest of the supply is accounted for by ten smaller suppliers each with 2–3 percent market share, then this could be an indication that the ten smaller companies should be considered fringe companies, who are simply followers to the larger companies. (OECD, 1999)

For examples, Table 4.4 depicts the market share of Internet retailing companies (e-platforms) based on the retail value or the retail selling price (excluding sales tax). As per the share criterion mentioned before, the market shares of selected developing countries are relatively much more dominant as compared to the selected developed countries. This picture represents the presence of oligopoly form of market in selected developing countries relative to the developed world. The table also includes the annual growth of market shares of companies which shows that on an average, the growth of top players remained positive over the last 3–4 years which indicates the presence of oligopoly form of market in the near future.

The share analysis done for the Internet retailing companies (e-platform) assumes the relevant market as all e-tail platforms that

Table 4.4 Share of Top Five Internet Retailing Companies (B2C) Based on Retail Value (Retail Selling Price Excluding Sales Tax)

Selected Developing Countries (Value in Percentage)

China	India	Indonesia	Malaysia	Brazil	Thailand
Alibaba Group Holding Ltd 43.5 (-1%)	Flipkart Online Services Pvt Ltd 39.5 (15%)	Alibaba Group Holding Ltd 21.6 (NA)	Alibaba Group Holding Ltd 29.9 (NA)	Lojas Americanas SA 21.3 (NA)	Alibaba Group Holding Ltd 17.1 (NA)
JD.com Inc. 20.2 (16%)	Jasper Infotech Pvt. Ltd 30.2 (38%)	XL Axiata Tbk PT 9.2 (NA)	Amazon.com Inc. 23.5 (-4%)	Mercado Libre SRL 14.1 (2%)	Charoen Pokphand Group 16.3 (37%)
Suning Commerce Group Co Ltd 3.1 (0%)	Amazon.com Inc. 12.1 (116%)	Rocket Internet GmbH 4.5 (17%)	Apple Inc. 6.7 (-6%)	Casino Guichard-Perrachon SA 12.4 (-2%)	Amazon.com Inc. 7.7 (-5%)
Vipshop Holdings Ltd 2.7 (22%)	Dell Inc. 2.8 (-40%)	Giosis Group 3.8 (20%)	Dell Inc. 6 (-20%)	Magazine Luiza SA 4.4 (5%)	Apple Inc. 4.1 (-9%)
GOME Electrical Appliances Holding Ltd 1.6 (21%)	Rocket Internet GmbH 1.1 (-22%)	Bhinneka Mentari Dimensi PT 3.2 (-3%)	Rocket Internet GmbH 5.3 (-1%)	Netshoes Comércio Ltd 4 (14%)	Big C Supercenter PCL 4 (NA)
Total share of top five cos 71.1	Total share of top five cos 85.7	Total share of top five cos 42.3	Total share of top five cos 71.4	Total share of top five cos 56.2	Total share of top five cos 49.2

Selected Developed Countries (Value in Percentage)

Japan		Canada		France		Germany		UK		US	
Amazon.com Inc	20.2 (2%)	Amazon.com Inc	10.2 (-12%)	Amazon.com Inc	10.7 (7%)	Amazon.com Inc	40.8 (3%)	Amazon.com Inc	26.5 (4%)	Amazon.com Inc	33 (6%)
Rakuten Inc	20.1 (-1%)	eBay Inc	6.4 (-14%)	Casino Guichard-Perrachon SA	9.9 (6%)	eBay Inc	15 (-1%)	eBay Inc	10.1 (-1%)	Walmart Stores Inc.	7.8 (8%)
Softbank Corp	8.9 (9%)	Apple Inc.	3.4 (-11%)	E Leclerc	7.5 (8%)	Otto Group	11.2 (-3%)	Tesco Plc	6.6 (-7%)	eBay Inc.	7.4 (-10%)
Apple Inc.	4.6 (-3%)	Wal-Mart Stores Inc.	3.2 (17%)	Vente-privee. com SAS	5.3 (-3%)	Apple Inc.	3.6 (5%)	Home Retail Group Plc	4.1 (-7%)	Apple Inc.	4.7 (-4%)
Seven & I Holdings Co Ltd	3.7 (46%)	Best Buy Co Inc.	1.6 (-20%)	Auchan Group SA	3.8 (-5%)	Zalando SE	3.1 (10%)	John Lewis Partnership Plc	3.5 (4%)	Valve Corp	1.8 (9%)
Total share of top five cos	57.5	Total share of top five cos	24.8	Total share of top five cos	37.2	Total share of top five cos	73.7	Total share of top five cos	50.8	Total share of top five cos	54.7

Source: Authors compilation based on Euro Monitor database.

Note: Values in brackets are the CAGR of Company Share from 2013-2016.

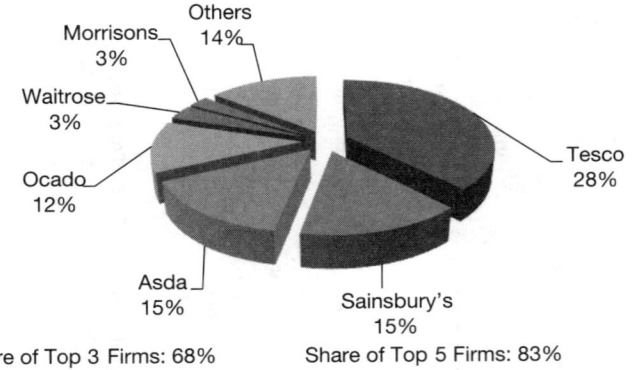

Share of Top 3 Firms: 68%   Share of Top 5 Firms: 83%

Figure 4.2 *Market Share of Firms Dealing in Online Grocery in United Kingdom*

Source: Compiled by authors based on the study by USDA Foreign Agriculture Service (2017).

are selling heterogeneous products under different market segments. A similar analysis can also be done by narrowing down the definition of the relevant market; however, such analysis is difficult to conduct due to the non-availability of relevant data and information. The e-platforms are not segregated enough with respect to specific segment of a market/industry. For instance, see Figure 4.2 for market share of firms dealing in online grocery in the United Kingdom. The figure clearly depicts the high concentration of firms, where top three firms account for 58 per cent of market share and top five firms account for 73 per cent of market share. This type of market clearly represents oligopoly form of market structure based on the share and the concentration criterion.

However, as explained earlier, segregating the firms into further sub-segments with respect to particular category of products or services is difficult as many e-platforms deal in heterogeneous products and services (e.g., same grocery items can be ordered from Amazon as well as on the Tesco).

While exploring the market share of e-platforms operating in other areas, high market share and concentration of few companies/platforms were found to be common among all (see Figure 4.3). This

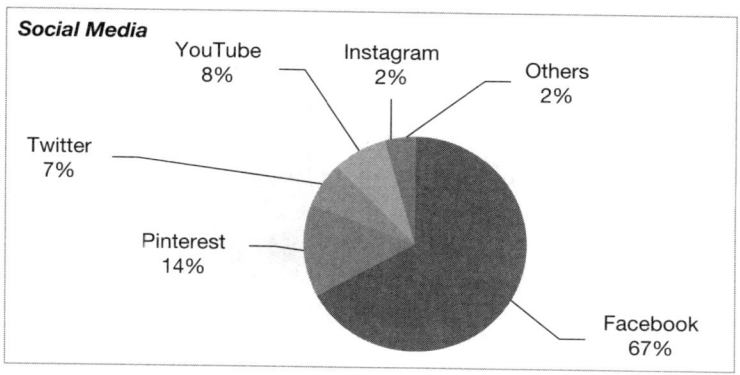

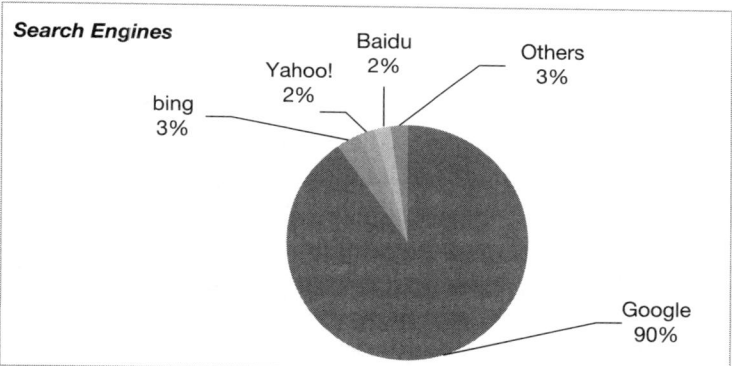

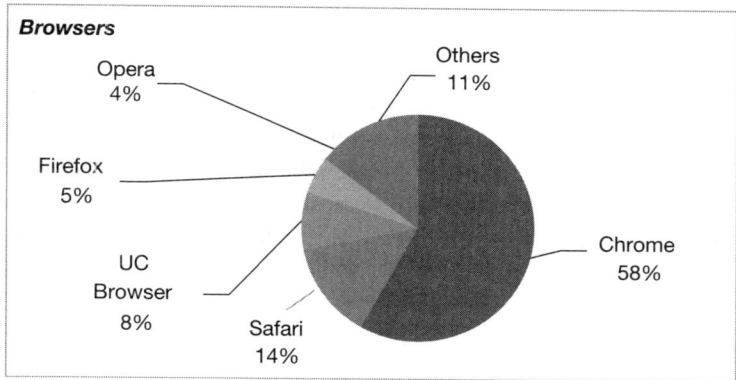

Figure 4.3 *How Dominant Are E-Platforms?*

Segment-wise global market share (value in %).

Source: Authors compilation based on the database of Statista.com (2018).

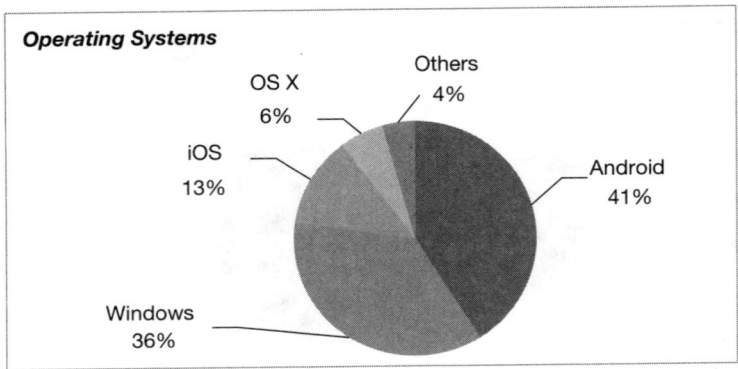

Figure 4.3 *Continued*

again fulfils one of the conditions of oligopoly market structure and raises the concern for competition authorities around the globe to check for the presence of dominance and subsequently for the abuse of dominance in the relevant market.

4.5.1.1 Market Concentration of E-Platforms

Another aspect to check the presence of dominance or oligopoly market is to look for the market concentration of undertakings in the market. Market concentration is one of the criteria that helps in segregating the markets in different forms, for instance, monopoly represents highest concentration (usually one firm is having 90–95% or more market share). In case of a perfect competition, concentration of the firms is recorded to be the lowest. In case of the oligopoly form of market, the concentration is somewhere between the perfect competition and monopoly but is closer to the monopoly. There are different methods through which market concentration can be calculated, such as Lerner Index, N-firm concentration ratio, Hirschman Herfindahl Index (HHI), Rothschild Index, etc. Among these, HHI is the most commonly used index.

$$HHI = \sum_{i=1}^{N} S_i^2$$

where S_i is the market share of firm I, and N is the number of firms.

US Department of Justice and the Federal Trade Commission consider a market with an HHI as follows:

1. HHI < 1,500 as un-concentrated market
2. 1,500 < HHI > 2,500 as moderately concentrated market
3. HHI > 2,500 as highly concentrated market

The HHI value 0 indicates perfectly un-concentrated market, and HHI value of 10,000 indicates pure monopoly (to compare the above value with respect to Internet retailing e-platforms, see the values in parentheses in Figure 4.4).

To segregate the market on the basis of the HHI value, Venuvinod (2011) suggest that 'an industry is considered competitive with an HHI smaller than 0.2, oligopolistic with HHI between 0.2 and 0.6, and monopolistic with HHI above 0.6'. Figure 4.5 depicts the HHI value of Internet retailing companies (B2C e-platforms) in selected developing and developed countries; the HHI value indicated is the average of years 2014–2016. It is clearly visible from the figure that in case of the selected developed countries, the overall market concentration is recorded to be low as compared to the selected developing countries. Among the selected developing countries, the highest concentration is recorded for India (0.27) and China (0.23); whereas, for the developed countries, Germany has the highest concentration of Internet retailing companies which also falls into the oligopoly market structure criterion, as its HHI value is greater than 0.2.

Apart from the HHI value, growth in the market concentration and HHI value over a period of time are also important determinants of market structure. Figure 4.5 depicts the compound annual growth rate of HHI from 2010 to 2016. The growth in the value of HHI was recorded positive for almost all the countries except Canada, where the concentration over a period of time has decreased. The highest growth in the HHI value in developing countries set was recorded for Indonesia and India. Whereas, for developed countries set, it was the highest for USA and Germany. Based on the historical change in the concentration level, it could be said that the market structure for

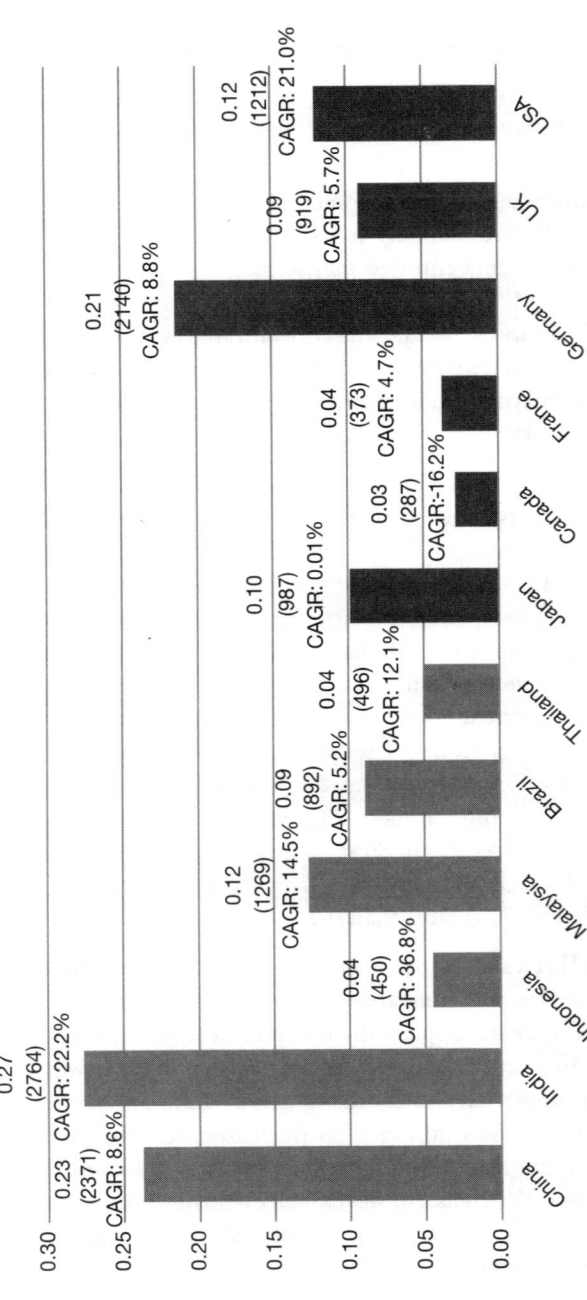

Figure 4.4 *Concentration/HHI of Internet Retailing Companies (B2C E-Platforms) in Selected Countries*

Source: Authors compilation based on Euro Monitor Data base

— HHI value on top of the bar ranges from 0 to 1.
— HHI value in bracket () ranges from 0 to 10,000.
— CAGR Value is the growth in the HHI value from 2010 to 2016.

Selected developing countries average = 0.53   Selected developed countries average = 0.36

Note: The HHI value indicated is the average of 2014-2016.

Internet retailing e-platforms may become oligopolistic for most of the countries in the near future.

However, to explore the market structure of the e-platforms further and its challenges with respect to competition, it would be essential to look into the existing barriers to entry faced by new entrants.

4.5.2. Barriers to Entry under E-Commerce Market

In this section, we discuss the possible presence of entry barriers in the e-commerce market for a new entrant and try distinguishing these from the barriers to set up a fully functional e-commerce market in an economy. Barriers to establish a fully functional e-commerce market can be broadly divided into three types:

1. *Lack of socio-economic development.* Many developing countries have inactive e-commerce markets because of poor consumer confidence in technology, lack of personal contact and language barriers (Lawrence & Tar, 2010). This is primarily because they see shopping as a personal and not a virtual experience.
2. *Infrastructural barriers.* Success of an e-commerce market fundamentally requires the presence of basic infrastructure. However, many countries still face problems such as poor access to technology (computers and connectivity to Internet), limited bandwidth and poor telecommunications (Lawrence & Tar, 2010). For instance, in many developing nations, the cost of computers and Internet connectivity far surpasses the monthly wage of the average earning person (Kommerskollegium, 2012).
3. *Political barriers.* The sheer absence of national Internet provision and regulation policy in many countries means that the government is not involved in Internet provisions (Lawrence & Tar, 2010).

Apart from these three barriers, there are a few barriers faced by a new player while entering the e-commerce/e-platform market. These barriers are generally different from what is seen in the traditional markets and, in some cases, are considered as anti-competitive practices. An attempt has been made to explain some of the strategies used by the e-platform owners to deter new entry into their markets. The strategies are then supported by case studies on some of the e-platform players. One of these strategies is 'divide and conquer'. Segal and Whinston (2000), in their research work, explained a crucial concept of naked exclusion[6] with the strategy of 'divide and conquer'. In analysis of this strategy, they consider an industry (with some assumptions) in which a new entrant needs a minimum level of sales to be viable in the market. In this case, if the incumbent firm wants to deter the entry of the new entrant, they need to convince just one buyer to stay with the incumbent and not switch to the new entrant (say by providing some incentive to this buyer). Therefore, the only buyer that turns away from the new entrant prevents the new entrant from reaching its viable level of sales. Hence, deterring any new entry and creating an entry barrier. This makes the incumbent the only available seller in the market from whom all other buyers are forced to make their purchases even if the incumbent sells at monopoly prices.

The final buyers are worse off in this case of monopoly than they would have been under the presence of a second efficient supplier (duopoly). Hence, the incumbent only needs to compensate the buyer that chooses to stay with them and turns away from the new entrant. This compensation, therefore, becomes the 'price' the incumbent must pay to monopolize the market.

Internet-based companies are vastly driven by discounts and competitive pricing, where consumers opt for the platforms with best offers and least prices. Therefore, customer loyalty is missing in this sector. However, some e-platform owners have devised ways in which they hook a section of their consumer base such that they do not switch over to their competitors (see a case study on Zomato).

---

[6] It can be defined as the ability of the incumbent firm to deter entry by writing exclusionary contracts (not able to ignore offers) so that the consumers stay with the incumbent firm rather than shifting to the new entrant.

Case Example: Zomato

Zomato has launched Zomato gold that offers two kinds of subscription to its customers—gold for dinning out and gold for nightlife. Under gold for dinning out, customers get complementary dishes across the menu with every meal they order at a partner restaurant on a plus one basis. Similarly, with the gold for nightlife, Zomato offers customers up to two complementary drinks (*The Pioneer*, 2018).

With the lure of these complementary dishes and drinks, customers choose to become Zomato gold members. Once a customer becomes a member, they would voluntarily want to extract maximum utility of the price paid to avail Zomato gold services. In this process, the customer involuntarily hooks themselves to choose services provided by Zomato gold over any other competing food app. Both instances consequently reach to the same natural reaction of hooking a customer close to Zomato and away from the competing rivals like Swiggy.

Further, the ready availability of a subscribed application reduces a consumer's chances of installing applications or visiting sites of other close competitors providing similar services. Thus, with the launch of Zomato gold services, it has succeeded in creating a group of loyal customers in the form Zomato gold members who, even when provided with the services of the next efficient seller (Swiggy), would choose to avail Zomato's services.

However, a relevant point over here is that the final buyers from Zomato are a mix of Zomato gold members and non-members. While the Zomato gold members avail complementary dishes, the non-members pay more to avail same services from same partner restaurants. Further, Zomato closes its membership for short duration, which stocks up their supply against their increasing demand and projects Zomato gold memberships as a 'closed niche membership'.

The study by Segal and Whinston (2000) further explains the fact that a single buyer, while deciding which seller to buy from, only considers his/her own pay off and not that of the entire market. Therefore, this customer (loyal groups), by choosing the incumbent firm over the new entrant, would disable the new entrant from reaching its viable level of sales, thereby creating an entry barrier. This drives the new entrant into losses and, consequently, out of the market.

4.5.2.1. Data as a Barrier to Entry

Brick and mortar stores can only collect data (regarding buyer preference, social status, regular purchases) from their immediate buyers. However, e-platform owner's start collecting consumer data even before the purchase is made by using information based on their scrolling and surfing. This data is further aggregated across all firms and consumers on the platform. The final data in the hands of e-platform owners is thus larger and more efficient than the smaller datasets available with the brick and mortar stores. The efficiency gains of larger data often reduce the diminishing returns[7] to zero or even negative, leading to economies of scope[8] (Martens, 2016).

Economies of scope can also be extended by applying machine learning to these datasets (Martens, 2016). Martens in his study had stated that 'machines can discover patterns in the datasets which are beyond the cognitive capacity of humans, moreover, the algorithms learned from one dataset can then be applied/extended to another set of data, generating economies of scope'.

---

[7] According to Stigler (1964), 'As equal increments of one input are added; the inputs of other productive services being held, constant, beyond a certain point the resulting increments of product will decrease, i.e., the marginal product will diminish'.

[8] Economies of scope describe situations in which the long-run average and marginal cost of a company, organization or economy decreases due to the production of similar complementary goods and services. The output of item A, therefore, reduces the cost of producing item B (Investopedia).

Case Example: Facebook

Facebook can channelize data from the use of its services, which can be broadly divided into applications such as WhatsApp or Instagram and the third-party websites and applications. If a third-party website has embedded Facebook products such as the 'like' button or 'Facebook login' or 'Facebook Analytics', then user data will automatically be transmitted to Facebook as soon as the user visits the third party's website. These data can be merged from the user's Facebook account even when the user has disabled web tracking in his/her browser (Schneider, 2018). These conditions, although not justified, provide Facebook access to bigger datasets, enabling it to analyse existing users and reach newer users, even across parallel social networking sites (Instagram) and chat rooms (WhatsApp).

Even in the presence of non-rivalry and potential excludability of data, there are vast data asymmetries between the e-platforms. The firms that initially succeeded in setting up online portals would always have a perennial advantage over others. Moreover, not all data in the data markets are tradable. In addition to this, there are considerable costs to acquire/collect data. These costs help the existing firms to erect substantial entry barrier against new entrants and maintain their market dominance by limiting their competitor's access to data (Martens, 2016).

Case Example: General Search Engines

First, setting up a general search engine requires considerable amount of time and resources. An example is Microsoft. Every year, Microsoft invests significant sum of money into R&D and the development and maintenance of latest version of general search engines under the brand name 'Bing'. Other companies have stated that the R&D cost and the large quantity of data needed to develop an effective search engine acts as a prominent barrier to entry (ref (286), ECC's Antitrust Procedure) as it leaves the new entrant with no choice except to match the level of investments by the existing firms. For instance, Google's worldwide capital investment in their general search services increased from $0.8 billion in 2009 to $9.9 billion in 2015.

Since 2007, a number of companies such as Yahoo and Ask.com have abandoned the national market for general search services in favour of third-party technology due to their inability to compete against market giants (ref (298), ECC's Antitrust Procedure). Also, many new start-ups have either left the market or have started providing complementary services that market giant (Google) doesn't provide (ref (299), ECC's Antitrust Procedure). Moreover, there has been only one significant entry into the national markets of general search services since 2007—Microsoft's 'Bing' (ref (300), ECC's Antitrust Procedure).

4.6. Economic Implications of Change in Market Structure of E-Platforms

It can be said with certainty that the e-commerce/e-platforms companies have positively affected different sectors of the economy, which led countries to attain higher GDP growth rates and enhanced cross-border B2C e-commerce trade (Terzi, 2011). A study by Anvari and Norouzi (2016) estimated that the e-commerce and R&D expenditure had a positive and significant impact on GDP per capita in selected 21 countries, mostly developed. Similarly, numerous studies have highlighted the potential benefits of e-commerce/e-platforms companies on an economy. However, the flipside of this is to look at the dismissive aspect of expanding market for e-platform/e-commerce companies, specifically on the developing world. It is well known that the e-commerce markets in the developing countries are not mature enough when compared with those in the developed countries.

Figure 4.5 clearly depicts the variance between the selected developed and developing countries, where the Internet retailing as a percentage of total retailing and Internet penetration as a percentage of total population of selected developing countries are far less as compared to the selected developed countries. Although, the average growth of Internet retailing as a percentage of total retailing of selected developing countries is relatively higher than that of their counterpart. Alyoubi (2015) in his study highlighted that the Internet economy has worsened the gap between the developed and the developing

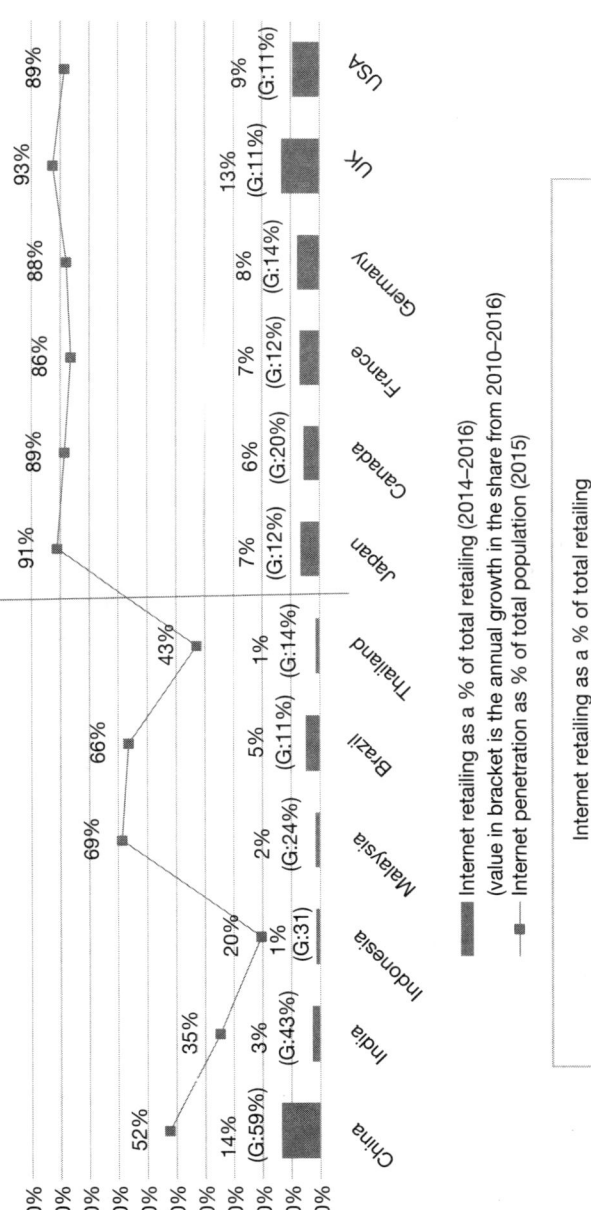

Figure 4.5 *Internet Retailing as a Percentage of Total Retailing and Internet Penetration as Percentage of Total Population*

Source: Authors compilation based on Euro Monitor Database and Internet Live Stats Data; International Telecommunication Union, United Nations Population Division, Internet and Mobile Association of India (IAMAI), World Bank.

nations, 'as the digital divide has revealed sharp disparities between the countries which are equipped with information, and those which are not'. Another study with respect to the impact of e-commerce on the economy of Egypt and USA explained that 'although the e-commerce is considered a significant instrument for development to the Egyptian economy. Trade over the Internet has not been quickly adopted in Egypt because there are a number of barriers that have mitigated e-commerce to properly takeoff' (El Gawady, 2005).

Some studies on the changing market structure of e-platforms have also highlighted the adverse impact on the SMEs. Rahayu and Day (2015), in their study, argue, 'the adoption of e-commerce by SMEs, especially in developing countries, is still very far behind the adoption by large companies'. The study further suggests by taking the case of Indonesian SMEs that they are forced to adopt e-commerce as a business model and those who hesitate are left behind. It has also been evident that SMEs around the globe use Internet, information and communication technologies (ICT) for production and commercial purposes; however, on an average, they have limited understanding of the potential benefits of e-commerce/e-platforms (OECD, 2017). A study by Mukherjee (2017) summarizes that the Indian SMEs are generally of low-web nature, and only around 5 per cent of them have their own website, while their counterparts in the same category own 53 per cent and 46 per cent in the United Kingdom and the USA, respectively. As per the OECD (2017) and United Nations (2016), SMEs account for around 45 per cent of total employment in the developing countries and are the major contributors to value creation, and any impact on the SMEs could significantly affect most of the developing economies, especially their employment and poverty levels.

Apart from the implication for the developing countries, some evidences with respect to the challenges for SMEs in e-commerce adoption were also found among the developed countries. For example, MacGregor and Vrazalic (2004) in their study on the comparative analysis of SMEs in Wollongong (Australia) and Karlstad (Sweden) found that 'SMEs in Australia lag significantly behind their Swedish counterparts in E-commerce adoption' and that the 'SMEs need to be re-educated about the benefits of E-commerce because this type of technology is still perceived by SMEs as being unsuitable to the way they do business'. To explore the implications of changing market structure of e-platforms on the economy, it would be relevant to discuss implications with respect to the key characteristics of market structure.

4.6.2. Expanding 'Market Share' and Its Implications on Fair and Healthy Competition

It is a general misconception that high market share or dominance of few firms in a market leads to the deterioration of healthy competition. High concentration level or high market share of few firms in a specific market does not imply that there is a threat to competition. To be a threat to competition, abuse of dominance has to be proved against a dominant company or a group of companies. In the case of Internet retailing companies and other e-platforms, there have been evidences that raise concern with respect to the abuse of dominance by the e-platforms. For instance, studies by LaVecchia and Mitchell (2016) and Khan (2016) discuss the monopolizing behaviour of Amazon.inc and how it has been using its dominant position to abuse its power in the USA through different methods. Recently, the government of France also filed a case against Amazon in Paris Commercial Court for abusing its dominant position with some suppliers. A similar situation was also seen in China where a report published by China Labs (an Internet research company) highlighted the exercise of monopoly power by three companies: Tencent Holding Ltd., Baidu Inc. and Alibaba Holding Group Ltd. The report by China Competition Research Centre (Fels, Wang, & Su, 2011) stated, 'the three companies hold monopoly positions in the instant messaging, search engine, and e-commerce sectors, respectively, which poses challenges to the interests of Internet users, the prosperity of the Internet industry, and government regulation'.

Rahman (2019) in one of his articles has also talked about monopoly power and the abuse of power by the e-platforms. With respect to all the big e-platforms players such as Google, Facebook, Uber, Airbnb, etc., he said, 'Users are locked into a single platform, which then leverages this user base and vast store of underlying data to grow even bigger, colonize adjacent markets, and eventually, once other competitors are no longer a threat, raise prices'. Recently Alphabet Inc.-owned Google also faced a fine of €2.42 billion by the European Commission for breaching EU antitrust rules. Google in this case was accused of abusing its dominant position with respect to its search engine (comparison shopping services), where it gave illegal advantage to its own product.

Table 4.5 shows a phenomenal increase in the market share (annual) of e-tail portals and a subsequent decrease in market share of offline retail businesses across six countries. Although, it is difficult

Table 4.5 *Annual Change in the Market Share of Companies in Overall Retailing, 2013–2016*

		China		India		Thailand
Internet retailing	Alibaba Group Holding Ltd	36%	Flipkart Online Services Pvt Ltd	82%	Alibaba Group Holding Ltd	NA
	JD.com Inc.	65%	Amazon.com Inc.*	112%	Charoen Pokphand Group	10%
	Suning Commerce Group Co Ltd	7%	Jasper InfoTech Pvt Ltd	26%	Amazon. com Inc.	0%
	GOME Electrical Appliances Holding Ltd	8%	Dell Inc.	0%	Apple Inc.	NA
Supermarket/ direct retailers*	China Resources Holdings Co Ltd*	−13%	Future Group	0%	Seven & I Holdings Co Ltd	6%
	Auchan Group SA	−4%	Reliance Group	0%	Big C Supercenter PCL	NA
	Walmart Stores Inc.	−11%	Tata Group	0%	Central Group	4%
	Carrefour SA	−21%	Avenue Super marts Ltd	14%	Home Product Center PCL	5%

	UK		USA		Germany	
Internet retailing	Amazon.com Inc.	16%	eBay Inc.	4%	Amazon. com Inc.	7%
	eBay Inc.	12%	Apple Inc.	0%	eBay Inc.	3%
	Tesco Plc	*-2%*	Valve Corp	NA	Otto Group	0%
	John Lewis Partnership Plc	2%	Amazon. com Inc.	31%	Apple Inc.	10%
Supermarket/ direct retailers*	Walmart Stores Inc.	*-4%*	Wal-Mart Stores Inc.	*-0.30%*	Aldi Group	*-1%*
	Wm Morrison Supermarkets Plc	*-3%*	Trader Joe's Co	0.00%	Edeka Zentrale AG & Co KG	1%
	Aldi Group	9%	Publix Super Markets Inc.	0.00%	Schwarz Beteiligungs-GmbH	*-0.50%*
	Co-operative Group Ltd	*-1%*	Wegmans Food Markets Inc.	0.00%	Rewe Group	2%

Note: *Companies included in the 'supermarket/direct retailing' category are those that have their majority business in the supermarket/direct retailing sector, and it doesn't mean that they are not into online retail at all.

Source: Authors compilation based on data from euro monitor.

to segregate the companies operating in both online and offline area, Table 4.5 still tries to justify the scenario closely. The table depicts the scenario of a significant shift from brick and mortar to the online shopping through e-platforms. For instance, Amazon share has grown substantially in India, the USA and the United Kingdom, scooping in largest increase in annual share over the last 3 years. The building up of consumer confidence on the online platforms is year-by-year reducing the footfalls to the offline retail shops. This signifies a tectonic shift in the way consumers' shop.

A report by Dutta, Nimbekar and Sood (2016) in association with the Retailers Association of India stated that the share of e-tailing would jump more than five times by 2019, and, during this period, the share of brick and mortar retail was likely to fall from 17 per cent to 13 per cent. Thompson (2017) in his study has reported nine retail bankruptcies in 2017 in the USA. Apart from this, J. C. Penny, RadioShack, Macy's and Sears have each announced more than 100 store closures.

Based on some recent evidences, it could be said that, with the increasing market share of few large e-commerce companies around the world, there is a need to look into the challenges associated with them, specifically with respect to fair and healthy competition in the economy.

4.6.3. Changing Market Structure and Barriers to Entry Faced by the E-Commerce Start-ups

New e-commerce start-ups market generally face different barriers to enter a market. These barriers to entry include lack of initial capital or seed funding, lack of physical infrastructure like end-to-end logistics platform, government regulations, competition from existing players, etc. The intensity of these barriers may differ for different countries. For example, for a country like China, government policy acts as the strongest barrier; however, for a country like India, lack of capital can act as a barrier. With the dominance of selected companies and subsequently with the increase in the cases of abuse of dominance, as discussed in the previous section, the barriers to entry for a new player or a start-up have also increased. These start-ups, especially in the developing countries, face tough competition from their foreign competitors. These big foreign players often use lethal strategies, such as predatory pricing, operating at loses initially to gain market, etc., to drive out small and new players from the market. It was also observed that the e-commerce start-ups operating in the developing countries often face very high expense to sales ratio with very low ARPU (average revenue per user) as compared to their counterpart, which again acts as a barrier for cash-strapped start-ups to survive in the market.

Apart from the barriers discussed above, another phenomenon that acts as a barrier for start-ups to enter the market is the trend in the

Table 4.6 *Number of Start-ups Acquired by Some Big Players*

Firm	Age of Firm: 0–5 Years	Age of Firm: 6–7 Years	Age of Firm: 8–10 Years	Age of Firm: Above 10 Years
Amazon	*21*	13	11	15
Facebook	*49*	4	1	3
Google (Alphabet Inc.)	*126*	26	13	18
Microsoft	*67*	21	28	32
Apple	*39*	10	10	12
Tencent	*127*	18	20	35

Source: Authors calculations based on the Bloomberg Data on M&A.

Notes: The number of firms mentioned here are for those whose year of incorporation was available on various internet sources and the period of investigation varies across companies. For Amazon, the period is from 1998 to March 2018; for Facebook, it is from 2007 to January 2018; for Google, it is from 2001 to May 2018; for Microsoft, it is from 1987 to May 2018; for Apple, it is from 1988 to April 2018; and for Tencent, it is from 2008 to May 2018.

The data is based on the age of the target firm at the time of merger/ acquisition.

mergers and acquisitions (M&A) of new e-commerce firms by the big and established players. Table 4.6 tries to explain this scenario closely. It can be seen (Table 4.6) clearly that majority of the M&A by the big players took place for new entrants in the market. For instance, out of 57 M&A by the Facebook in a given period, 49 were to acquire the firms that were 0–5-years old. Although the basket of these target firms acquired by these players includes firms that are their direct and indirect competitors, firms that fall into their value chains and firms that are from different domains, but if the above scenario continues for a longer period of time, this could create a potential threat for start-ups to enter the market and survive. Such M&A trends are found to be common among other big players as well. The researchers around the globe also argue that this trend of M&A of technological start-ups can have a negative impact on innovation and R&D (see Cassiman & Ueda, 2006)

The pricing strategy followed by some of the dominant players in the e-platform market has also added to the barriers of entry faced by the new players. It has been found that big players follow the strategy of cutthroat price competition. For instance, a study by Bergen, Kauffman and Lee (2005) found that, as compared to traditional retail outlets, online portals adjust their prices more frequently throughout the year. They examined two online book retailers during 2003–2004 and found that Amazon changed prices for its books every 222 days, whereas Barnes and Noble changed its prices every 56 days.

Pricing strategy of dominant e-platform owners with respect to third-party retailers has also raised concerns for the survival of third-party retailers. These third-party retailers pay a price proportional to their sale to the e-platform owners. However, it has been noticed that the e-platform owners actually extract more than just fee and payments from these third-part retailers (LaVecchia & Mitchell, 2016). Such pricing strategies by dominant players again raise concerns for new players in the markets and may lead to the lack of level playing field for new entrants in the market. This lack of level playing field due to changing market structure and the increase in the barriers to entry faced by start-ups can become fatal for the future prospects of start-up culture around the globe.

4.7. Conclusion

The chapter has briefly touched upon the various aspects of market structures of e-platforms and tried to find the implication of changing market structure of e-platforms on the fair and healthy competition in the economy. In the initial sections, the chapter tried to analyse the concept of relevant market for e-platforms. However, establishing relevant market for e-platforms seems quite difficult mainly due to their complex business model and the unavailability of the relevant data and information to conduct such analysis. Although it is based on different decisions of competition authorities around the world, the concept of the relevant market for e-platforms is evolving as it differs on case-to-case basis.

To identify the type of the structure present in the e-commerce markets, the chapter analysed the aspects such firm's market share or market concentration and barriers to entry faced by new entrants. While exploring the market share of e-platforms in different segments, it was found that majority of these segments were dominated by few big players with their market share ranging from 50 per cent to 90 per cent. This type of market concentration of firms clearly shows the presence of monopoly or the oligopoly market share in their respective segments/category. Country-wise analysis with respect to the market concentration of e-tail platforms has shown that, for selected developed countries, the market is currently not that much concentrated as in case of the developing nations; however, it can be said that, due to a significant growth in the market share, a few firms (mainly Amazon Inc. and eBay) may lead their market for e-tail platform to become oligopoly in the near future. It has been found that, with the increasing market share of few big e-tail firms in the developing countries, the challenges for small players and new entrants (including the large number of SMEs in the developing countries) to compete with few large players have also increased.

Few dominant e-platform portals are also found to establish certain barriers, such as legal barriers, infrastructure bottlenecks, M&A, unethical practices, etc., for the new firms to enter the online portal. Further, big players follow divide and conquer practices and data mining to expand their market dominance and later exploit markets with this dominant position. Such behaviour violates the provision of equal playing field between the firms. These issues hold severe meaning if the country in question is a developing nation with poor political will, underdeveloped legal jurisprudence and insufficient information technology infrastructure. The chapter argues that the rise of the Internet economy might worsen the gap between the developed and the developing nations. For the e-platform players around the globe have immense potential either to reduce or widen the gap of economic equality. A positive effect seems possible, only if the developing countries are given sufficient policy space to develop their national strategies for e-platforms/e-commerce players that are customized to their situation and resources.

References

Alyoubi, A. A. (2015). E-commerce in developing countries and how to develop them during the introduction of modern systems. *Procedia Computer Science*, *65*, 479–483.

Anvari, R. D., & Norouzi, D. (2016). The impact of e-commerce and R&D on economic development in some selected countries. *Procedia–Social and Behavioral Sciences*, *229*, 354–362.

Belousova, A. (2010). *Relevant market: The application to the e-commerce area in the EU.*

Bergen, M. E., Kauffman, R. J., & Lee, D. (2005). Beyond the hype of frictionless markets: Evidence of heterogeneity in price rigidity on the Internet. *Journal of Management Information Systems*, *22*(2), 57–89.

Boshoff, W. H. (2006). Quantitative techniques in competition policy – The Elzinga-Hogarty Test. Research note 3. https://econex.co.za/wp-content/uploads/2015/04/econex_researchnote_3.pdf

Cassiman, B., & Ueda, M. (2006). M&A and innovation: A conceptual framework. In B. Cassiman and M. G. Colombo (eds.), *Mergers and acquisitions.* Edward Elgar Publishing.

Dutta, S. S., Nimbekar, A., & Sood, A. (2016). *Think India think retail 2016.* Mumbai: Knight Frank India Pvt Ltd.

El Gawady, Z. M. (2005). The impact of e-commerce on developed and developing countries case study: Egypt and United States. In International Conference of Globalization, Technology and Sustainable Development, United Arab Emirates University, World Association for sustainable Development, Al Ain, UAE.

Fels, A., Wang, X., & Su, J. (2011). *China competition bulletin.* China Competition Research Centre. http://www.iolaw.org.cn/web/pdf/2011/6China_Competition_Bulletin_February_2011.pdf

Hagiu, A. (2009). Multi-sided platforms: From microfoundations to design and expansion strategies. *Harvard Business School Strategy Unit Working Paper*, (09–115).

Khan, L. M. (2016). Amazon's antitrust paradox. *Yale LJ, 126*, 710.

Kommerskollegium. (2012). *Everybody is in services: The impact of servicification in manufacturing on trade and trade policy.* Direction Nationale du Commerce.

Koutsoyiannis, A. (1975). *Modern microeconomics.* Springer.

LaVecchia, O., & Mitchell, S. (2016). *Amazon's stranglehold: How the company's tightening grip is stifling competition, eroding jobs, and threatening communities.* Washington, DC: Institute for Local Self-Reliance.

Lawrence, J. E., & Tar, U. A. (2010). Barriers to e-commerce in developing countries. *Information, Society and Justice Journal*, *3*(1), 23–35.

MacGregor, R., & Vrazalic, L. (2004). Electronic commerce adoption in small to medium enterprises (SMEs). A Comparative study of SMEs in Wollongong (Australia) and Karlstad (Sweden), University of Wollongong.

Margolis, S. E., & Liebowitz, S. J. (1998). Path dependence. In *New Palgrave Dictionary of Economics and Law*. London: Palgrave MacMillan.

Marshall, A. (2009). *Principles of economics: Unabridged eighth edition*. Cosimo, Inc.

Martens, B. (2016). An economic policy perspective on online platforms. Working Paper 5, Institute for Prospective Technological Studies Digital Economy.

Mukherjee, S. (2018). Challenges to Indian micro small scale and medium enterprises in the era of globalization. *Journal of Global Entrepreneurship Research, 8*(1), 28.

Nguyen, D. D., & Kira, D. S. (2001). Market structure, competition, and equilibrium in electronic commerce setting.

OECD. (1999). Policy round-tables oligopoly 1999. https://www.oecd.org/daf/competition/1920526.pdf

OECD. (2017). Enhancing the contributions of SMEs in a global and digitalised economy. In *Meeting of the OECD Council at Ministerial Level, Paris* (Vol. 7, No. June, p. 2017).

Rahayu, R., & Day, J. (2015). Determinant factors of e-commerce adoption by SMEs in developing country: Evidence from Indonesia. *Procedia–Social and Behavioral Sciences, 195*, 142–150.

Rahman, K. S. (2019). Curbing the new corporate power. *Boston Review*. http://bostonreview.net/forum/k-sabeel-rahman-curbing-new-corporate-power

Robinson, J. (1969). *The economics of imperfect competition*. Springer.

Schneider, G. (2018). Testing Art. 102 TFEU in the digital marketplace: Insights from the Bundeskartellamt's investigation against Facebook. *Journal of European Competition Law & Practice, 9*(4), 213–225

Segal, I. R., & Whinston, M. D. (2000). Exclusive contracts and protection of investments. *RAND Journal of Economics, 31*(4), 603–633.

Slot, P. J., & Farley, M. (2017). *An introduction to competition law*. Bloomsbury Publishing.

Smith, A. (1937). *The wealth of nations [1776]*.

Stigler, G. J. (1964). A theory of oligopoly. *Journal of Political Economy, 72*(1), 44–61.

Terzi, N. (2011). The impact of e-commerce on international trade and employment. *Procedia–Social and Behavioral Sciences, 24*, 745–753.

The Pioneer. (2019). Zomato offers gold subscription for Indian customers: Know Everything in Five Facts. https://www.dailypioneer.com/2018/impact/zomato-offers-gold-subscription-for-indian-customers-know-everything-in-five-facts.html

Thompson, D. (2017). What in the world is causing the retail meltdown of 2017? *The Atlantic, 10*(04).

Tirole, J. (2017). *Economics for the common good*. Princeton University Press.

United Nations. (2016). World economic situation and prospects. https://www.un.org/en/development/desa/policy/wesp/wesp_current/2016wesp_ch1_en.pdf

Venuvinod, P. (2011). *Technology, innovation and entrepreneurship Part II: My Firm (Vol. 2).*

Zhang, Q., & Wang, Y. (2018). Struggling towards virtuous coevolution: Institutional and strategic works of Alibaba in building the Taobao e-commerce ecosystem. *Asian Business & Management, 17*(3), 208–242.

CHAPTER 5

Foreign Investment in Indian E-Commerce Sector and Its Drivers

Rahul Nath Choudhury and
Pravin Jadhav

5.1. Introduction

With the adoption of the New Economic Policy, the Indian economy underwent a structural change in 1991. The economy moved from a highly state-controlled regime to an open, liberal and market-friendly regime. The prime objectives of the policy change were to integrate the domestic economy with the rest of the world and to attract foreign direct investment (FDI). Policymakers believed that an open and liberal regime would attract a considerable volume of FDI which will provide the domestic industry much-needed capital infusion. Since then, the scope of FDI has expanded gradually from manufacturing to the services and infrastructure sectors. Along with other segments in the service sector, the e-commerce industry was opened for 100 per cent FDI in 2000 on the condition that the companies engage only in B2B activities.[1] Currently, the service sector attracts the highest foreign inflows and the e-commerce industry is a major contributor.

India's journey towards e-commerce industry started with the establishment of baazee.com in 2000, which was acquired by the American e-commerce giant eBay in 2004 and India received its first FDI in this sector (*The Indian Express*, 2004). From 2004 to 2008, eBay had no significant rival in the Indian market. The scenario changed with the entry of Flipkart.com, a company in the same sector promoted by two Indians. Since then, the e-commerce sector in India has witnessed a remarkable growth. It reportedly grew at a rate of more than 34 per cent CAGR between 2009 and 2014 (PwC, 2015). Currently, the sector is growing at the year-over-year rate of 25 per cent. The major players such as Flipkart and Amazon have consistently reported higher revenues (Sen, 2017). The total size of the industry was reported to be $14.5 billion in 2016 and was expected to grow to $80 billion by 2020 (FT Bureau, 2017). The *Global Payments Report*, published annually by Worldpay, suggests that India will become the second largest market, overtaking the USA by 2034 (ANI, 2016). The vast, growing Indian market has attracted global e-commerce players such as Amazon, eBay and Alibaba. Foreign investment in the Indian e-commerce industry has soared from $2.9 billion in 2014 to $4.4 billion in 2017 (up to September).[2] All the investment flown into Indian e-commerce sector was in the form of private equity (PE).

Almost all the companies operating in the sector have received some amount of foreign investment. Some of the companies have even changed their business format to comply with the existing Indian laws (Choudhury, 2015). Curiously, not many studies have explored the question of how and why the Indian e-commerce industry has

---

[1] Press note no 2, 2000 Series. DIPP, Ministry of Commerce and Industry, Government of India. B2B, is a type of transaction that exists between businesses, such as one involving a manufacturer and wholesaler, or a wholesaler and a retailer. In this type of business transaction end user of the goods and services sold are not involved.

[2] As per the data compiled from Venture Intelligence 2017. The data for only IT and ITES sector is considered.

grown phenomenally so fast. In the case of e-commerce, there is considerably less evidence on what determines investment patterns, especially in lower-income countries such as India. Raipuria (2000) studied e-commerce in the context of opportunities for Indian export. He argued that it is essential for a business to survive and grow in a competitive world. Satapathy (1999) discussed various proposals made by or within the World Trade Organization (WTO) and their implications regarding e-commerce. Anuradha (2018) explored various forms of WTO disputes pertaining to services commitments. Government policies governing the e-commerce sector are not very clear and robust. There are also debates on whether to include it in the purview of the WTO. Agarwal and Wu (2000) examined various factors influencing the growth potential of e-commerce in emerging economies from a multi-theoretical perspective, while Gupta (2017) investigated the role of government policies in determining the growth of the e-commerce sector in India. A similar study was conducted by Viswanathan and Pick (2005) comparing India and Mexico. It focused on the policy and institutional variables that might affect the diffusion of the e-commerce sector. Kuthiala (2003) explored the opportunities and challenges that India faces in adopting e-commerce. Analysing the secondary data, the study outlines the potential gains that India can make in the global market by adopting e-commerce.[3]

Analysing the investment structure in the Indian e-commerce sector, one can understand that most of it is in the form of market-seeking investment. It is a big-size, growing consumer class that has encouraged foreign players to exploit their advantage over the Indian firms.

Upon discussion of all the afore-mentioned literature, several research questions arise: Why foreign investors are so keen on investing in India? What are the factors behind this remarkable growth? It is in this regard that this study tries to identify the potential determining factors that are driving the growth of this sector and attracting foreign investment in such a short span of time.

---

[3] For a review of the literature on the e-commerce sector, see Vaithianathan (2010).

The rest of the chapter is structured in the following manner. Section 2 analyses the trend of investment in the Indian e-commerce industry. In Section 3, we discuss the major determinants, while Section 4 describes the methodology and data source of the study. This includes sampling methods, discussion of variable selection, mathematical model and data sources. Section 5 provides the result and findings of both primary and secondary analysis. Section 6 points out the limitations of the study. Finally, in Section 7, the study makes the concluding remarks.

5.2. Trends in Investment Flow

The investment made by PE firms is playing a pivotal role in the growth of the Indian e-commerce sector. Statistics suggest that around 400 investments were made by PE firms in this growing sector between 2007 and 2014. In 2013, PE firms invested $617 million, with 31 deals in this sector. The number of deals increased to 40 with a total investment of $4,402.23 million in 2017. These investments poured into businesses of various sizes and in different segments of the sector. The Indian e-commerce giant Flipkart alone received $4,000 million, of which $2,500 million came from the Japanese investor Softbank in August 2017. Later in 2018, Flipkart was acquired by American retail giant Walmart for approximately $16 billion. Flipkart's investment was followed by another e-commerce brand, Paytm. The trend in foreign PE investment in the Indian e-commerce sector is given in Figure 5.1.

PE investment has grown almost steadily with some variation since 2002. Figure 5.1 shows there was a steep increase in 2013 followed by a sharp fall in 2016 which again jumped in 2017. The major reason for this unusual increase was the capital infusion in Flipkart. This extraordinary large volume of investment shook the entire trend of investment. The fall during 2016 was obvious as the market returned to the normal stage and no such huge investment was made as it happened in 2014. All these make it worth investigating what leads to such a huge volume of funds in this sector. This is attempted in the next section of the chapter.

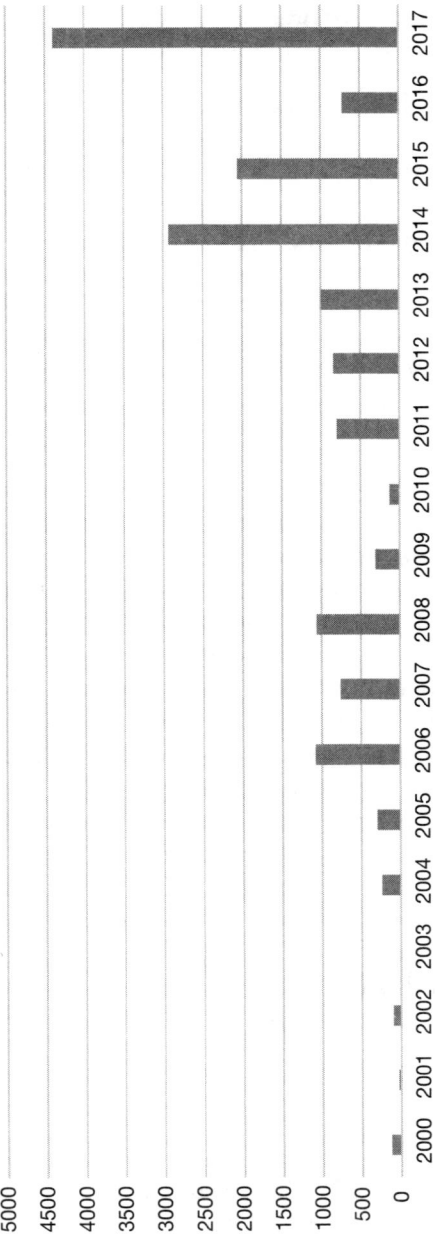

Figure 5.1 *Trends in Foreign PE Investment in Indian E-Commerce Sector, 2000–2017*

Source: Author's calculation from Venture Intelligence Database, 2018.

5.3. Major Determinants

There are various factors that play a decisive role in the growth of a sector in an economy. The persistent growth of the Indian e-commerce sector has attracted foreign investors. Today, the majority shares of almost all the companies operating in the industry are held with foreign investors (Banerjee, 2016). E-commerce sector experienced the boom in India for various reasons such as rapid adoption of modern technology by Indian consumers, increase in the number of Internet users, innovative and different business models and alternative payment options offered by e-commerce companies, etc. (Pal, 2017). This shows the importance of information and communications technology (ICT) in enabling a conducive platform for investment in a short period of time.

People now, especially in urban areas, are growing accustomed to making online purchases. Today, in any Tier 1 or Tier 2 city, we can purchase almost everything from fruits and vegetables to high-end jewellery without visiting a brick-and-mortar store. The government's policies to promote digitalization and the digital transaction have helped this industry to grow. The Indian government has strongly encouraged the development of Internet and information technology through various incentives, including exempting the industry from burdensome regulations and controls (Gupta, 2017; Miller, 2001). There are things we can no longer do unless we go online. For instance, it has become mandatory to file income tax returns online; shares and debentures cannot be bought in physical form; and cash transactions are not possible beyond a certain limit. Most of the commercial banks are promoting online transactions and offering discounts or privileges when we use the online banking system. The evolution of digital wallets, gift cards and other similar online payment methods have helped the e-commerce sector grow. We elaborate on this in the following subsections.

5.3.1. Internet Penetration

A study by Cisco found that 373 million people in India, or 28 per cent of the population, were connected to Internet in 2016 (IANS, 2017).

The figure is even higher, according to the report *Internet in India 2016* issued by the Internet and Mobile Association of India (IAMAI, 2016) and IMRB International. It says the number of Internet users in India went up from 278 million in October 2014 to 432 million in December 2016. Of them, 269 million (62.3 per cent) were from urban India and 163 million (37.7 per cent) from rural India. The report says that 51 per cent of the urban users (137.19 million) use Internet every day while 90 per cent of the urban users (242 million) use Internet at least once a month. On the other hand, in rural India, 78 million users, or around 48 per cent, use Internet every day while 140 million, or around 83 per cent, use Internet at least once a month (Pai, 2017). According to a report by Telecom Regulatory Authority of India (TRAI), 60 million new Internet users were added in 2016, and around 100 million users (existing plus new) took up broadband connections.

5.3.2. Mobile Penetration

Currently, India is the biggest consumer of mobile phones in the world (ANI, 2016). Almost half of the country's population now subscribes to a mobile service. According to a report prepared by the GSMA in 2016, India has 616 million active unique mobile subscribers. Mobile broadband connections are growing at a rate of 15 per cent per year. A Confederation of Indian Industry report estimates that, in 6 years, around 600 million people will be accessing Internet through mobile phones (Mishra, 2015). The GSMA report estimated that over 400 million SIM connections would be added by 2020, bringing the connections' penetration to just over 100 per cent.

5.3.3. Cost of Mobile Data

The cost of mobile Internet plans plays a big role in encouraging e-commerce activities in India. There has been a continuous fall in the prices of mobile data in India since its launch. Department of Telecommunication (DoT) claims India to have the cheapest mobile data in the world in 2018. DoT also reported that mobile Internet rates plunged by 93 per cent while data usage per user surged by over

25 times in three years to 2017. It also reported that mobile data consumption in India is now the highest in the world at 1.3 million GB per month—more than combined data usage in the USA and China.

The data in Table 5.1 shows the tremendous growth in all the factors that determine the performance of the e-commerce sector. Number of internet users have outstandingly increased from only 19 million in 2010 to 510 million in 2017. Data reveals that there was a sudden jump in the number of Internet subscribers from 22 million in 2011 to 164 in 2012. This is mainly due to the introduction of mobile Internet at pan India level. However, to date, it is only 41 per cent of the total mobile users of the country. This means that only 41 per cent of the mobiles used in India is having active Internet connection. Sharp fall in the prices of mobile and the emergence of a few domestic mobile manufacturing companies and easy import of low-cost mobiles from China have revolutionized the market.

Drop in call rates and the availability of smartphones at lower prices and on monthly instalments have boosted mobile sales and usage. Data plans in India cost only half as much as in China and are merely one-third of the price in the USA (ANI, 2016). As the data in Table 5.1 depicts, the cost of Internet which was as high as $16.67 in 2010 has dropped to less than a dollar in 2017. This has facilitated traffic to e-commerce websites in India. Accessing e-commerce websites through mobile phones has increased significantly in the country in recent times. At present, mobile commerce represents nearly 50 per cent of online retail sales in India, compared with around 48 per cent in China and 34 per cent in the USA. According to a recent report by research firm Forrester, nearly half, $12 billion, in yearly online sales in India takes place through mobile phones, which were set to overtake PC-based sales in 2016 and reach $51 billion by 2020. Myntra, a fashion retailer owned by Flipkart, saw 90 per cent of its traffic and 70 per cent of its sales from mobiles before famously abandoning its PC-based site altogether (Srivastava, 2016). Another e-commerce firm, Snapdeal, also gets much of its business over the phone—50 per cent of its sales orders come through its mobile app (Singh, 2014).

Table 5.1 Select Factors Determining E-Commerce Growth

Year	PE Investment ($ million)	No of Mobile Users (million)	No of Internet Users (million)	Cost of the Internet ($)	GDP per Capita Current Prices ($)	Share of Internet Users in Total Mobile Users (%)	Growth Rate of Mobile Users (%)	Growth Rate of Internet Users (%)
2010	129.43	811.59	19.67	16.67	1,345.77	2.4	38.8	21.6
2011	799.01	919.17	22.86	10.00	1,461.67	2.5	13.2	16.2
2012	842.42	867.8	164.81	4.20	1,446.98	19.0	−5.58	621.0
2013	998.72	904.51	251.59	4.18	1,452.19	27.8	4.23	52.7
2014	2,933	969.89	302.35	4.48	1,576.00	31.2	7.22	20.2
2015	2,057	1,033.63	342.65	3.77	1,606.03	33.2	6.57	13.3
2016	725.87	1,170.18	462.0	1.32	1,717.47	39.5	13.21	34.8
2017	4,402.23	1,220	510.0	0.32	1,939.61	41.8	4.25	10.4

Source: Venture Intelligence, TRAI, World Bank and media reports.

The development of mobile applications used for shopping has contributed immensely to the sales of e-commerce companies. A shopping app on a mobile device helps a person shop from anywhere, anytime. Shopping with a mobile app is easier and faster than shopping using a desktop computer. E-commerce companies have come up with user-friendly applications. This has resulted in increased sales for e-commerce companies. Flipkart has been following a 'mobile first' approach, and 70–75 per cent of its total traffic is already coming from its mobile app (Sanjai & Dalal, 2015).

Cash on delivery or paying at the time of delivery of the goods purchased online is another significant reason for the increased sales of the e-commerce companies. As reported by *Business Today*, citing a study by Ernst & Young, cash on delivery accounts for 50–80 per cent of the online transactions in India (Das, 2014). An increase in the number of credit card users is another reason for the exponential growth in the sales of e-commerce companies. Faster and on-time delivery of goods, the ability to deliver goods in rural/remote areas and the emergence of exclusive logistic companies for delivering goods sold by e-commerce companies have also pushed up their sales volume.

An econometric analysis covering these factors is conducted in the next section, which starts with describing the methodology applied in the analysis.

5.4. Methodology

In order to verify the theoretical reasons behind the phenomenal growth of the Indian e-commerce sector and the foreign investment flows into it, we adopted a two-tier methodology with primary as well as a secondary survey. First, we conducted a primary survey to understand the perception of the consumers during the online purchase of various goods and services. After a thorough review of the literature, a structured questionnaire was designed. Initially, a pilot survey was conducted and, based on the responses, we finalized our questionnaire. The final questionnaire for the survey is divided into three sections. The first section consists of questions about demographic information of the respondents such as age, sex, income, etc., while in the second section, questions related to reasons and pattern of their online purchase were asked. The final section of the questionnaire inquired about the challenges they face during an online purchase.

5.4.1. Sampling

As mentioned above, a pilot survey was conducted before finalizing the questionnaire. The pilot survey covered a sample size of 50 with 5 respondents in each city. The final survey covered a sample size of 1,000 respondents in 10 cities in the northern region of the country.

Data was collected from Delhi, Chandigarh, Jaipur, Lucknow, Noida, Gurgaon, Agra, Patiala, Jalandhar and Amritsar. The locations for the survey were selected strategically to get a better representation of the entire north Indian region. The survey was conducted in various colleges, shopping malls and other business and recreation centres. Data was collected from the respondents across age groups. The first phase of data was collected during November and December 2018, while the final phase of the survey was conducted in February and March 2019. The time period of the survey was strategically selected considering two major Indian festivals of Holi and Diwali and English New Year. This is because these two festivals are highly celebrated across the northern region of India and most of the people buy during these festivals. Further, e-commerce companies also offer deep discounts during this period to woo their customers. Notably, special discounts are offered to the customers during Flipkart's Big Billion Day and Amazon's Great Indian Sale.

Upon collection, scrutiny and refinement of the data, we considered only those responses that were given by the people who have purchased an item in the last quarter.

5.4.2. Secondary Survey

In the second phase of the analysis, we studied an extensive list of literature exploring the determinants of investment in an economy or in a sector of an economy. Studies pertaining to the e-commerce sector were also consulted. However, there is hardly any research study analysing the determinants of the inflow of investment in the e-commerce sector in India. Therefore, we consulted a few media articles and studies conducted by renowned private consulting firms such as PwC and Deloitte while selecting the appropriate determinant variables for the study.

Based on the various theoretical and descriptive trend analyses, we model that the significant foreign investment inflows in e-commerce depend on mobile subscription and Internet penetration, reflecting ICT usage and purchasing power of the consumers which is reflected by GDP per capita. In functional form, it is written as follows:

$$PE = f(MP, IP, GDP) \qquad (1)$$

where MP is number of mobile users, IP is number of Internet users and GDP is GDP per capita in India.

We use multiple linear regression on a log-log model. We use ordinary least squares (OLS) regression estimation technique to assess the relationship and impact of the independent variables on the dependent variable. The model functional form is given in Equation 2.

$$lanc_{et} = \alpha + \beta_1 lnMS_t + \beta_2 lnIS_t + \beta_3 ln\ GDP_t \epsilon_t \qquad (2)$$

Here, $PE_{it} =$ PE inflow in the e-commerce sector in India during the time period t. MS refers to the number of mobile subscribers, IS refers to the number of Internet subscribers in India during the time period t and GDP refers to the GDP per capita in India during the time period t.

5.4.3. Sources of Data

The data set used in the econometric model discussed above consists of three variables namely, PE investment in the Indian e-commerce sector, total number of mobile users and Internet subscribers in India. The time period considered is from 2000 to 2017. All the data collected and used are on an annual interval. The selection of the time period was strictly based on the availability of reliable and continuous data.

The annual reports published by TRAI were consulted for compiling data on mobile and Internet subscribers. However, due to non-availability of TRAI's annual reports before 2005, data were extracted from Indiastat.com for the same variables. Indiastat.com is a well-known data provider in India. It provides secondary-level socio-economic statistical information about India, its states and regions and is widely used by Indian academia.

The data on GDP per capita was collected from the World Development Indicators published by the World Bank.

Another database, Venture Intelligence, was relied upon to collect data on PE investment in the Indian e-commerce sector. Venture Intelligence is one of the leading sources of information and analysis on private company financials, transactions (PE, venture capital and merger and acquisition) and their valuations in India. This database is used extensively by transaction industry practitioners, entrepreneurial companies, educational institutions and the media.

All the analyses were carried out using the statistical software called EViews. It is a statistical package for Windows, used mainly for time series oriented econometric analysis. It is developed by Quantitative Micro Software.

5.5. Estimation Results and Discussion

5.5.1 Results of Primary Survey

5.5.1.1. Reasons for Buying Online

The results of the primary survey gave us a clear idea on the perception of the consumers of online stores. Although a large section of the consumers faces a few challenges in purchasing online, they are happy until they get the same item at a cheaper rate compared to the brick and mortar store. The data from the primary survey (the table below) shows that most of the buyers buy online mainly because of discounts and low prices than the traditional stores.

Reasons	Percentage
Cheaper than offline stores	75
Get heavy discounts	82
Saves time	69
All the above	61

Mode of payment. The proverb 'cash is the king' still finds a place in the Indian e-commerce sector. In fact, it is not only India but also all the South Asian countries have the same experience (Choudhury, 2019). Our result shows that 87 per cent of Indian consumers still prefer to pay when the product is delivered at their doorstep. This is happening in a situation when various efforts are undergoing from both the government and the online platforms to influence people to shift towards digital payment system. Companies are offering various discounts to influence their consumer to opt for digital payments. However, they still need to cover a long distance.

A growing section of the customers has started using mobile wallets. Although it is a very recent phenomenon, it is increasing rapidly. During our discussion, respondents reveal that they get additional discounts for making payments through different mobile wallets. It is to be noted that most of the prominent online sellers have started their online payment services in the form of mobile wallets. Flipkart facilitates its customers to make payments through PhonePe while Amazon does it through Amazon Pay.

Mode	Percentage
Credit card	21
Debit card	53
Mobile wallet	32
Cash on delivery	87

Value and type of the product. We categorize goods and services ranged up to ₹2,500 as low-value, ₹2501–5,000 as medium-value and anything above ₹5,000 as high-value items. Our survey reveals that most of the (67 per cent) customers still hesitate to buy high-value items from online stores. Customers (62 per cent) are also hesitant of buying non-branded or lesser known brands. A major reason cited for this was that they fear if product delivered does not function properly (primarily in case of electronics) or does not fit them (in case of expensive apparels). Their hesitation also comes from the post-delivery hassles that they need to face in case of exchanging or returning the item.

Our survey finds that most of the people (73 per cent) buy apparels, electronic products such as mobile phones, music systems, etc., from online stores. Movie tickets and travel tickets are the highest purchased services from online stores. The practice of buying grocery items from online stores are also picking up in small towns.

Type of Item	Percent
Apparels	73
Electronic items	76
Tickets	91
Grocery	27
Other household items	39

Challenges in online shopping. One interesting thing that comes out of the survey is that trust or faith is still a big issue in the e-commerce sector in India even when it is growing at a tremendous rate. It poses a serious challenge to online sellers. It is the only trust that is stopping customers to buy high-value goods and services and non-branded items from these online stores. Standard and quality of the goods is also a concern for them, especially in the case of grocery items.

Consumers are also sceptical of using their credit and debit cards during their online shopping. Majority of them think that it will be difficult to get the money back if they make any mistake during the transaction. Some of them are also doubtful of the security system of the shopping websites. Many of the respondents have also complained about having received duplicate or wrong items against their order.

It is pertinent here to share that many of such incidences have been reported widely in various parts of India.

Based on the above evidence, it is suggested that online sellers should take these complaints seriously and initiate adequate measures to solve the issue. Faith should be built among the consumers about the safety of the websites, be it for security during a transaction or delivering right and original product. The companies should devise policies to eliminate the hassles faced by the customers in case of returning or exchanging the goods. Cases of cheating and fraud by the customers have also been reported in some cases. The government should formulate a policy that helps to hold the offender responsible and punish them accordingly. All these are of urgent need considering the growth potential and jobs that are associated with the sector.

5.5.2. Results of Secondary Analysis

In this model, first, we checked the stationarity of the data by the unit root test. Internet penetration and mobile penetration are not stationary at the first level. They are found to be significant at the second level, so we take second level for our interpretation. GDP per capita is found stationary at the second level. According to the estimated model reported in Table 5.2, 1 per cent increase in GDP per capita will increase PE inflow by 5.59 per cent. The result is found to be statistically significant at 1 per cent level. Similarly, 1 per cent increase in Internet subscribers will increase PE by 4.06 per cent, statistically significant at 1 per cent level. A 1 per cent increase in mobile penetration is negatively associated with investment and statistically significant at 1 per cent level. This result indicated that the use of mobile in India is more that increment in PE investments.

The econometric results reveal that both GDP per capita and Internet access have a positive impact on the level of PE inflow. Based on R^2, we can argue that the OLS model has been able to explain 72 per cent of the variation in the dependent variable based on the selected independent regressors. The negative relation between investment and mobile penetration suggests that higher mobile subscription has not been able to lead more users to purchase online.

Table 5.2 OLS Estimation Results, 2000–2017

Variable	Coefficient	Std Error	Prob
GDP	5.59	2.15	0.0223
Internet penetration	4.06	1.65	0.0293
Mobile penetration	−5.59	2.31	0.031
C	−2679.26	1180.1	0.0408
R-squared	0.723153	Mean dependent var	976.8553
Adjusted R-squared	0.659265	SD dependent var	1171.017
SE of regression	683.5525	Akaike info criterion	16.09481
Sum squared resid	6074171.	Schwarz criterion	16.29086
Log likelihood	−132.8059	Hannan–Quinn criter.	16.11430
F-statistic	11.31909	Durbin–Watson stat	2.741614
Prob (F-statistic)	0.000628		

Note: HAC standard errors, bandwidth 1 (Bartlett kernel); *denotes significance at the 10 per cent level.

Thus, based on the regression model, it is found that ICT and purchasing power has a major influence on investment by foreign companies in the e-commerce sector in India. The major driver of investment is the increased penetration of mobile subscription in the recent period.

5.6. Limitations of the Study

The study is conducted at a time when there is a serious dearth of literature in this field and only a few academic studies have been conducted on the subject matter (Basu & Jones, 2003; Chattopadhyay, 2003). The Indian e-commerce sector has grown so rapidly that it has given hardly any time to policymakers to understand its various dimensions. Academics or researchers have also not been able to come out with many conclusive studies. In this regard, this is a preliminary attempt to contribute to this emerging area of study. Being a preliminary study of an emerging and unexplored area, the study has a few limitations.

In the case of a primary survey, the study covers only a few cities and a sample size of only 1,000 consumers. Although conducting a research study with a sample of this size is considered statistically significant, it is merely a small fraction of the total online consumers of India. As the primary survey for the study was conducted in the urban centres only, it fails to capture the perception of the consumers from the semi-urban and rural areas. And with the Internet revolution, consumers from semi-urban and rural areas have increasingly participated in the modern form of shopping through electronic gadgets.

The prime limitation is the availability of data. Among many determining factors for the rapid growth of the Indian e-commerce sector, data are available only for three variables, namely mobile penetration, Internet penetration and per capita GDP. Data for the same variable is also not available from the same source. In addition, figures for the same variable vary significantly among different sources. Moreover, the available data is not for a prolonged period and is not robust in nature. Considering that there are only three variables in the econometric analysis and that too for a period of only 16 years, it does not provide any conclusive results. The e-commerce sector in India is only about 10–12 years old (although there were a few companies operating even before that period) and the data for this sector is not properly maintained. With the 10–12 years of annual data, it is very difficult to conduct a conclusive study. These are some of the major reasons behind an inconclusive result of the econometric analysis.

5.7. Concluding Remarks

The e-commerce sector in India has witnessed remarkable growth in recent years. Both Indian and foreign companies are competing in this sector. The noteworthy growth has also attracted many PE investors, both Indian and foreign. In this regard, the study attempted to analyse the factors helping the sector achieve and maintain a consistent growth rate in such a short period. In particular, the study is an attempt to explore the major factors playing a determining role in attracting foreign investment in the form of PE in the Indian e-commerce sector. We use regression analysis and use mobile subscription and Internet penetration as significant determinants of foreign PE in e-commerce. Among the factors we considered in the econometric model, both Internet usage and GDP per capita have a positive impact on investment. However, the effect is statistically significant in the case of GDP per capita.

The negative correlation between the number of mobile subscribers and PE investment reflects that although people are having mobile phones, they are not using the same for online shopping. The number of mobile users is substantially high, but, among them, smartphone share is not very significant. The statistical results suggest that increase in the number of mobile users is not contributing to the growth of online shopping. However, all the major online firms have claimed to have a higher share of their sale through mobile applications. The reflection of a negative relation between e-commerce growth and mobile subscribers is probably due to the short period of the data. Shopping through a mobile application is a very recent phenomenon and is not captured in the time series data.

The result reveals that the deep penetration of Internet networks has helped users go online shopping, and this has created an incentive structure for foreign players to invest and expand business opportunities in India. The increased use of smartphones and the widespread use of mobile applications for shopping have also helped the e-commerce companies increase their sales volume and raise their growth rate. Cash on delivery, catering to remote locations, and timely and fast delivery of goods and services have also helped these companies increase sales and sustain growth.

References

Agarwal, J., & Wu, T. (2015). Factors influencing growth potential of e-commerce in emerging economies: An institution-based N-OLI framework and research propositions. *Thunderbird International Business Review, 57*(3), 197–215.

ANI. (2016, December 05). India set to become world's largest e-commerce market. *Business Standard.*

Anuradha, R. V. (2018). Technological neutrality: Implications for services commitments and the discussions on e-commerce. Working paper CWS/WP/200/51, Centre for WTO Studies, Indian Institute of Foreign Trade, New Delhi.

Banerjee, S. (2016). FDI Guidelines for e-commerce. *Economic & Political Weekly*, *51*(36), 21.

Basu, S., & Jones, R. (2003). E-commerce and the law: A review of India's Information Technology Act, 2000. *Contemporary South Asia*, *12*(1), 7–24.

Chattopadhyay, R. (2003). The Internet and postcolonial development: India's transnational reality. *Contemporary South Asia*, *12*(1), 25–40.

Choudhury, R. N. (2015). *India's FDI policy on e-commerce: Some observations.* Discussion paper, DN2015/03, Institute for Studies in Industrial Development, New Delhi.

Choudhury, R. (2019). E-commerce and developing countries: The South Asian experience. *South Views*, 173. https://us5.campaign-archive.com/?u=fa9cf387 99136b5660f367ba6&id=3fb4cb574b

Das, G. (2014, February 16). Cash-on-delivery: Necessary evil. *Business Today.*

FT Bureau. (2017, January 31). E-commerce in India: From 180% in 2015, growth crashes to 12% in 2016 at $14.5 bn. *The Financial Express.*

Gupta, P. (2017). Proposed e-commerce disciplines@ WTO: Implications for government programmes and digital initiatives in India. CWS Working Paper 42, Centre for WTO Studies, Indian Institute of Foreign Trade, New Delhi

IAMAI. (2016). *Internet in India 2016.* New Delhi: IAMAI.

IANS. (2017). Internet users in India to double by 2021: Cisco report. https://yourstory.com/2017/06/india-internet-users-report/

Kuthiala, S. K. (2003). E-commerce in India: Challenges and choices. *Journal of Services Research*, *2*(2), 139.

Miller, R. R. (2001). Leapfrogging? India's information technology industry and the Internet. World Bank. http://documents.worldbank.org/curated/en/596841468750845 416/Leapfrogging-Indias-information-technology-industry-and-the-Internet

Mishra, M. (2015, February 13). 5 factors that will drive e-commerce growth. *Business Standard.*

Pai, V. (2017, March 03). 37% of Internet users in Dec'16 came from rural India: IAMAI. *Medianama.* https://www.medianama.com/2017/03/223-iamai-internet-india-2016-report/

Pal, K. H. (2017). National report on e-commerce development in India: Inclusive and sustainable industrial development. Working Paper Series, WP 15, UNIDO, Vienna.

PwC. (2015). Ecommerce in India: Accelerating growth. https://www.pwc.in/assets/pdfs/publications/2015/ecommerce-in-india-accelerating-growth.pdf

Raipuria, K. (2000). Electronic commerce: Opportunities for Indian exports. *Economic and Political Weekly*, 3260–3265.

Sanjai, P. R., & Dalal, Mihir. (2015, August 28). Flipkart, Myntra users go mobile; desktop still key for online travel firms. *The Live Mint.*

Satapathy, C. (1999). WTO Work Programme on Electronic Commerce: A developing country perspective. *Economic and Political Weekly*, 2771–2776.

Sen, A. (2017, January 02). Flipkart pares losses, boosts revenue at its largest unit. *The Live Mint.*

Singh, A. (2014, May 05). Goodbye e-commerce, hello m-commerce? 50% of Snapdeal's sales come via mobile; Flipkart tries to catch up. *Firstpost.*

Srivastava, M. (2016, April 04). Mobile phones to dominate online sales medium in India: Report. *The Live Mint.*

The Indian Express. (2004). 'eBay buys Bazee for 230 Crore'. New Delhi, 24 June.

Vaithianathan, S. (2010). A review of e-commerce literature on India and research agenda for the future. *Electronic Commerce Research, 10*(1), 83–97.

Viswanathan, N. K., & Pick, J. B. (2005). Comparison of e-commerce in India and Mexico: An example of technology diffusion in developing nations. *International Journal of Technology Management, 31*(1–2), 2–19.

CHAPTER 6

Valuation of E-Commerce Companies and Their Funding Patterns[*]

Akanksha Garg

6.1 Introduction

E-commerce (electronic commerce or EC) can be defined as buying and selling of goods and services, or the transferring funds or data, over an electronic network, primarily the Internet. These business transactions occur either as B2B, business-to-consumer, consumer-to-consumer or consumer-to-business. The terms 'e-commerce' and 'e-business' are often used interchangeably. The term 'e-tail' is also sometimes used in reference to transactional processes for online shopping (Rouse, 2019). Globally, the digital payment space is being driven by four mega trends that are expected to dramatically

---

[*]The data presented in the chapter is subject to the limitations of secondary data.

affect the future of this industry. These are (a) the ongoing digital/technology revolution, (b) entry of non-traditional players, (c) more demanding customer expectations and (d) 'enabling' regulations (Shah et al., 2016). Digital wallets, payment banks and Unified Payments Interface (UPI) are expanding in a big way. India has witnessed an exponential growth in the area of digital payment in recent times. With ever-increasing Internet and mobile penetration, the country is all set to witness a massive surge in the adoption of digital payments in the coming years (Das, 2016). Mobile has become an integral part of everyday life for almost everyone. The evolution in communication technology is not only making life easier for the end users but also providing opportunities for the government to connect with the citizens and provide better governance. Currently, India is the second largest telecom market in the world with 1.17 billion subscribers, out of which 1.14 billion use wireless means of communication (Indian Brand Equity Foundation [IBEF], 2018b). The use of mobile Internet is growing sharply. The number of users accessing Internet services on mobile was expected to reach 3 billion by 2020, covering 65 per cent of the world's adult population, as compared to approximately 1.9 billion in 2015 (Shah et al., 2016). Owing to these developments, e-commerce industry was worth $35 billion (as on September 2018) and is expected to grow at 25 per cent in the next five years in India. Being supported by rising incomes and surge in Internet users, it has the potential to grow more than four folds to $150 billion by 2022 (IBEF, 2018a). This rapid pace is powered by the confluence of favourable political, economic, social and demographic factors in India. For example, the changing spending behaviour of Indians, increasing Internet penetration, excessive use of social media and rapidly increasing online payments. The initiatives taken by the Government of India, including Digital India, Skill India, Start-up India and Make in India, and regulatory reforms such as 100 per cent foreign direct investment (FDI) in B2B e-commerce businesses and in multi-brand goods and services under marketplace model have given impetus to e-commerce industry to flourish (as cited in IBEF, 2018a). In the present study, five e-commerce companies are considered to identify the difference in their valuation. Out of these five e-commerce companies, two (i.e., Flipkart and Paytm

Mall) are unlisted and three (i.e., Infibeam Avenue, Info Edge and Justdial) are listed companies. Three methods—enterprise valuation, venture capital and discounted cash flow (DCF)—are used in the present study for the valuation of these e-commerce companies. It has been found that DCF method is not a viable valuation method for loss-making high-revenue e-commerce firms. Rather, venture capital method helps in valuing the firm based on revenues, as this method works well for loss-making companies and gives more comparable results. For valuation of listed e-commerce companies, we use enterprise value (EV) multiple which help in valuing the firms. The results are then compared on profitability and EV to identify the financial and fundamental strength of the listed and unlisted companies. On their comparison, a profitability and investment matrix is deduced that depicts how an e-commerce start-up moves from seed funding to public funding.

6.2 Overview of E-Commerce Industry

6.2.1 E-Commerce Industry in India

The Indian e-commerce industry is still in a nascent stage. The businesses in this sector are growing, driven by a combination of rising Internet penetration, a drop in data access costs, a shift to smartphones and a flow of credit to consumers and micro enterprises. Such parameters demonstrate the industry's growth potential. However, the rapid progress of this industry in India shows no signs of slowing down. Growth of this magnitude is to raise several operational, regulatory, legal and financial issues. This has led to the emergence of issues related with data protection, privacy, competition law, etc. Enormous efforts are infused to enhance customer's online experience and high levels of cash burn on promotions, advertisements and discounts for customer acquisition. An AlphaWise Survey (paywall) conducted in December 2014 established that the Internet users with less than two years of activity were doing fewer online transactions than those over five years of experience. This will mark an inflexion point in online shopping and result into continuous demand of capital from investors.

According to Aswath Damodaran (2009a), the life cycle graph of young companies such as Flipkart and Paytm Mall is currently at the point of inflexion owing to overloaded funding and expansion in their effort to reach the rural untapped segment. According to its life cycle stages and as the results show in the DCF valuations, the losses are yet to grow many folds.

The life cycle of a young or start-up firm initiates from the stage of idea generation (refer Figure 6.1) where there are zero revenues and negative operating income, no operating history, no comparable firms, the product is untested and do not have an established market. The valuation of firms at this stage is entirely on expected future growth. As the firm gradually gains some presence of its product in the market, revenues start to generate and firms enter into the next stage of its life cycle. The revenues in this stage are small but increasing and increasing at a faster rate while the operating losses are even

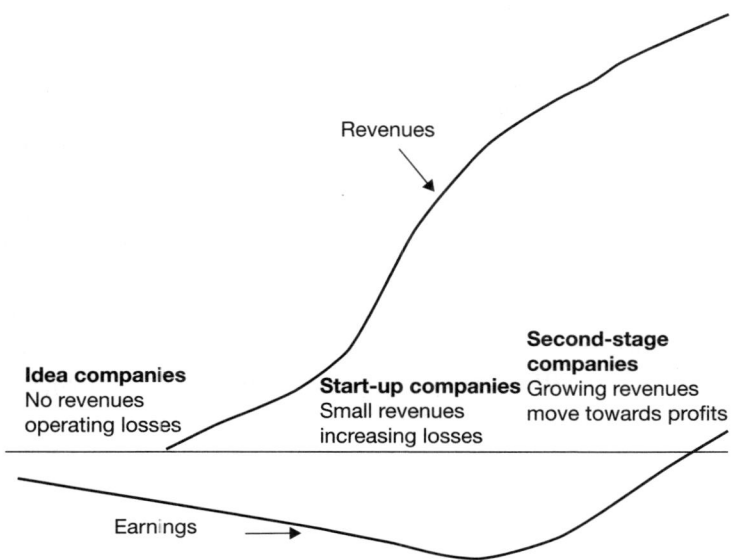

Figure 6.1 *Different Stages of Growth during Life Cycle of Young or Start-up Companies*

Source: Damodaran (2009a).

Box 6.1 Recent Trends in Venture Capital and Private Equity Investments

E-commerce industry in India witnessed 21 private equity and venture capital deals worth $2.1 billion in 2017 and 40 deals worth $1,129 million in the first half of 2018 (as cited in IBEF, 2018a). The number of deals in this space decreased from 91 in FY16 to 60 in FY17.

However, the scale of investments increased from $1.5 billion in FY16 to $4.7 billion in FY17. The US-based e-commerce giant Amazon has invested about $1 billion in its Indian arm so far in 2017, taking its total investment in its business in India to $2.7 billion (as cited in IBEF, 2018a). There has been overwhelming funding by US VCs and private equity firms into the Indian unicorns with some revenue such as Flipkart, Snapdeal, Ola, Zomato, etc., with the expectation to gain windfall gains in future. Potential deals in this space includes Chinese phone manufacturer, Xiaomi Corporation, planning to invest about $1 billion in 100 Indian start-ups over the coming 5 years, with an aim to make an ecosystem of apps surrounding its smartphone brand (Khaitan & co., 2015).

higher and continue increasing as the revenues increases. Once the firm establishes a sizeable position in the market with the increase in revenues, although at a decreasing rate, the firm starts to minimize its losses first and then finally starts generating profits. The growth of such firms is dependent on macroeconomic forces such as demographic changes, growth of the economy or of few specific sectors, technological changes that calls for innovation, etc. Despite of such risky and unpredicted life cycle, such young start-ups manages to get investments from venture capitalists (VC) and private equity (PE) firms. Why VCs/PEs invest in young start-ups? How do they value these firms to make investments?

6.2.2. Gross Merchandise Value (GMV): An Irrational Valuation Metrics

Currently, the e-commerce companies are valuing themselves high using GMV metric. Such overshot valuations have raised concerns for investors in companies being overvalued. Today, Flipkart's valuation is over $15 billion (₹100,000 crores) higher than the market value of Tata Motors, which is worth a mere ₹95,000 crores. India's largest aluminium company, Hindalco, values only ₹16,000 crores, whereas Snapdeal, merely a 5-year-old company, is valued at ₹35,000 crores (as cited in Merchant, 2015).

These e-commerce unicorns hyped GMV as the sole performance indicator of the e-tailing companies. GMV is the aggregate of all products sold through e-commerce platform. For example, a service aggregator or e-payment providers would use GTV which is aggregate of all services provided or payment transactions undertaken through e-commerce platform.[1] Likewise, e-commerce retailers are using GMV as its revenue for valuation of their firms, but in reality their revenue (which consists of commission and listing or advertising fees charges to vendors) is a mere fraction of GMV. This is the primary reason why GMV (or GTV) is used to eliminate the vast difference in revenue between online marketplaces and the direct service models for the same value of goods (or services) sold over the platform. GMV is not a true reflection of company's valuation as same is not reflected in financial statements of the company and also the actual revenue is only a fraction of GMV, for such businesses as e-commerce companies utilize up to 90 per cent of funds raised into customer acquisition only, therefore, incurring huge expenses which are not reflected in GMV calculation (as cited in Chawla, 2016). GMV-based valuation methods essentially imply that it is more optimal to compare market share rather than financial or operational performance (Khaitan & co., 2015). This gives some very strange valuation results for Flipkart. It was reported to have a GMV of $4 billion for the calendar year 2014 and was valued by venture capital investors at $11 billion by the end of 2016, and, now in another round of funding, it has raised $700 million at a valuation of $15 billion (Khaitan & co., 2015). The focus of Flipkart has been on fetching high volumes of sales than profitability, which is required to absorb high promotional, logistics and other fixed costs. It's is shocking to see such a rapid increase in the value of a heavily loss-making firm. Can we consider GMV as a robust metric for the valuation of e-commerce young start-up firms? If not, then how to discover the right valuation of such firms?

---

[1] https://economictimes.indiatimes.com/industry/services/retail/all-you-want-to-know-about-gross-merchandise-value/articleshow/33361672.cms

For companies in e-tail or e-commerce space, an initial public offering (IPO) would be a more accurate price discovery mechanism. Recently the e-commerce giant, Alibaba registered a global record IPO for $25billion at a valuation of $220 billion in September 2014. By the end of December 2014, Alibaba's GMV was $270 billion that accounts for 80 per cent of all total online purchase and nearly 7 per cent of total retail sales in China. Despite being an absolute leader and global leader in terms of value of transactions, Alibaba has been valued at less than 1.0x of its GMV at IPO when the revenues were $6.14 billion and pre-tax profits of $4 billion (Verma et al., 2015). While e-commerce companies in India are valued three times of their GMV that are not even profitable. The justification to such overvaluation could be the assumed aggressive growth targets which is only leading to GMV and valuations mismatch and will sooner or later bring down the GMV multiple.

6.2.3. Valuation Bubble: Another Dotcom Bubble

History does not repeat itself, but it rhymes. There are many similarities between present Indian e-commerce industry and the Dotcom bubble of 2000, which can be understood from the following:

1. In both cases, investors have unclear profitability model,
2. Investors pumped funds merely on expected revenues,
3. Valuations are based on best case growth scenarios with untested market models and
4. There are no tangible assets.

It is uncertain that the Indian infrastructure comprising of Internet reach, transportation, security and payment solution would be able to match this pace to facilitate the projected growth in e-tailing. However, other counterparts of e-commerce that do not involve in physical delivery of products, such as online ticketing, information and service aggregation, look more robust.

These segments have not witnessed similar aggressive valuations, for example, MakeMyTrip, the market leader in online tourism, has 48 per cent share of online travel in India. Its reported revenue was nearly $300 million for the FY 2014 (and losses of $14.5 million), with a market capitalization of merely $800 million (Khaitan & co., 2015). Therefore, VCs and PE investors after the series of seed funding look for exit through public offering or through secondary deals.

6.3. Objective of the Study

The objective of the study is to identify

- Which valuation method is more robust for the valuation of loss-making start-up private firms?
- Whether unlisted e-commerce firms are fundamentally sound?
- What is the investment pattern of VC firms?

6.4. Valuation Techniques Adopted for Young Start-up Firms

6.4.1. Venture Capital Method and Enterprise Valuation Method

The most likely valuation methods that can be used for valuing young start-up firms are enterprise valuation, venture capital and DCF methods. By evaluating the EV or free cash flows of firms, the true value of these firms can be ascertained.

6.4.1.1. Enterprise Valuation Method

In the enterprise valuation method, evaluators identify the true worth of the firm by using the earnings before interests, depreciation, tax and amortization (EBITDA) multiple, earnings before interests and taxes (EBIT) multiples and revenue multiples. Enterprise valuation is the net amount of total assets less cash and bank balances. It is worth mentioning here that enterprise valuation method is applicable for listed companies (Behrmann, 2016). The following multiples are used:

EBITDA Multiple = EV/EDITDA

EBIT Multiple = EV/EBIT

$$\text{Revenue Multiple} = \text{EV/Sales}$$

Calculation of EV:

$$\text{EV} = \text{Equity} + \text{Debt} + \text{Cash Reserves}$$

where

$$\text{Equity} = \text{Total Market value of Equity}$$

$$\text{Debt} = \text{Total Market value of Debt}$$

$$\text{Cash Reserves} = \text{Bank, Cash balances and cash equivalents}$$

Calculation of earnings before interest taxes, depreciation and amortization (EBITDA)

$$\text{EBITDA} = \text{Net Income} + \text{Interest} + \text{Taxes} + \text{Depreciation and}$$
$$\text{Amortization}$$

6.4.1.2. *Venture Capital Method*

This is the most common valuation method used by investors while funding unicorns. This method uses the common factors needed for valuation, that is, relative valuation, value of equity claim, growth assets and discount rates. This process has four steps:

Step 1. Estimating the expected revenues and earnings in future $T(n)$, typically for 3–5 years. This is normally the time period by which the VCs plan to exit the business.

Step 2. Evaluate the equity value at the end of the forecasted period by multiplying the expected earnings for $T(n)$ with the earning multiple (p/e) of a publicly traded firm in this sector. Similarly, to calculate the value of entire business the expected revenues in $T(n)$ are multiplied with the revenue multiple.

$$\text{Equity Value} = \text{Expected Earnings}_{\text{year N}} \times \frac{P}{E} \text{ (Relative)}$$

Or

$$\text{Equity Value} = \text{Expected Sales}_{\text{Year N}} \times \frac{EV}{Sales} \text{ (Relative)}$$

Step 3. The EV is discounted at the target rate of return which are high enough to perceive the risk associated in the business and the likelihood of the survival of the firm.

$$\text{Present Value of EV} = \frac{EV_{\text{Year N}}}{1 + \text{Target Rate of Return}}$$

Table 6.1 summarizes the target rates of return demanded by VCs in different stages of life cycle.

It can be ascertained that these target rates of return have survival risks built into them as the business moves up the stages of life cycle the chances of failure drops off and the risk associated with it decreases (Damodaran, 2009a).

Step 4. VCs gain a percentage of shares in the business in return for the capital they bring to the firm. To make a decision on what proportion of the firm they have can be arrived at by post-money valuation (Damodaran, 2009a).

$$\text{Proportion of Equity to VC} = \frac{\text{New Capital}}{\text{Post} - \text{Money Valuation}}$$

Table 6.1 VC Target Rates of Return: Stage in Life Cycle

Stages of Development	Target Rate of Return (%)
Start-up	50–70
First stage	40–60
Second stage	35–50
Bridge/IPO	25–35

Source: Damodaran (2009a).

where

1. Post-money valuation = Pre-money valuation + new capital
2. Pre-money valuation = EV today

A lot of literature concerning valuation techniques in general is available; Aswath Damodaran can be described as the current guru of valuations. In his research paper (Damodaran, 2009a), he examined the best way to value young companies. He explains not only the start-up life cycle and the different valuation methods but also their limitation that can be employed to assess their valuation. He also highlighted the kind of errors analysts make in valuing emerging market companies (Damodaran, 2009a). Eoin Whelan and Fergal McGrath (2002) suggested the costs dynamics of e-commerce companies for an indigenous Irish corporation. A research paper by Festel, Wuermseher, and Cattaneo (2013) presents the methodology for the valuation of 16 early stage start-ups in the field of biotechnology, nanotechnology, medical technology and clean technology along with a comprehensive comparison of different options for early stage investors.

6.4.2. Discounted Cashflow Method

Under DCF method, the future cash flows expected to earn from the project or proposal are discounted at the internal rate of return to ascertain the value of equity.

> Stage 1: Estimation of future cash flows
> Stage 2: Estimate of discount rate
> Stage 3: Estimation of present value and adjusting for survival
> Stage 4: Valuing equity claims in business

Peter Easton (1985) aims to provide empirical evidence to the fundamental links between accounting data and contemporaneous security prices. He argued that there is a strong link between security prices and the present value of future dividends (Easton, 1985). A research paper titled "The Validity of Company Valuation using DCF Methods" closely examines the theoretical and practical aspects of DCF valuation method. In this research, it was found that assumption play a vital role in DCF valuation method, as even the slightest change in valuation can change the results (Steige, 2008). Start-up valuation by VCs is an empirical study that examines the VCs valuation by factors identified in the strategy theory as important to firm performance. The attractiveness of the industry, the skills of the founder and the top management team as well as external relationships on new venture significantly and positively affect its valuation by VCs when it seeks venture capital financing in its early stage of development (Miloud, Aspelund, & Cabrol, 2012). The pricing on Internet stocks is the case of research department at IESE Business School wherein they illustrate the facts and cases on supply and demand for Internet stocks and the valuation methods used that reflects the pricing of Internet stocks (Estrada & Blakely, 1999). The only online retailing that was pioneered during the burst of dotcom bubble is Amazon (Christensen, Raynor, & McDonald, 2015). Clayton Christensen (1990) coined the term 'radical innovation', that is, innovation that disrupted traditional economic mechanisms, and argued that this kind of disruptive innovation is more prominent in start-ups than in the more established firms. DCF valuation and the multiple valuation used for valuing mature companies are irrelevant for valuing start-ups because they lack their profitability history for a reasonable forecast (Desaché, 2019). Behrmann (2016) suggested a valuation technique to be used for Internet companies by comparing the results and accuracy of different valuation techniques.

The chapter further studies the best valuation technique in the emerging market like India and what valuation method to be used at different stages of a firm's life cycle.

6.5. Valuation of Unlisted Retail Companies

In present study, we are taking into account two unlisted retail e-commerce companies: Flipkart and Paytm Mall.

6.5.1. Flipkart's Valuation

Flipkart is currently the market leader in online retail segment of e-commerce because of its high revenue volumes. Thus, it is important to analyse its true value as claimed by the company based on GMV metric. Instead of valuing the company on GMV multiple (EV/ GMV), we are valuing it on revenue multiple.

6.5.1.1. Enterprise Valuation Method

Enterprise valuation method uses peer multiples to arrive at the EV. It's a relative valuation method which makes it more comparable and helps in identifying whether the company is rightly valued or its valuation is inflated.

The current reported revenue of Flipkart for 2018 is ₹21,615 crores (as cited in Peermohamed, 2018)

$$\text{EBIT Multiple (peer)}^* = 81.35$$
$$\text{Revenue Multiple (peer)}^* = 15$$
$$\text{EBITDA Multiple (peer)}^* = 46.23$$
$$EV = Revenue\ Mulitple \times Sales$$
$$= ₹3,24,225 crores$$

*It is the average of listed peer companies: Info Edge, Infibeam and Justdial.

To calculate the EV for Flipkart, we need EBIT and EBIDTA values of company. Since, it is a loss-making company, the EBIT and EBIDTA values are negative. This makes EV calculation infeasible using EBIT and EBIDTA multiples. We can only use Revenue multiple to arrive at Flipkart's EV.

6.5.1.2. VC Method

In May 2018, Walmart acquired 77 per cent stakes in Flipkart by investing ₹107,890 crores, valuing at $20.7 billion (as cited in *Financial Express*, 2018) Using VC method, we ascertain the expected revenues that the Walmart is expecting in next 5 years. As the e-commerce firms are incurring losses, we are not expecting that the firm will earn any profits in next 5 years. We come to the following results:

Table 6.2 *Venture Capital Method*

Valuation	Results
Proportion of equity to VC	77%
Post money valuation	140,139 crores
Enterprise value (*n*=5)	173,351 crores
Expected revenue	11,300 crores
Enterprise value today	32,231.96 crores

Assumption

1. Target rate of return=40 per cent. Based on VC's stages of life cycle. Currently, Flipkart falls in the first stage.
2. EV/Sales=15. The average peer multiple of the listed counterparts.
3. N=5 years

Walmart is expecting only 52 per cent of current revenue in the next 5 years. These calculations are based on the current valuation of Flipkart at $20.7 billion. The results are based on author's analysis for more details refer Table 6.2.

6.5.1.3. DCF Method

According to the December 2018 reports by IBEF (2018b), online retail sales in India was expected to grow by 31 per cent to touch $32.7 billion in 2018, led by Flipkart, Amazon India and Paytm Mall where Flipkart holds 39.5 per cent share (as cited in Satish Meena, 2018), that is, ₹87,690 crores ($12.9 billion). As per IBEF (2018b), the online retail market was expected to grow by 29.2 per cent CAGR (Compound Annual Growth Rate).

Assumptions

1. Market growth rate=30 per cent
2. Market share expected to grow in 10 years=60 per cent
3. Expected revenue growth of Flipkart=30 per cent, based on previous year's growth rate in revenue (Nair, 2018)

4. It is assumed that in the next 5 years company will not generate any profits.
5. Pre-tax operating margin for the next 5 years will grow at −10 per cent, for next two years at −5 per cent and thereafter at 5 per cent. (Assumption is based on sources; as cited in Nair, 2018)
6. Current Flipkart market share = 40 per cent
7. Total market share in 2018 = ₹2,220 billion (IBEF, 2018b)
8. Flipkart revenue in 2018 = ₹216.5 billion (as cited in Peermohamed, 2018)
9. Flipkart losses in 2018 = ₹20.6 billion (as cited in Peermohamed, 2018)

These accumulated losses are added to the current year loss to ascertain gross loss before tax for the subsequent years. Since the cash flows are negative, that is, company is unable to generate profits for next 10 years, it's not feasible to ascertain the present value of cash flows. The results are found by the author during the analysis, for details refer Table 6.3.

6.5.2. Paytm Mall Valuation

According to the Bloomberg Quint, Paytm Mall, the online retail platform of India's biggest digital-payments brand, expended nearly ₹5 crore a day in the year ended March 2018 to gain market share as it competes with the likes of Amazon and Walmart-backed Flipkart. The company reported net losses of ₹1,787 crores on GMV of only ₹744 crores while, in fiscal year 2017, its revenue was just ₹7.35 crores and ₹13.63 crores. The company now holds 14 per cent share in e-commerce e-tail market (as cited in Sharma, 2018). We chose Paytm Mall for the study because of its recent funding from VCs and its growing popularity among online customers.

6.5.2.1. Enterprise Valuation Method

Enterprise valuation method uses peer multiples to arrive at the EV. It's a relative valuation method which makes it more comparable and helps identify whether the company is rightly valued or the valuation is inflated.

Table 6.3 Discounted Cash Flow Calculation

Year	YOY Market Growth Rate	Total Market In ₹ (billion)	Market Share	Estimated Revenue in ₹ (billion)	Pre-tax Profit Margin	Estimated Earnings Before Tax in ₹ (billion)	Gross Loss before Tax* in ₹ (billion)	Taxes	PAT (FCF F) in ₹ (billion)
2018	30	2220	40	216.5	-10%	-20.6	-20.6	0	-20.6
2019	30	2886	42	281.45	-10%	-28.145	-48.745	0	-48.745
2020	30	3751.8	44	365.885	-10%	-36.5885	-85.3335	0	-85.3335
2021	30	4877.34	46	475.6505	-10%	-47.5651	-132.8986	0	-132.8986
2022	30	6340.542	48	618.3457	-10%	-61.8346	-194.7331	0	-194.7331
2023	30	8242.705	50	803.8493	-10%	-80.3849	-275.118	0	-275.118
2024	30	10715.52	52	1045.004	-5%	-52.2502	-327.3683	0	-327.3683
2025	30	13930.17	54	1358.505	-5%	-67.9253	-395.2935	0	-395.2935
2026	30	18109.22	56	1766.057	5%	88.30285	-306.9907	0	-306.9907
2027	30	23541.99	58	2295.874	5%	114.7937	-192.197	0	-192.197
2028	30	30604.59	60	2984.636	5%	149.2318	-42.96515	-30.0756	-12.88955

The current reported revenue of Paytm Mall for 2018 is ₹774.8 crores.

$$\text{EBIT multiple (peer)}^* = 81.35$$

$$\text{Revenue multiple (peer)}^* = 15$$

$$\text{EBITDA multiple (peer)}^* = 46.23$$

$$EV = \text{Revenue multiple} \times \text{Revenue (sales)}$$

$$= ₹11,622 \text{ crores}$$

*It is the average of listed peer companies: Info Edge, Infibeam and Justdial.

To calculate the EV for Paytm Mall, we need EBIT and EBIDTA values of company. Since, it is a loss-making company, the EBIT and EBIDTA values are negative. This makes EV calculation infeasible using EBIT and EBIDTA multiples. We can only use revenue multiple to arrive at Paytm Mall EV.

6.5.2.2. VC Method

Recently, SoftBank funding into Paytm Mall raised company valuation to many folds. SoftBank infused ₹3,000 crores, valuing Paytm Mall close to $2 billion (₹13,200 crores) (as cited in Bansal and Chanchani, 2018). SoftBank gained 21.13 per cent stakes in it after the final round of funding (as cited in Sharma, 2018). Using VC method, we will identify what value and revenue the SoftBank expected of Paytm Mall.

Assumptions

1. Target rate of return = 40 per cent. Assuming the firm is in the first stage of venture capital life cycle.
2. EV/Sales = 15. The peer multiple of the listed counterparts (NDTV Profit, 2019).
3. $N = 5$ years

The result shows that SoftBank estimated Paytm Mall's true worth to be only ₹111.97 crores, that is, $1.64 billion, today and revenues

Table 6.4 *Venture Capital Method*

Valuation	Results
Proportion of equity to VC	21.13%
Post money valuation	14,197 crores
Enterprise value (*n*=5)	60,224.57 crores
Enterprise value today	11,197.82 crores
Expected revenue	3,925.98 crores
Expected revenue	5.07 times

to be ₹3,925.98 crores in the next 5 years. This is quite an optimistic expectation as their registered revenue in fiscal year 2017–2018 was ₹774 crores. It's true that company is incurring huge losses but holds some market share in the e-tail segment, and payment bank Paytm is the market leader, which is one of its sister companies. Down the time horizon, customers' acquisition is expected to triple. Thus, they took 5 times of their total revenues as the expected revenues as being the market leader in payment bank, Paytm Mall has the benefit of customer retention thus less cash burn is expected on customer acquisition. The results are found by the author during the analysis, for details refer Table 6.4.

6.5.2.3. DCF Valuation

The DCF valuation will help us identify the year when profitability in e-commerce companies can be expected.

Assumptions

1. Market growth rate=30 per cent; same as taken for Flipkart
2. Market share expected to grow in 10 years=34 per cent
3. Expected revenue growth=30 per cent; based on peer growth rate in revenue
4. It is assumed that in the next 9 years company will not generate any profits.

5. Pre-tax operating margin for the first 2 years will grow at −200 per cent then at −150 per cent for next 2 years, at −100 per cent for next 2 years, at −50 per cent for another 2 years, at 10 per cent for the next 2 years and at 5 per cent thereafter.
6. Total market share in 2018 = ₹2,220 billion (IBEF, 2018b)
7. Paytm Mall revenues in 2018 = ₹774.8crores (as cited in Ahuja, 2018)
8. Paytm Mall losses in 2018 = ₹1,787 crores (as cited in Ahuja, 2018)

Since the cash flows are negative, that is, company is unable to generate profits for the next 10 years, it's not feasible to ascertain the present value of cash flows. As the companies are incurring losses, free cash flows (FCFFS) can't be discounted at negative internal rate of return (IRR) rate. Thus, further steps in DCF valuation cannot be calculated for both the firms. This deduces that DCF valuation method is not the appropriate valuation method for e-commerce start-ups that are generating losses irrespective of their high revenues. The results are found by the author during the analysis, for details refer Table 6.5.

6.6. Valuation for Listed Companies

The data on revenue for following companies is collected from NDTV profit on which enterprise valuation method is used to identify their correct valuation.

EV of listed companies using Revenue multiple for following listed e−commerce companies are explained below:

1. Infibeam Avenues (EV) = ₹7,930.95 crores
2. Info Edge (EV) = ₹1,4043.62 crores
3. Justdial (EV) = ₹2,923.82 crores

The listed companies have market value in line with profitability, see Table 6.6. We are not applying EBITDA and EBIT multiples because the EV obtained from these multiple cannot be used to compare the EV results of unlisted companies. We have not used venture capital method because the companies are more than 20 years old and are not

Table 6.5 Discounted Cash Flow Calculation for Paytm Mall

Year	YOY Market Growth Rate	Expected Total Market in ₹ (billion)	Expected Revenue in ₹ (billion)	Expected Pre-tax Profit Margin	Expected Earnings before Tax in ₹ (billion)	Gross Loss Before Tax* In ₹ (billion)	Taxes	PAT (FCFF) In ₹ (billion)
2018	30	2220	7.748	−200%	−17.87	−17.87	0	−17.87
2019	30	2886	10.0724	−200%	−20.1448	−38.0148	0	−38.0148
2020	30	3751.8	13.09412	−150%	−19.6412	−57.65598	0	−57.65598
2021	30	4877.34	17.02236	−150%	−25.5335	−83.18951	0	−83.18951
2022	30	6340.542	22.12906	−100%	−22.1291	−105.3186	0	−105.3186
2023	30	8242.705	28.76778	−100%	−28.7678	−134.0864	0	−134.0864
2024	30	10715.52	37.39812	−50%	−18.6991	−152.7854	0	−152.7854
2025	30	13930.17	48.61755	−50%	−24.3088	−177.0942	0	−177.0942
2026	30	18109.22	63.20282	−10%	−6.32028	−183.4145	0	−183.4145
2027	30	23541.99	82.16366	−10%	−8.21637	−191.6308	0	−191.6308
2028	30	30604.59	106.8128	5%	5.340638	−186.2902	0	−186.2902

Note: *These accumulated losses are added to the current year loss to ascertain Gross Loss before Tax for the subsequent years.

Table 6.6 *Different Ratios of Listed E-Commerce Companies*

Company/Ratios	Infibeam Avenues	Info Edge	Justdial
P/sales	26.10	15.5	3.81
P/B	3.13	9.36	3.19
EV/EBITDA	90.78	35.21	12.70
EV/Sales	25.93	15.34	3.74
EV/EBIT	179.85	49.12	15.09
P/E	197.85	107.44	20.79
Market price	43.55	1,595.55	476.65
Book value per share	47.13	170.48	138.80
Operating profit growth	56.53	35.77	17.12
Revenue (sales) (₹ in crores)	305.86	915.49	781.77
Market cap (₹ in crores)	2,889.02	19,484.00	3,213.40

Source: NDTV Profit (2019).

in stage of VCs funding. Thus, VC method cannot be applied in it. We have not used DCF valuation method because of time constraints. Therefore, enterprise valuation method is the most suitable one to ascertain the true value of a firm for its peer comparison.

6.7. Findings

After using VC method and DCF valuation method for the valuation of unlisted e-tail companies, we can conclude on the basis of results that DCF method is not the best suitable method for loss-making e-commerce start-ups as the profit margins are very low. DCF calculations are entirely based on profits (cash flows). On the other hand, in VC method, one has the option to calculate the value of the firm either through profits or through revenues, as these loss-making firms have very high sales volume and they have yet not captured the entire Indian retail market. A company in this segment should generate very high volumes of sales to push themselves towards profits. In 2018, the online retail market share was only 2.9 per cent of the retail segment (IBEF, 2018b). On the other hand, we calculated the EV of listed

Table 6.7 *Enterprise Value under Different Valuation Methods (in ₹ crores)*

	Listed Companies			Unlisted Companies	
Company	Infibeam Avenues	Info Edge	Justdial	Flipkart	Paytm Mall
Enterprise valuation	7,930.95	14,043.62	2,923.82	324,225	11,622
Venture capital	NA	NA	NA	32,231.96	11,197.82

e-commerce firm using the given EV/sales multiple. These company's EVs are in line with their profits. Refer the details in Table 6.7.

The EV for unlisted companies is higher than listed companies. The enterprise valuation method results for listed and unlisted company are still comparable, whereas venture capital method results are misleading because Flipkart is valued at ₹32,231.96 billion while Paytm Mall at just ₹11,197.82 billion. VC method is not applicable to listed companies. The reason for VCs valuing loss-making companies more than their profit-making counterpart is the fact that Indian online retail segment is yet to expand its market share. India is still in the stage of Internet penetration which gives favourable conditions for companies such as Flipkart and Paytm Mall to capture larger chunks of retail market in near future. While, according to enterprise valuation method, Flipkart has the highest value, Info Edge comes second, and Paytm Mall stands third. We can say that this is due to their market share in the online retail segment. However, the fundamental side of such companies is little weary. The comparison below shows the fundamental gaps between the listed and unlisted companies.

6.7.1. Comparison between Listed and Unlisted Companies

1. The listed counterparts of e-commerce companies have robust fundamental financials. Therefore, they are well mitigated towards

downside market and other risks and to save themselves and their investors in the moment of turmoil.

2. Unlisted companies majorly focused on customer acquisition by way of heavy discounts, cashback and excessive advertisements and load their financials with heavy losses in order to gain market share in online retail in India.

3. Listed companies are profitable and giving average returns to its investors while unlisted companies are demanding more funding to gain more market share than focusing on increasing profitability.

4. The valuation and analysis of company financials is easier to deduce and quantify.

6.7.2. VC or PE Strategy for Investments

VC or PE strategy for investments have been to invest in young company(s) so as to create a brand, then scale it in next 3–5 years, attract more investors by rich valuations, and finally exit through IPO or acquisition. But it is not that easy for VC/PE firms to exit through IPO, as non-profitable companies are not allowed to issue IPO. VC/PE will be facing more challenges as Indian customers prefer cash on delivery over direct online payments (PTI, 2018). Because of these factors, e-commerce space has heated up in India and the valuations that these companies are getting are very rich in order to attract more investors.

Based on the valuation and comparison of the listed and unlisted online companies, it is evident that the profits in e-tailing segment of e-commerce start to emerge after more than two decades of the company's establishment. The players and VCs aim to earn profits from their venture, but, in the initial stages, they need to acquire customers and have substantial market share that will generate higher profits in the future. As e-tailing in India is more of a service provider or trading business model, the profits are majorly based on revenues because it's a commission-based model. The valuation of a commission-based trading company merely on GMV values is more irrational. Thus, instead we can use DCF and VC methods to arrive at expected number of

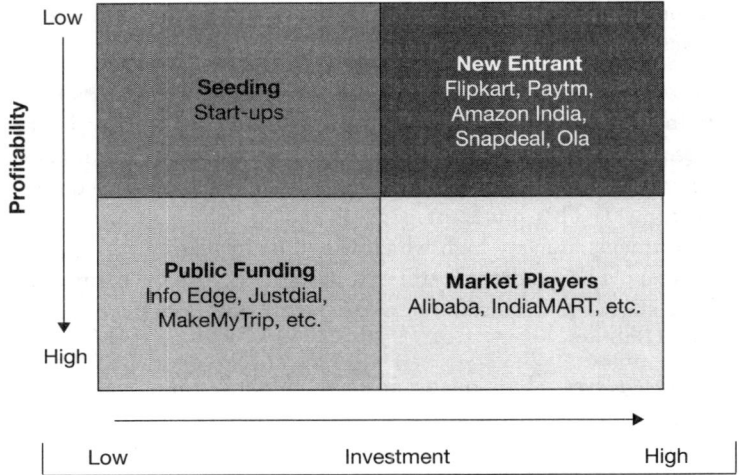

Time Horizon for each Quadrant is 5 years

Figure 6.2 *Investment vs Profitability Matrix*

years needed to book profits and the amount of funding required for such firms.

Based on the deduction, it's been identified that companies in e-commerce sector incur losses in their initial years of seeding phase and the losses start increasing as it enters the new phase. Once they have substantial market share, the losses reduce and profits start to emerge and then finally e-tailers call for IPO.

The matrix shown in Figure 6.2 is deduced based on the DCF valuation of the online firms. The matrix is scaled with profitability on vertical side and investment on horizontal side. The whole matrix is divided into four quadrants which are explained as under:

Seeding. In this quadrant, the companies need low investment and normally incur losses or almost nil profits. This quadrant may have low revenues or no revenue at all. This is because the company is still an idea and in its formation stage. Start-ups are the key players in this quadrant, which use different revenue and business model along with marketing strategies to acquire customers. The red colour of this quadrant depicts the losses and gradual increase in investment on the time horizon.

New entrant. In this quadrant, the e-commerce companies have to inject huge investment while the companies are incurring heavy losses. By this quadrant, the start-ups have gained a little market share and have very high revenues from their base of acquired customers. This quadrant is again red in colour as losses and investments are very high which would be increasing for another 10 years. The quadrant is still new entrant because the companies have started to acquire some market share and become visible in the economy.

Market players. This quadrant starts to show some stability in e-commerce companies. It's coloured yellow because the losses gradually start decreasing on the scale of time horizon and the investment injected also starts moving towards lower side from high side of the matrix. The companies in this quadrant are market players, as they have high customer base, customers' trust and reliability, and their market share also increases.

Public funding. This is the last quadrant wherein every company wants to fall into. The e-commerce firms will go for IPO to raise funds from public and such funds will be taken by shareholders (VC firms) as their capital gain for their investment in such companies rather than being invested in the company for further expansion or business operations.

6.8. Conclusion

The analysis of actual revenues of e-commerce firms and their massive losses clearly shows that valuations are running ahead of themselves in order to attract more investors for funding. Therefore, are now shifting their focus from 'high valuation companies' to 'sustainable, scalable and profitable companies'. The valuations for unlisted e-commerce companies clearly show that there are no signs of profits in the coming next 10 years as companies are spending 80–90 per cent of funds from their investors in customer acquisition. Therefore, despite of funds flooding in Indian e-commerce retail segment, the e-commerce sector is sunk in losses for at least another 10 years. The reasons for funding by VCs attributed to are as follows:

- Lucrative untapped rural market
- Internet penetration is expected to grow at 45 per cent
- World's largest young population
- Online retail sales in India is expected to grow at 31 per cent (IBEF, 2018b)

Due to all these above mentioned favourable economic and demographic factors, VC and PCs having been flooding funds in ecommerce unicorns despite of heavy losses. But the question is how long they will remain invested and bear the burden of losses. According to venture capital method, the last stage for them to exit the company is by bringing IPO. That means transferring their burden of losses by diluting their share in market. The shares by then become so popular and demanding in the market that they are issued at extremely premium prices. This premium pricing will pocket profits for VC and PEs in these companies. And after the listing, if the fundamentals are weak, any negative news in the market will blow the value of these companies that will result in heavy losses to small investors.

It's the time to be cautious and to adopt wait-and-watch strategy to see the growth graph of these e-tailing companies in e-commerce sector. Although the segment is not new to the world and we have seen Amazon in losses for more than a decade, the VCs expect that the segment have potential to generate profits but after acquiring large market share and later in investment cycle.

References

Ahuja, A. (2018). Paytm Mall's loss rises 150 times to ₹1,787 crore in FY18. *Livemint*, 29 October. https://www.livemint.com/Companies/2qbxHBT Eys8gGM6uU83wcK/Paytm-Malls-loss-rises-150-times-to-1787-crore-in-FY18.html

Bansal, V., & Chanchani, M. (2018). SoftBank in talks with Paytm Mall for a ₹3,000 crore round. *Economic Times*, 6 March. https://

economictimes.indiatimes.com/small-biz/startups/newsbuzz/softbank-in-talks-with-paytm-mall-for-a-rs-3000-crore-round/articleshow/63179689.cms

Behrmann, G. (2016). *Internet company valuation: A study of valuation methods and their accuracy* (BSc Thesis). https://www.researchgate.net/publication/303767594

Chawla, H. (2016). Inside Flipkart's reversal of fortunes. *Livemint*, 28 April. https://www.livemint.com/Companies/7zVXid1PdH2YwxKAzVIbaP/Inside-Flipkarts-reversal-of-fortunes.html

Christensen, C. M., Raynor, M. E., & McDonald, R. (2015). What is disruptive innovation? *Harvard Business Review*, *93*(12), 44–53.

Confederation of Indian Industry. (2016). *Digital: A revolution in the making in India.* Deloitte. https://www2.deloitte.com/content/dam/Deloitte/in/Documents/technology-media-telecommunications/in-tmt-digital-revolution-in-making-cii-noexp.pdf

Damodaran, A. (2009a). Valuing young, start-up and growth companies: Estimation issues and valuation challenges. http://people.stern.nyu.edu/adamodar/pdfiles/papers/younggrowth.pdf

Damodaran, A. (2009b). Volatility rules: Valuing emerging market companies. www.stern.nyu.edu/~adamodar/pdfiles/papers/emergmkts.pdf

Das, U. (2016). *Digital: A revolution in the making in India.* https://www2.deloitte.com/content/dam/Deloitte/in/Documents/technology-media-telecommunications/in-tmt-digital-revolution-in-making-cii-noexp.pdf

Desaché, G. (2019). *How to value a start-up?* http://www.vernimmen.net/ftp/Research_paper_V3.pdf

Easton, P. D. (1985). Accounting earnings and security valuation: Empirical evidence of the fundamental links. *Journal of Accounting research*, 54–77.

Estrada, J., & Blakely, B. (1999). The pricing of internet stocks. https://papers.ssrn.com/sol3/papers.cfm?abstract_id=195630

Festel, G., Wuermseher, M., & Cattaneo, G. (2013). Valuation of early stage high-tech start-up companies. *International Journal of Business*, *3*(18), 216–231.

Financial Express. (2018). Walmart buys Flipkart, finally: US giant picks up 77% stake in Indian e-tailer for $16 billion: 5 key things. https://www.financialexpress.com/industry/its-official-walmart-picks-up-77-stake-in-flipkart-for-16-billion/1160541/

IBEF. (2018a). E-commerce. https://www.ibef.org/download/Ecommerce-March-2018.pdf

IBEF. (2018b). Indian Brand Equity Foundation. https://www.ibef.org/industry/ecommerce.aspx

Khaitan & co. (2015, September). *ERGO perspective.* Mumbai: Khaitan & co.

Meena, S. (2018). By acquiring Flipkart, Walmart gets access to the Indian market — For a premium. *Forrester*, 15 May. https://go.forrester.com/

blogs/by-acquiring-flipkart-walmart-gets-access-to-the-indian-market-for-a-premium/

Merchant, M. (2015). Why start-ups like Flipkart are worth more than Tata Motors. *Dailyo.* https://www.dailyo.in/business/flipkart-snapdeal-ola-tata-motors-general-motors-amazon-e-commerce-foodpanda-jet-airways/story/1/5939.html

Miloud, T., Aspelund, A., & Cabrol, M. (2012). Startup valuation by venture capitalists: An empirical study. *Venture Capital, 14*(2–3), 151–174.

Nair, R. P. (2018). When will, and can, Flipkart reach this important milestone? *Your Story,* 15 February. https://yourstory.com/2018/02/flipkart-break-even-ebitda/

NDTV Profit. (2019). Info Edge (India) Ltd. 12 January. https://www.ndtv.com/business/stock/info-edge-_naukri/financials-ratio

Peermohamed, A. (2018). Flipkart India unit's FY18 losses zoom 742% in spite of 39% rise in revenue. *Business Standard,* 29 October. https://www.business-standard.com/article/companies/flipkart-india-unit-s-fy18-losses-zoom-742-in-spite-of-39-rise-in-revenue-118102800636_1.html

PTI. (2018). PE/VC investments, exits hit record in 2017 at $26.8b, $13 billion *Financial Express,* 15 January. https://www.financialexpress.com/market/pevc-investments-exits-hit-record-in-2017-at-26-8b-13-billion/1016341/

Rouse, M. (2019). E-commerce (electronic commerce. https://searchcio.techtarget.com/definition/e-commerce

Shah, A., Kaushik, V., Roongta, P., Jain, C., & Awadhiya, A. (2016). *Digital payments 2020: The making of a $500 billion ecosystem in India.* India: The Boston Consulting Group.

Sharma, N. (2018). Paytm Mall lost nearly ₹5 crore per day last fiscal to catch up with Amazon, Flipkart. *Bloomberg Quint,* 29 October. https://www.bloombergquint.com/technology/paytm-mall-lost-nearly-rs-5-crore-per-day-last-fiscal-to-catch-up-with-amazon-flipkart#gs.vvY05yA7

Steige, F. (2008). The validity of company valuation using discounted cash flow methods. A seminar paper. https://arxiv.org/ftp/arxiv/papers/1003/1003.4881.pdf

Whelan, E., & McGrath, F. (2002). A study of total life cycle costs of an e-commerce investment. A research in Progress. *Evaluation and Program Planning, 25*(2), 191–196.

CHAPTER 7

E-Commerce Taxation
An Unsettled Agenda

Pralok Gupta, Shreyansh Singh and Sunayana Sasmal

7.1. Overview

The expansion of e-commerce activities in India and other countries has led to the start of discussions on taxing such activities. The move from physical to digital is overwhelming, and countries are scrambling to tax the companies that are making large amounts of profits. However, by the virtue of the remote nature of doing business exacerbated by the digital economy and ruled by various platforms, it has become easy for corporations to get away with paying a meagre amount in taxes. A company like Uber that plans its taxation intelligently, finds it easy to legally remain untaxed in a jurisdiction where it high profit generation; instead, it finds a channel to pay taxes in a tax haven, usually where they are headquartered (Govindrajan et al., 2019). Ireland is a popular destination for the purpose, bearing a low corporate tax rate of 12.5 per cent (Regan, 2019). Governments are frustrated when big corporations with first-mover advantage and network effects can run havoc in the traditional economic model prevalent in the country, affecting changes in consumption patterns and employment while avoiding taxes. Therefore, a number of countries have been deliberating the need to make these companies fulfil the underlying philosophy of taxation, that is, to contribute to the growth and development of the place where profits are being generated.

Given the virtual nature of these activities and the absence of physical connect between buyers and sellers, taxation of e-commerce transactions is a complex issue. The e-commerce taxation can be understood from three perspectives. First, domestic taxation on e-commerce firms and goods and services sold on e-commerce platforms. Second, taxation of income of digital firms including e-commerce platforms. While the Goods and Services Tax (GST) is applicable on purchases made on online platforms, there exists a regulatory void with regard to taxation of online entities and their activities. Third, taxation on cross-border e-commerce transactions, called custom duty.

Traditionally, it has been believed that income of the corporations must be taxed at source, complimented by recipient countries' imposition of consumption taxes. Not departing from that entirely, a number of countries have moved to imposing consumption taxes in the form of value-added tax (VAT) or GST on cross-border supplied services, irrespective of having a digital services tax (DST) in place alongside. These taxes are imposed on the sale of electronic or digital services by online providers and platforms to consumers. The bone of contention is jurisdiction from where the taxes should be collected. With the rising challenges of the digital economy, the OECD offered its guidance in the form of VAT/GST Guidelines in 2017, whereby it suggested that the destination principle be adopted. In both cases of B2B and B2C transactions, the tax should be collected where the final recipient of the service resides. It was recommended that for B2C services, the service provider must register and charge VAT in the country of residence of the consumer, whereas, for B2B, the service recipient should make a self-assessment through a reverse-charge mechanism (OECD, 2017a).

Both the developed and the developing countries, such as South Korea, Singapore, Canada, Australia, Bangladesh, Chile, India, etc., have amended their indirect tax structures since then, to start collecting VAT/GST on the imported digital services (Terada-Hagiwara, Gonzales, & Wang, 2019). However, not all practices have been adopted in absolute concurrence with the suggestions of the OECD. For example, South Africa amended its law in 2014 to mandate registration of non-resident service supplier in the country to collect VAT and, in 2019, increased the threshold required for registration as well as the taxable services (South Africa National Treasury, 2019).

Thus, taxation of digital economy and related transactions is an emerging issue that has remained unsettled for both developed and developing countries. Against this backdrop, this chapter covers important taxation issues in the context of e-commerce and digital economy at large. Section 2 of the chapter discusses e-commerce taxation in India with applicability of GST for e-commerce transactions as well as equalization levy imposed by the Government of India. Section 3 presents the OECD approach for taxation of digital economy. Section 4 highlights the experiences of selected countries in implementing policies for taxing digital economy. Section 5 discusses e-commerce taxation in the context of the WTO moratorium on custom duties on electronic transmissions. Section 6 concludes the chapter.

7.2. E-Commerce Taxation in India

The interim report of a market study on e-commerce in India conducted by Competition Commission of India reveals issues, such as deep discounting, algorithm opaqueness in search rankings, and increasing dependence of brick and mortar establishments on e-commerce platforms, which are jeopardizing the competition in the market and disrupting the traditional businesses (Competition Commission of India, 2019). Such deep discount schemes and the disruption of traditional businesses are partly because these new-age businesses escape taxes that the traditional businesses are subjected to. It is due to the nature of e-commerce that these entities can conduct businesses and be operational without any physical presence in India for the purposes of taxation (Sharma & Gupta, 2019). Further, the savings thus accrued can be used for other purposes, for example, to provide discounts that lure consumers and, in the long run, adversely affect the competition.

In order to correct this anomaly, India has introduced multiple measures to tax the digital economy in order to make e-commerce players equalize the unfair tax advantage. It has introduced taxation measures in the form of both indirect taxes and direct taxes. In the following sub-sections, we discuss the measures India has implemented in its domestic taxation framework.

7.2.1. Framework under GST

7.2.1.1. Taxation of Online Information and Database Access or Retrieval Services

Prior to December 2016, the Online Information and Database Access or Retrieval (OIDAR) services provided by a service supplier located outside India were not taxable since the place of provision of such services was the location of service provider, that is, outside the taxable territory. In December 2016, the amended Place of Provision of Services (PoPS) Rules, 2012[1] came into effect which made location of service recipient as the place of provision of services and thus nullified the unfair tax advantage enjoyed by the online platforms not based in India. This, together with the Integrated Goods and Services Tax (IGST) Act, 2017[2] marked a practical shift in India's digital taxation policy. The IGST Act defines OIDAR as follows:

> Online information and database access or retrieval services means services whose delivery is mediated by information technology over the internet or an electronic network and the nature of which renders their supply essentially automated and involving minimal

[1] http://www.servicetax.gov.in/htdocs-servicetax/st-rules-placeof-provsn-services

[2] http://gstcouncil.gov.in/sites/default/files/IGST.pdf

human intervention and impossible to ensure in the absence of information technology. (IGST Act, Section 2(17))

As per the definition, for any service to qualify as OIDAR, it must satisfy the following tests. First, it should be mediated by information technology over the Internet or an electronic network. Second, it is automated and impossible to ensure without information technology. The illustrative list followed by the definition includes online advertising, e-books, cloud services, online gaming, supply of digital content, that is, movies, music other intangibles over the Internet, digital data storage, etc. It is to be noted that a website that allowed free access for viewing images and charged a fee for downloading images is also covered under OIDAR and thus liable to pay tax.[3]

The transaction relating to OIDAR services falls within the tax net when the recipient of OIDAR services is located in India or, in other words, the place of supply of service is in India, irrespective of the fact that the service supplier is not located in India.[4] The IGST Act also provides that in case of OIDAR services being supplied by a service provider not based in India to a business entity in India, the reverse charge mechanism would be applicable and the business entity (registered person) in India is liable to pay the tax.[5] The IGST Act, 2017 shifts the liability to pay applicable tax to overseas OIDAR service supplier in cases where the recipient of OIDAR services is a 'non-taxable online recipient'.

The IGST Act, 2017 also requires that, for tax compliance and other necessary procedures, the overseas service supplier or its representative should register under the Simplified Registration Scheme. Further, it also provides that the overseas supplier can appoint a representative if it doesn't have a physical presence or a representative

[3] Photolibrary India Pvt Ltd. v. Commissioner of Service Tax, Mumbai, 2017 (7) G.S.T.L. 386 (Bom.).

[4] Section 13(12), Integrated Goods and Services Tax Act, 2017.

[5] National Academy of Customs, Indirect Taxes & Narcotics, Online Information Data Base Access and Retrieval (OIDAR) GST (Goods & Services Tax), Directorate General of Taxpayer Services, Central Board of Excise and Customs.

in India for the payment of tax. It is to be noted that OIDAR suppliers based in India have to file regular GST returns whereas OIDAR suppliers located outside India are required to file GST 5A returns.

A ruling delivered by the Authority on Advance Rulings (AAR), Karnataka,[6] provides further clarity on few issues, as it specifically states that the supplier of OIDAR services has to charge applicable GST on individual consumers who are not receiving such services for the purposes of commerce, industry or any other business or profession. Additionally, the burden to prove that such OIDAR services received by individual consumers were for purposes other than commerce, business, etc., lies with supplier of OIDAR services.

7.2.1.2. Taxation of Radio Cabs and Accommodation-related Services

The Central Goods and Services Tax (CGST) Act, 2017[7] provides the power to the government to specify services for which the e-commerce operator is liable to pay the tax. Pursuant to this, a notification[8] was released on 28 June 2017 which stated that e-commerce operators are liable to pay tax for two types of services:

- Providing radio taxi that uses General Packet Radio Service (GPRS) or Global Positioning System (GPS) for tracking.
- Providing accommodation services to the consumers in hotels, guesthouses, etc., except where the person supplying service through the e-commerce platform has an aggregate turnover of more than ₹2,000,000 and is liable for registration under the CGST Act, 2017.

This notification effectively covered ride-hailing e-commerce operators such as Uber, Ola, etc., and online websites providing accommodation

---

[6] M/s. Springer Nature Customer Service Centre GmBh, The Authority on Advance Rulings (AAR), Karnataka Advance Ruling No. KAR ADRG 70/2019. https://gst.kar.nic.in/Documents/General/AAR70SPRINGNATURE.pdf

[7] http://www.gstcouncil.gov.in/sites/default/files/CGST.pdf

[8] Notification No.17/2017-Central Tax (Rate), dated 28 June 2017.

services such as Oyo, Make My Trip, etc. This position was also further affirmed by an advance ruling by the Appellate Authority on Advance Rulings (AAAR), Karnataka,[9] which clarified that the e-commerce operator was liable to pay the tax for the amount paid by the passenger to the driver for the trip.

7.2.2. Equalization Levy

The Finance Act, 2016[10] introduced the concept of 'equalization levy' in the Indian tax system which was aimed at remedying the limitations arising in case of the business income of foreign digital service suppliers that operate in India without any 'permanent establishment' (PE) because of the very nature of e-commerce platform and the economy. The equalization levy on online or digital advertisement services is equal to 6 per cent of the total amount to be paid for such services. According to the Finance Act, 2016, service recipients who are Indian residents or non-residents who have PE in India shall deduct the equalization levy from the amount payable to a non-resident service supplier which doesn't have PE in India when the aggregate value of service is more than 1 lakh rupees in the previous year. In March 2020, India enacted the Finance Act, 2020[11] which effectively broadened the scope of equalization levy. The Act imposes a 2 per cent levy on the amount of 'consideration' received by an e-commerce operator for services it provides to: (a) an Indian resident; or (b) to a non-resident for sale of advertisement meant for an Indian resident or a customer who accesses the advertisement though internet protocol address located in India; or (c) sale of data, collected from an Indian resident or from a person who uses internet protocol address located in India or (d) to a person who buys such goods or services or both using internet protocol address located in India.

---

[9] M/s. OPTA Cabs Pvt. Ltd, The Appellate Authority on Advance Rulings (AAR), Karnataka Advance Ruling No. KAR/AAAR/04/2018–19. http://gst-council.gov.in/sites/default/files/appellate-order/OPTACABS.pdf

[10] http://www.cbic.gov.in/resources/htdocs-cbec/fin-act2016.pdf

[11] Part VI, The Finance Act, 2020,http://egazette.nic.in/WriteReadData/2020/218938.pdf

The 2 per cent equalisation levy is not to be charged in cases where the e-commerce operator has a PE in India in connection to the services being provided, or the e-commerce operator is already covered under the purview of equalisation levy for online or digital advertisement services, or where the annual sales or turnover from such services is less than two crore rupees. Interestingly, the equalization levy provided under the Finance Act, 2020 is to be paid by e-commerce operator directly as prescribed under the Act.

7.2.3. Significant Economic Presence (SEP) and Business Connection

The Finance Act, 2018[12] amended the Income Tax (IT) Act, 1961 and inserted a new section to the IT Act to levy income tax on companies, digital service suppliers which are not based in India. As per this section of the IT Act, for the imposition of income tax, the taxable income should arise through a 'business connection' in India. Prior to the amendment, the business connection was not broad enough to be applicable to companies and service supplier non-residents in India. Through amendment, it was specified in the IT Act, 1961[13] that SEP shall constitute business connection. The SEP is deemed to be established when:

- Transaction is conducted by a non-resident in India in respect of goods, services or property (including download of data and software) if the total payments arising from such transactions exceeds the threshold amount during the previous year or
- Soliciting of business activities or engaging in interaction through digital means with a prescribed number of users takes place in India.

The non-resident cannot escape its tax liability by claiming that the agreement for such transactions is entered outside India thus, beyond the jurisdiction; they have a residence or place of business in or outside India; or they supply services in or outside India. The Finance Act,

---

[12] http://egazette.nic.in/writereaddata/2018/184302.pdf
[13] https://www.incometaxindia.gov.in/pages/acts/income-tax-act.aspx

2020 deferred the application of SEP provisions to 1st April, 2022 to be applied for the assessment year 2022–2023. The memorandum provides that the policy decision was taken in light of the continuing discussion in G20-OECD BEPS project.[14]

Thus, India has started implementing tax on digital economy in the past few years. Although India has incorporated certain changes in its domestic laws and legislations to bring e-commerce players under the purview of tax net, the effectiveness still remains to be seen. It is likely that some of the measures introduced may not achieve the purpose because of the Double Taxation Avoidance Agreements (DTAA). Further, it can be reasonably concluded that tax imposed on e-commerce operator can be conveniently passed on by them to the consumers and businesses using their platforms. This can raise the costs of services for the consumers and will further increase the costs for the service suppliers (like drivers on a radio taxi app).

7.3. OECD on Taxation in Digital Economy

With the advent of multinational corporations with areas of operation spanning worldwide, rules were sought to tax the companies at source while ensuring that the home country did not impose double taxation. In this area, the Organisation of Economic Co-operation and Development (OECD) has been at the forefront of formulating taxation principles. The OECD, in its 'Model Tax Convention on Income and on Capital' has laid down that tax could not be collected on profits derived from business in another country unless attributable to a PE (OECD, 2017b). The OECD Model Tax Convention defines PE as, 'a fixed place of business through which the business of an enterprise is wholly or partly carried on' but would not mean a place for maintenance of stocks of goods for storage, display, delivery or processing, purchasing of goods or merchandise, collection of information. Therefore, traditionally, the nexus of physical presence was absolutely necessary to be able to impose taxes.

---

[14] Memorandum to the Finance Bill, 2020. https://www.indiabudget.gov.in/doc/memo.pdf

This, for obvious reasons, creates a hurdle for countries in taxing e-commerce corporations when their business models utilize the benefits of the Internet and cloud hosting and thereby avoid tax by not having the requisite nexus. The questions that have arisen in the digital economy therefore relate to whether websites can be considered to be PE, and how to bring the e-commerce companies operation remotely under domestic tax brackets. The definition of PE has been considered worth of an amendment for this purpose.

This led the OECD to formulate measures against tax avoidance by base erosion and profit shifting (BEPS), on the insistence by the G20 member countries. The project began in 2015 with a view to tackle taxation issues arising out of digitalization (OECD, 2015). In order to create a singular road map and prevent different unilateral arrangements by countries, the OECD has attempted to set standards on the issue and provide coherence to future practices. An inclusive framework was created whereby participating nations could come together with the OECD to recommend and implement changes in their taxation laws regarding nexus and profit allocation (OECD, 2018).

In 2019, the inclusive framework has identified three proposals on methods of taxations open to public consultation (OECD, 2019a). These are as follows:

- *User participation proposal.* Aimed at businesses with high dependence on user involvement such as social media, search engines and marketplaces. It proposes that 'an amount of profit be allocated to jurisdictions in which those businesses' active and participatory user bases are located, irrespective of whether those businesses have a local physical presence'.
- *Marketing intangibles proposal.* Aimed at a larger number of businesses, whereby through either remotely or a limited local presence, they develop a user/customer base and other marketing intangibles.
- *SEP proposal.* It says that digitalization of the economy and other technological advances have enabled business enterprises to be heavily involved in the economic life of a jurisdiction without a significant physical presence, rendering the nexus requirement irrelevant.

In October 2019, with the inputs of governments, business, civil society, academia and the general public, the OECD secretariat furnished a new 3-tiered taxation proposal, that drew upon earlier three proposals. It was called a 'unified approach' for formulating new nexus rules based on sales thresholds and profit allocation going beyond arm's length (OECD, 2019b). It was welcomed by many countries as it aligns with their desire to bring e-commerce corporations under the tax ambit. However, the work on this will continue as countries being a part of this multilateral instrument must now have consensus on making changes in the Model Tax Convention as well as domestic legislations. In the meanwhile, several countries have begun implementing 'digital taxes' by amending their income tax legislations or new domestic indirect taxes on 'digital products' (KPMG, 2019a).

7.4. Taxation on Digital Economy: Selected Countries' Experiences

7.4.1. The European Union

In early 2018, the European Commission released two proposals related to taxation on digital economy, both set to go into effect in 2020 (European Commission, 2018a; 2018b). If they are to come into effect, they will require several changes at the continental level with effects on relationships with rest of the world. The two proposals are as follows:

- An 'interim' 3 per cent DST on gross revenues (i.e., turnover) derived from activities in which users are deemed to play a major role in value creation (arising out of social media, online marketplaces, online advertising, data collection).
- Corporate tax on 'significant digital presence' with nexus and profit allocation.

Both these proposals were faced with several protests and roadblocks, and therefore both were put on hold for the time being until a common solution is arrived at the OECD (Reuters, 2019). However, there have been several efforts at the individual country level to impose digital taxes.

7.4.2. France

Inspired by the Commission's failed efforts, France also began deliberating on digital taxes with culmination in the French legislature passing a Bill in July 2019 imposing a 3 per cent DST, applying retrospectively from 1 January 2019 (KPMG Insights, 2019). It has also been called the 'GAFA Tax', as those are the corporations being brought under the scanner. The tax is targeted at only two kinds of services:

- Intermediary services except the supply of digital content, communication services and qualifying payment services, when the user concludes a transaction or accesses the service in French territorial limits.
- Provision of services to advertisers based on data collected about users while accessing the digital interface, provided the user whose data has been collected is located in France.

The Bill has established thresholds of revenue generated such that when revenue in excess of the threshold is generated, the total amount of revenue generated in France is liable to be taxed. However, the GAFA tax is not deductible from corporate income tax, which is an added benefit under the UK legislation which follows next.

On prima facie, this legislation is not discriminatory between countries; the tax is expected to affect big technological giants with considerable market shares in France. As it predominantly affects the US companies, the USA has threatened to retaliate with tariffs on specialized French imports of wine and cheese (Burchard, 2019). However, reportedly both countries have negotiated an agreement whereby France's digital service tax will be in force only until an agreement is arrived at the OECD in 2020. In the meanwhile, the USA has been conducting a Section 301 investigation on the French DST and has clarified their intent to investigate the taxes of Italy, Austria and Turkey as well. On 2 December 2019, the United States Trade Representative (USTR) published the Section 301 Report which found that the French tax is unreasonable, discriminatory and burdens the US commerce. It proposed imposition of additional duties of up to 100 per cent on certain French products having an approximate value of $2.4 billion (USTR, 2019). However, subsequently, due to the talks between France and USA, there is a temporary suspension of the collection of taxes till the end of 2020 (KPMG Insights, 2020).

7.4.3. United Kingdom

On lines similar to those adopted by France, from April 2020, the UK has introduced a 2 per cent DST on businesses that provide a social media platform, search engine or an online marketplace to UK users, which also includes carrying on associated online advertising business (HM Revenue and Customs, UK, 2020). This differs from France's plan, which taxes those advertising activities that derive data from the user located in France. In the UK system, the advertisement simply needs to be viewed by a user in UK. In this context, the UK taxation appears to subscribe to the first of the three proposals submitted at the OECD, which focuses on taxing businesses by the virtue of involvement of users in the creation of value of service and brand.

The taxation methodology remains similar to that of France, whereby revenue when generated above predetermined thresholds will be taxable in its entirety. The legislation tries to maintain a balance by providing for a safe harbour approach allowing for alternate calculation; by exempting the first 25 million pounds earned in UK from tax; by allowing it to be deducted from corporate income tax, provided the cost is incurred wholly and exclusively for purposes of trade; by stating that the tax is an interim solution only and will be replaced by the multilaterally agreed tax under the aegis of the OECD. However, the introduction of the tax has led to the retaliation threats from the USA in the form of increased import tariffs on cars from the UK (Elliott & Mason, 2020).

7.4.4. Italy

In the midst of a probe against Netflix for underreporting taxable activities in Italy, the Italian government declared its intentions of imposing a DST of 3 per cent on digital services in December

2018 (EY Indirect Tax Alert, 2019). Due to protests, the idea was discontinued in the wait of a multilateral solution, but it gathered momentum in late 2019. The Italian Budget Law 2020 paved the way for a DST, different from the one earlier proposed (EY Tax Alert, 2020). Charged on an annual basis at a rate of 3%, Italy imposes the tax on online advertising, intermediation through social media, online marketplaces and data collection when the user is located in Italy or a transaction is concluded in the tax period in Italy. This tax has also been defined as an indirect tax; hence, it will be outside the purview of double taxation treaties.

7.4.5. Other EU Members

Post the French DST, a number of other EU countries have proposed such Bills with sunset clauses. Spain has recently approved a draft DST legislation imposing tax of 3% (Bloomberg Tax, 2020), advocating a very similar method of taxation of digital services, as put forth by Italy. However, Spain uses the terms 'location of device', and this may lead to increase in fraudulent activities involving redirecting or disguising the geo-localization of devices (Díaz-Súnico, 2019).

In Belgium as well, in 2019, a DST of 3 per cent was proposed on the services of online advertising, intermediation through social media, online marketplaces and data collection (BDO Belgium, 2019). Hungary has an 'advertisement tax' on advertisements in Hungary or in the Hungarian language, whereby depending on advertisement sales revenue, progressive rates of taxation were established. It was aimed at media service providers, publishers, advertising media owners and printed materials for advertising purposes. The Austrian Parliament also introduced the *Digitalsteuerpaket*, a 5 per cent tax on revenue generated by advertising (EY Tax Insight, 2019), provided the advertisement is viewed by a device with an IP address proving its use in Austrian limits and that it addresses Austrian users. It came into effect from 1 January 2020. On March 1 2020, Turkey also introduced a levy of 7.5 per cent tax on revenue generated by certain activities in the digital economy (Özer & Pat, 2020). The revenue must be generated by digital advertising services or in sale of or use of any audio, visual or digital content in digital media, social media, online marketplaces and intermediary services. Countries such as Finland, Sweden and Denmark have stated in a joint statement that they would prefer to wait for a multilateral solution and hence would not be adopting interim digital taxes (Sweden Ministry of Finance, Sweden, 2018).

7.4.6. United States of America

The USA has vehemently opposed several countries' unilateral impositions of digital taxes. They have maintained that they oppose any taxation system that singles out any particular digital company, fearing that the maximum effect will be on American companies (Sanger & Thomas, 2018). The EU tax has been called a de facto 'discriminatory tariff' that violates WTO law (Hufbauer & Lu, 2018). The US Senate Committee on Finance wrote a letter to the European Council laying down their objections to the tax that seemed to override all commonly accepted principles of taxation and the assertion to be in the bounds of the OECD's final output on the matter (Senate Finance Committee, 2018). The thresholds established, nature of revenues taxable and the subtraction of VAT from the taxable base have been put forth as three main arguments for EU to discriminate against the US firms specifically. The USA positions itself that there are other ways to control BEPS and that it is an argument without backing to say that digital companies are undertaxed since these companies have to pay taxes at other stages in conducting business (Congressional Research Service, 2019). The EU tax ultimately did not get implemented; however, this puts the individual countries that have implemented such taxes at risk of US retaliation and legal action under WTO law.

7.5. WTO Custom Duty Moratorium on Electronic Transmissions[15]

Electronic commerce was introduced into the WTO during the Third Ministerial Conference of the WTO held in 1998, when members agreed to continue their current practice of not imposing

---

[15] This section of the chapter is based on Das (2019).

customs duties on electronic transmissions. The moratorium was considered temporary in nature; however, since then it has been extended periodically by consensus at the subsequent WTO ministerial meetings. In recent times, certain WTO members are of the opinion that the moratorium should be made permanent and accordingly have started building pressure on other countries to agree to a permanent moratorium on customs duties on electronic transmissions.

There are a number of issues that need to be settled before any decision on permanent moratorium could be adopted at the WTO. First and foremost is the definition of electronic transmission. The terminology 'electronic transmissions' has not been defined at the WTO and hence the scope and coverage of electronic transmission is vague. Second, the use of terminology 'customs duties' suggests that the moratorium would be applicable only to goods traded through electronic transmissions across borders as custom duties are applicable only for goods. However, there are proponents who consider that the scope of the moratorium also extends to services trade. Third, it is also not clear whether the moratorium is applicable only in respect of carrier or it includes the content as well.

The issue of moratorium on custom duty on electronic transmissions is discussed widely in India. India has also made a few submissions at the WTO on the issue of e-commerce moratorium. In its first submission, India puts forth that a moratorium on customs duties on electronic transmissions could imply that customs duties are not imposed on products exported in digitalized form, even if the bound rate on the same product, if it is delivered in the physical form, is not zero.[16] Thus, a moratorium on customs duties on electronic transmissions could in effect undermine the existing schedule of tariff concessions of WTO members. India also raised the issue of scope of the e-commerce moratorium and pointed out that there is no agreed definition nor common understanding among the members of what is covered under 'electronic transmissions'.

[16] WTO document WT/GC/W/747 dated 13 July 2018.

In its subsequent submission in June 2019, India was of the view that as there is a difference of opinion between members on whether 'content' is covered in 'electronic transmissions', and the consequent significant implications this has for calculating revenue losses, it would be useful for the membership to arrive at a common understanding on this critical issue before the review of the e-commerce moratorium.[17]

A recent study by UNCTAD (2019) estimated that 85 per cent of the revenue loss on account of the moratorium on digitizable products is borne by the developing countries. The list of digitizable goods include cinematograph film; books, pamphlets, maps; newspapers, journals and periodicals; postcards, personal greeting message or announcement cards; other printed matter; video games; computer software; musical records, tapes and other sound or similar recordings; and other recorded media. According to this study, India is a net importer of digitizable products and the annual revenue loss being suffered by India on account of the moratorium has been estimated to be in the range of \$467–497 million. As more products get progressively digitalized, the revenue loss is likely to steadily increase in future.

7.6. Concluding Remarks

Other than developed countries, several developing economies have also signalled to the world their willingness to partake in the race for taxing e-commerce giants. India, as highlighted earlier, has amended the definition of PE to tax those who do not have a physical presence in the country, and the equalization levy which was fine tuned in 2020 is considered to be one of its kind digital tax and an unprecedented step towards taxing the digital economy. Indonesia has also amended the income tax system to introduce taxation of non-resident service providers on the basis of SEP criterion from April 2020 (Deloitte, 2020). In 2019, three African nations also joined the worldwide practise. Kenya's finance ministry received presidential assent to tax income derived from digital marketplaces,

---

[17] WTO document WT/GC/W/774 dated 4 June 2019.

defined as 'a platform that enables the direct interaction between buyers and sellers of goods and services through electronic means' (Republic of Kenya, 2019). The Nigerian Finance Act of 2020 introduced the concept of 'SEP' to reign in the fast growing digital economy (Komolafe & Chukwuani, 2020). Zimbabwe has amended the Finance Act to include a 5 per cent digital tax on revenues from foreign satellite broadcasters and e-commerce platforms supplied to local residents from suppliers domiciled outside of the country (KPMG, 2019b). In South America, Uruguay has also implemented a tax on revenue from intermediary services and services provided digitally through the Internet, technological platforms and computer applications, in the realm of audiovisual services (Uruguay Ministry of Economy and Finance, 2018). Chile has proposed to introduce a 10 per cent digital tax on digital services provided by foreign platforms (PWC, 2018).

Thus, it could be observed that the domestic taxation of digital economy in various geographies is still at an experimental stage. Many countries across the globe have initiated efforts to tax e-commerce transactions and many other countries are in a wait-and-watch situation learning from other countries' experiences. There appears to be differences in ideologies adopted by different countries in taxing the digital economy, and this may lead to contradictions in achieving the same goal. At the WTO, there is no consensus either on permanent moratorium or on imposing custom duties on electronic transmissions. Therefore, it could be said that e-commerce taxation remains an unresolved issue both within domestic context as well as international (WTO) contexts.

References

BDO Belgium. (2019). Belgium jumps on the bandwagon to tax Online Giants. https://www.bdo.be/en-gb/news/2019/belgium-jumps-on-the-bandwagon-to-tax-online-giants

Bloomberg Tax. (2020). Insight: Spanish Digital Services Tax—Here we go again. https://news.bloombergtax.com/daily-tax-report-international/insight-spanish-digital-services-tax-here-we-go-again

Burchard, H. (2019). Trump says tariffs on French wine depend on digital tax 'deal'. *Politico*, 26 August. https://www.politico.eu/article/trump-says-tariffs-on-french-wine-depend-on-digital-tax-deal/

Competition Commission of India. (2019). Market study on e-commerce in India: Interim observations. https://www.cci.gov.in/sites/default/files/whats_newdocument/Interimobservations_30August2019.pdf

Congressional Research Service. (2019). Digital services taxes (DSTs): Policy and economic analysis. https://fas.org/sgp/crs/misc/R45532.pdf

Das, A. (2019). Concept note for stakeholders' consultation on moratorium on customs duties on electronic transmissions in the WTO. FICCI, New Delhi, 6 November. http://www.ficci.in/past-event-page.asp?evid=24510

Deloitte. (2020). Indonesia Tax alert April 2020. https://www2.deloitte.com/content/dam/Deloitte/id/Documents/tax/id-tax-alert-en-apr2020.pdf

Díaz-Súnico, G. (2019). The new Spanish digital service tax: A strange combination of value creation and geolocalization. https://news.bloombergtax.com/daily-tax-report-international/insight-the-new-spanish-digital-service-tax-a-strange-combination-of-value-creation-and-geolocalization

Elliott, L., & Mason, R. (2020). UK to impose tax on tech giants but risks US tariffs on car exports. https://www.theguardian.com/business/2020/jan/22/uk-to-impose-tax-on-tech-giants-but-risks-us-tariffs-on-car-exports

European Commission. (2018a). Proposal for a council directive laying down rules relating to the corporate taxation of a significant digital presence. https://ec.europa.eu/taxation_customs/sites/taxation/files/proposal_significant_digital_presence_21032018_en.pdf

European Commission. (2018b). Proposal for a council directive on a common system for a digital services tax on revenues resulting from certain digital services. https://ec.europa.eu/taxation_customs/sites/taxation/files/proposal_common_system_digital_services_tax_21032018_en.pdf

EY Indirect Tax Alert. (2019). Italy introduces new Digital Services Tax. https://www.ey.com/en_gl/tax-alerts/italy-introduces-new-digital-services-tax

EY Tax Insights. (2019). Austrian government approves digital tax advertising bill. https://taxinsights.ey.com/archive/archive-news/austrian-government-approves-digital-advertising-tax-bill.aspx

EY Tax Alert. (2020). *The Italian Budget Law 2020, provides for the entry into force—as of 1 January 2020*. https://www.ey.com/en_gl/tax-alerts/ey-italys-digital-services-tax-enters-into-force-as-of-1%C2%A0january-2020

Govindrajan, V., Srivastava, A., Warsame, H., & Enache, L. (2019). The problem with France's plan to tax digital companies. *Harvard Business Review*. https://hbr.org/2019/07/the-problem-with-frances-plan-to-tax-digital-companies

HM Revenue and Customs, UK. (2020). *Policy Paper: Digital Services Tax*. https://www.gov.uk/government/publications/introduction-of-the-digital-services-tax/digital-services-tax

Hufbauer, G., & Lu, Z. (2018). The European Union's proposed Digital Services Tax: A de facto tariff. *Peterson Institute for International Economics.* https://www.piie.com/system/files/documents/pb18-15.pdf

KPMG Insights. (2019). France: Digital Services Tax (3%) is enacted. https://home.kpmg/us/en/home/insights/2019/07/tnf-france-digital-services-tax-enacted.html

KPMG. (2019a). Taxation of the digitalized economy developments summary. https://tax.kpmg.us/content/dam/tax/en/pdfs/2019/digitalized-economy-taxation-developments-summary.pdf

KPMG. (2019b), The Zimbabwe 2019 mid-term fiscal policy review. https://assets.kpmg/content/dam/kpmg/us/pdf/2019/08/tnf-zimbabwe-aug15–2019.pdf

KPMG Insights. (2020). *France: Draft administrative regulations, scope of digital services tax.* https://home.kpmg/us/en/home/insights/2020/03/tnf-france-draft-administrative-regulations-scope-digital-services-tax.html

Komolafe, D., & Chukwuani, O. (2020). *The impact of the Finance Act on digital taxation In Nigeria.* https://www.mondaq.com/nigeria/tax-authorities/903148/the-impact-of-the-finance-act-on-digital-taxation-in-nigeria

OECD. (2015). OECD/G20 base erosion and profit shifting project, explanatory statement. https://www.oecd.org/ctp/beps-explanatory-statement-2015.pdf

OECD. (2017a). *International VAT/GST Guidelines.* https://www.oecd.org/ctp/international-vat-gst-guidelines-9789264271401-en.htm

OECD. (2017b). *Model tax convention.* https://www.oecd.org/ctp/treaties/articles-model-tax-convention-2017.pdf

OECD. (2018). Tax challenges arising from digitalisation: Interim report 2018. In *OECD/G20 base erosion and profit shifting project.* https://www.oecd-ilibrary.org/taxation/tax-challenges-arising-from-digitalisation-interim-report_9789264293083-en

OECD. (2019a). Addressing the tax challenges of the digitalisation of the economy public consultation document. https://www.oecd.org/tax/beps/public-consultation-document-addressing-the-tax-challenges-of-the-digitalisation-of-the-economy.pdf

OECD. (2019b). Secretariat proposal for a 'unified approach' under Pillar One. https://www.oecd.org/tax/beps/public-consultation-document-secretariat-proposal-unified-approach-pillar-one.pdf

Ozer, Y., & Pat, H. (2020). *Turkey: Digital Service Tax enters into force on 1 March 2020.* https://www.mondaq.com/turkey/sales-taxes-vat-gst/892420/digital-service-tax-enters-into-force-on-1-march-2020

PWC. (2016). India introduces new equalization levy on online advertising revenue. https://www.pwc.com/us/en/services/tax/library/insights/india-introduces-new-equalization-levy-on-online-advertising-rev.html

PWC. (2018). Economic and policy aspects of digital services turnover taxes: A literature review. https://www.pwc.com/us/en/services/tax/library/insights/economic-and-policy-aspects-of-digital-services-turnover-taxes.html

Regan, A. (2019). Ireland is a tax haven and that's becoming controversial at home. *The Washington Post*, 15 April. https://www.washingtonpost.com/politics/2019/04/25/ireland-is-tax-haven-thats-becoming-controversial-home/

Republic of Kenya. (2019). The Finance Act 2019. In *Kenya Gazette Supplement*: *Acts, 2019*. http://kenyalaw.org/kl/fileadmin/pdfdownloads/AmendmentActs/2019/FinanceAct_No23of2019.PDF

Reuters. (2019). EU ditches digital tax plan, to work for global reform. *Reuters*, 12 March. https://www.reuters.com/article/us-eu-tax-digital/eu-ditches-digital-tax-plan-to-work-for-global-reform-idUSKBN1QT1HC

Sanger, C., & Thomas, R. (2018). New digital tax policies: What, when, where, how and by whom? *An excerpt from EY's global tax, policy and controversy briefing*, 22 (March). https://www.ey.com/Publication/vwLUAssets/EY-new-digital-tax-policies-what-when-where-how-and-by-whom/$FILE/EY-new-digital-tax-policies-what-when-where-how-and-by-whom.pdf

Senate Finance Committee. (2018). Letter to President of the European Council and President of the European Commission. https://src.bna.com/CCX

Sharma, A., & Gupta, N. (2019). Digital tax: The changing contours of tax structure in India. *SCC Online Blog* (Blog post). https://www.scconline.com/blog/post/2019/10/22/digital-tax-the-changing-contours-of-tax-structure-in-india/

South Africa National Treasury. (2019). Explanatory memorandum on regulations prescribing electronic services. https://www.sars.gov.za/AllDocs/LegalDoclib/ExplMemo/LAPD-LPrep-EM-2019-01%20-%20Explanatory%20Memorandum%20on%20Regulations%20prescribing%20electronic%20Services%2018%20March%202019.pdf

Sweden Ministry of Finance, Sweden. (2018). Global cooperation is key to address tax challenges from digitalization. https://www.government.se/statements/2018/06/global-cooperation-is-key-to-address-tax-challenges-from-digitalization/

Terada-Hagiwara, A., Gonzales, K., & Wang, J. (2019). Taxation challenges in a digital economy: The case of the People's Republic of China. Asian Development Bank, Brief No. 108. https://www.adb.org/sites/default/files/publication/504616/adb-brief–108-taxation-digital-economy-peoples-republic-china.pdf

UNCTAD (2019). Growing trade in electronic transmissions: Implications for the South. UNCTAD research Paper no. 29.

Uruguay Ministry of Economy and Finance. (2018). Decree of the President of Uruguay on 22nd May 2018. https://medios.presidencia.gub.uy/legal/2018/decretos/05/mef_1835.pdf

USTR. (2019). Report on France's Digital Services Tax prepared in the investigation under Section 301 of the Trade Act of 1974. https://ustr.gov/sites/default/files/Report_On_France%27s_Digital_Services_Tax.pdf

CHAPTER 8

E-Commerce Logistics
Operational Challenges and Strategic Issues[*]

Pritam Banerjee

8.1. Introduction

E-commerce is another word for the convenience of the modern consumer to shop remotely from anywhere in the world without having to visit a specific physical location and have the goods they have purchased delivered anywhere around the world without having to deal with complexities of the physical movement of their purchases. The gamut of services that provide for this convenience can essentially be clubbed under the logistics of e-commerce. In other words, without efficient, modern logistics, there would be no e-commerce.

Thus, the logistics of e-commerce would include services related to warehousing, transportation, both long-haul and last-mile services, and other value-added services (local packaging, labelling, invoicing and payment on delivery, among others). In the case of cross-border

---

[*]The opinions and ideas in this chapter are the sole responsibility of the author and are in no way attributable to his current or former employers.

e-commerce, it would also include regulatory compliance aspects related to customs and other types of clearance of goods at the border (i.e., customs brokerage services).

Since the focus of this edited volume is on the cross-border aspect of e-commerce, the subsequent discussion will remain focused on this element. However, brief discussions of domestic e-commerce from an Indian perspective, especially where policy, infrastructure or economies of scale aspects have a spillover on cross-border aspects of e-commerce, shall be woven into this discussion as well.

Before moving onto a detailed discussion on the logistics aspects of cross-border e-commerce, it is important to bring about a sense of the size and scope of this rapidly growing and evolving segment of the logistics industry. Unfortunately, there are no consistent numbers on the overall size of the logistics industry supporting e-commerce. There are several reasons for such lack of precise data. The first and foremost being the lack of precise numbers of the size of global cross-border e-commerce itself. In addition, the size of the logistics pie serving this cross-border element of e-commerce would itself depend on the services included in its ambit and the modes.

For example, one would have to consider whether such logistics services include all aspects of warehousing or should cross-border online payment services be included in its ambit. In terms of the means of transmission of goods, there would be questions about whether such logistics services be limited to courier and postal services that provide door-to-door services for individual small packages or it should include a wider definition of general freight (especially air freight), which is very commonly used in the case of certain models of cross-border e-commerce. These definitional challenges, which in turn are subject to the different business models of e-commerce, also have a bearing on the discussion of challenges and policy priorities for e-commerce logistics and are taken up in greater detail in subsequent sections.

Some broad assumptions would need to be made in our assessment of overall market size of logistics serving cross-border e-commerce. The first broad assumption would be that the overall average logistics

Table 8.1 Global Cross-Border E-Commerce, Regional Breakdown ($ billion)

Region	2014	2020
North America	67	176
Western Europe	73	216
Asia Pacific	71	476
Latin America	6	53
East and Central Europe	13	45
Africa and Middle East	5	26
Global cross-border e-commerce	235	992

Source: Accenture-Ali Research (2015).

cost is around 40 per cent of the overall transaction value for cross-border e-commerce.[1] The second broad assumption would be to include all modes of transmission (i.e., courier, postal and general freight) in the ambit of logistics of e-commerce, since all these modes of transmission play a critical role depending on the model of e-commerce being discussed.

The size of the global cross-border e-commerce market varies widely between different assessments and reports. For the purposes of this chapter, we would use the assessment made by one of the most comprehensive reports on cross-border e-commerce volumes, *Global Cross Border E-commerce Market 2020* (Accenture–AliResearch, 2015). Table 8.1 summarizes the broad numbers as per this report.

Based on the numbers in the table, if we assume the current market size by transaction value of global cross-border e-commerce to be around $900 billion and apply our assumption of the logistics being 40 per cent of overall transaction value of cross-border e-commerce (or 20% of the value ascribed to one country or region), then the size of the logistics industry supporting cross-border e-commerce globally

---

[1] This is based on the author's industry experience and discussion with industry stakeholders. This 40 per cent includes logistics expenditures in both the exporting and importing countries and the cost of transport between the two.

would be in the ballpark of $180 billion.[2] Moreover, given the phenomenal growth rates represented by the number in Table 8.1, the logistics of cross-border e-commerce would have quadrupled in size in just about five years.

The reported cross-border e-commerce numbers from India are more modest. According to the data reported by Invest India, cross-border e-commerce in India was valued at $500 million in 2015 and is expected to reach around $2 billion by 2020.[3] Using the same assumptions, cross-border e-commerce logistics would represent $180 million service industry.

8.2. Types of E-Commerce Transactions and Associated Logistical Models

E-commerce-related logistics are impacted by the general infrastructure and policy challenges of the modes of transportation, storage and distribution being used for that particular transaction, but they also face certain challenges that are peculiar to the e-commerce industry. In addition, the rising tide of e-commerce in turn has resulted in the creation of new challenges for the logistics industry and traditional means of regulation and policymaking that governed the movement of goods (Lieb & Lieb, 2016).

However, before delving into the critical elements of logistics of e-commerce and their associate policy aspects, it is important to start the chapter by reiterating the fact that logistics is essentially the ecosystem of services for transport, storage and distribution of goods that result from specific transactions between parties (Yang et al., 2010). It follows that the nature and type of these transactions will define the type of logistics that serve them. Any discussion on the

---

[2] Since $900 billion represent the overall size that includes both export and import, the actual volume of business and the transaction value are assumed to be half (since every transaction is double counted; i.e., exports of one is the imports into another), and thus 40 per cent is applied on $450 billion.

[3] https://www.investindia.gov.in/team-india-blogs/next-step-trade-cross-border-e-commerce

logistics aspects of e-commerce therefore cannot be done without first clearly underlining the different transactional types that exist for e-commerce and then distinguishing them. The three main transactional models for e-commerce are (a) direct selling model, (b) fulfilment model and (c) traders' inventory model. A discussion on peculiarities of the three models and the specific logistics modes and services that are used for them follows.

8.2.1. Direct Selling Transactions

This is the pure business-to-consumer (B2C) model, where a seller lists their inventory of goods on an e-marketplace portal and a buyer purchases and pays for it online. The seller arranges for purchased goods to be shipped and delivered to the buyer without any support from e-marketplace, dealing with all the transport- and distribution-related intermediaries themselves. Figure 8.1 provides a clear conceptualization.

While called B2C, the buyer might also be a small business making purchases online. In many cases the sellers are not a 'business' but an individual selling things online. Thus, these relationships could be business-to-business (B2B), consumer-to-business (C2B) or even consumer-to-consumer (C2C). The critical differentiators are that the transaction takes place directly between a buyer and a seller without

Figure 8.1 *Direct Selling Transaction Model of E-Commerce*

any intermediary getting involved at any stage in the process, and the transmission of goods takes place in the form of individual parcels for each buyer using courier or postal mode. The defining element of the logistics related to this model of e-commerce is that small individual parcels are transported directly from the sellers premises in one country to the buyers premises in another.

It needs to be noted that the e-retailer itself can be the seller in the direct selling model. This is the so-called 'inventory model' where the e-marketplace itself is the seller and owns the inventory listed in their e-marketplace portal. In India, the 'inventory' model is restricted for majority foreign-owned e-marketplaces.

A special case of direct selling transactions is the so-called 'third-party sales model'. Under this model of trade, the purchaser of goods and the final recipient are different. For example, an online seller in the USA lists goods on a US-based e-marketplace for Indian manufactured goods. Once a purchase is made by a US buyer, the Indian manufacturer arranges for the goods to be directly sent to the door of the US buyer. The payment for goods, however, has to come from the US-based online seller. The consignee who receives the goods and one responsible for payment and on whose name the invoicing is done are different. This gives rise to some specific regulatory challenges in the cross-border e-commerce context which would be discussed later.

8.2.2. Close-to-Market 'Fulfilment' Transactions

Like the direct selling model, a seller sells their inventory directly to an individual buyer through an e-marketplace. Unlike in the case for direct selling transactions, the e-marketplace also provides logistical and transactional support services. This means that the e-marketplace would arrange for the shipping, storage and distribution of the product domestically or cross-border. In many cases, in order to ensure that purchased goods reach customers quickly, the e-marketplace would store the seller's inventory closer to the market. For example, a seller of sandalwood furniture from Karnataka might like to have some of their inventory stored close to a location like Delhi from where they get frequent buyers in order to reduce the time of delivery to the buyer. The e-marketplace would provide this service.

In the case of domestic movement of goods, the ownership of inventory does not need to change; that is, goods are still held in the name of the seller. In the case of cross-border movement, there needs to be an official importer of record (IOR), that is, a commercial entity officially registered in the importing country required by customs rules. Since many online sellers would not want to be commercially registered in all countries they sell to, the online marketplace, or an affiliate, becomes the IOR, assuming all legal responsibilities and ownership for that inventory of goods. Figure 8.2 provides a graphical explanation for this model of e-commerce transactions.

The e-marketplace plays an important intermediary role in these types of transactions (Lewis, 2001). They arrange for the transport of goods between sellers' premises and the 'fulfilment centres' closer to locations where likely purchases are expected to happen, and assume the responsibility for the storage of goods, their security and quality, and the final distribution to the buyers' premises once a purchase actually takes place. In doing so, the e-marketplace also assumes the responsibility for invoicing and maintenance of legal record of transactions, and in many cases payment of domestic duties and charges related to such sales.

The role of the e-marketplace as an intermediary is even greater in the case of cross-border fulfilment models. In addition to the functions already discussed, the e-marketplace or their commercial affiliate assume the responsibility for the ownership of the goods once they cross international borders, and pay all duties, taxes and transaction fees associated with such imports. The e-marketplace charges a percentage of the sale proceeds to provide such services to the sellers.

A critical distinction is the preferred mode of transport and logistics services. Unlike in the case of direct selling, the fulfilment type of e-commerce transaction requires relatively large quantities (i.e.,

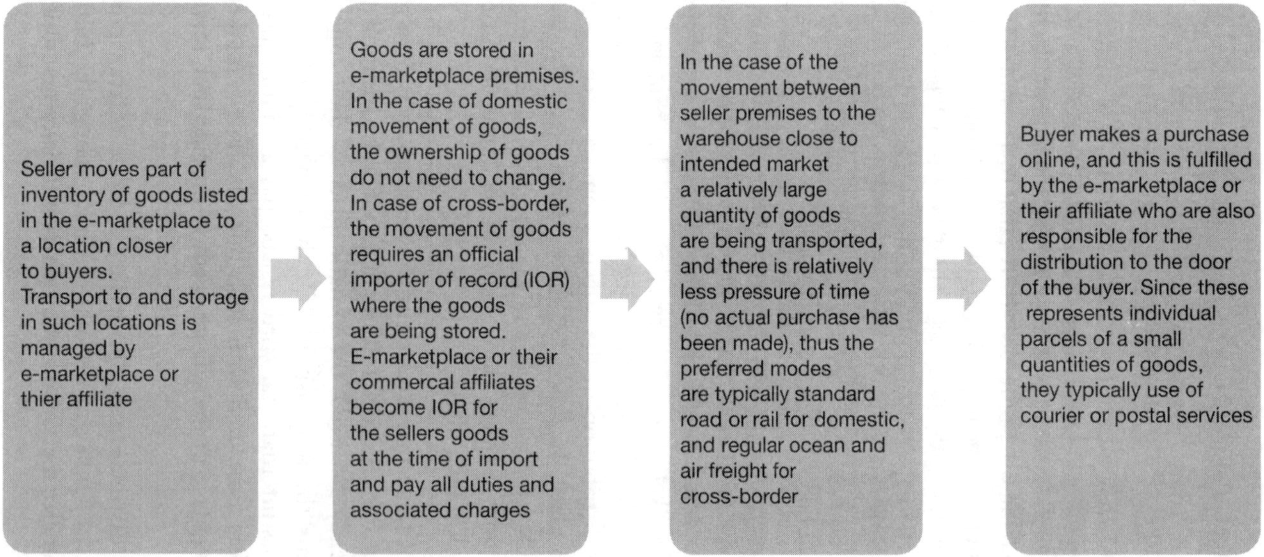

Seller moves part of inventory of goods listed in the e-marketplace to a location closer to buyers. Transport to and storage in such locations is managed by e-marketplace or thier affiliate

Goods are stored in e-marketplace premises. In the case of domestic movement of goods, the ownership of goods do not need to change. In case of cross-border, the movement of goods requires an official importer of record (IOR) where the goods are being stored. E-marketplace or their commercal affiliates become IOR for the sellers goods at the time of import and pay all duties and associated charges

In the case of the movement between seller premises to the warehouse close to intended market a relatively large quantity of goods are being transported, and there is relatively less pressure of time (no actual purchase has been made); thus the preferred modes are typically standard road or rail for domestic, and regular ocean and air freight for cross-border

Buyer makes a purchase online, and this is fulfilled by the e-marketplace or their affiliate who are also responsible for the distribution to the door of the buyer. Since these represents individual parcels of a small quantities of goods, they typically use of courier or postal services

Figure 8.2 Fulfilment Model of E-Commerce

number of units) to move between sellers' premises and the warehouse or 'fulfilment' centres close to target markets. Given the larger size of shipments, they typically use regular road or rail services for domestic trade. For cross-border trade, they typically use regular ocean freight (for goods that are lower cost per unit such as low-cost electronics or accessories) or air freight (for goods that are high cost per unit such as expensive fashion items or mobile phones).

Once a purchase is made, the goods are delivered from the nearby warehouse or fulfilment centre where the goods are being stored to the buyer's premises using courier or post just like in the case of direct sales.

Like in the case for direct selling, fulfilment transactions can also be based on a so-called inventory model where the e-marketplace or their affiliates source and sell products, that is, act as traders instead of just being a marketplace.

Thus cross-border e-commerce uses a mix of direct cross-border transmission of small parcels using time definite expedited logistic services such as courier or post, as well as more traditional ocean or air freight. Such expedited shipments of small units of goods can be provided by so-called private courier services such as DHL, FedEx, UPS, Blue Dart and Delhivery, or by postal operators with their courier, parcel and letter post services.

E-commerce also uses the more traditional movement of large quantities of goods using road, rail, air or ocean freight (typically containerized). Such traditional freight services (that include transport, clearance and storage close to the market) are provided by freight forwarders and third-party logistics service providers.

Table 8.2 summarizes the discussion on transaction type and the choice of logistics extant in the e-commerce industry today and introduces some of the key challenges and implications related to them. The following sections shall elaborate on the various dimensions of these challenges and implications and analyse their impact on the logistics that serves e-commerce.

Table 8.2 *Logistics Challenges Relevant to Different E-Commerce Models and Preferred Modes of Transmission of Goods*

Transaction Type	Long Haul	Last Mile	Use of Warehousing and Value-Added Services	Regulatory Implications
Direct selling	Private courier (international and domestic express delivery)		No	Domestic: Management of indirect taxation and compliance with E-Way Bill rules
	Postal		No	Cross-border: Differential treatment of low-value consignments using courier and postal channels by customs. Customs and other regulatory restrictions. Implications for availing export incentives and benefits and bank realization. Management of returns. Treatment of third-party transactions.
Fulfilment	Road freight	Courier or post	Yes	Domestic: Management of indirect taxation, E-Way Bill compliance, tax treatment of returns.
	Rail freight	Courier or post	Yes	
	Air freight	Courier or post	Yes	Cross-border: Management of returns. Managing remittances and bank realization. Using of special economic zones and free warehousing zones to store inventory.
	Ocean freight	Courier or post	Yes	

8.2.3. E-Commerce Logistics: Postal and Courier Services

Postal and courier services are integral to the e-commerce supply chain. This is due to the fact that irrespective of the transaction type (i.e., direct selling or fulfilment) there is a role for courier or postal services. The product sold online must arrive at the door of the buyer and typically must do so within some guaranteed/agreed upon timeline. Courier and postal services provide this service of moving many small consignments of goods to the door of the consumer within a definite time (i.e., the promise of time-definite delivery).

8.2.3.1. Hinterland Challenges: Common Issues for International and Domestic E-Commerce

Domestic e-commerce services for a large geography like India need to use air transport for long haul (500–600 km plus distances), given that they have a commitment of time-definite delivery, and this can only be met by air transport. Middle and short haul (last mile) is typically done by road. There have been some attempts to use railways network for long-haul or even some middle-haul services. However, relatively poor service reliability, especially service punctuality and cargo-handling capabilities (and quality management), is preventing greater use of the rail mode. Domestic courier and postal operators face significant regulatory and infrastructure challenges:

1. E-waybill-related challenges: The GST e-waybill, essentially a detailed declaration of goods being carried by transporters, was designed to replace the multiple state-level documents and create a national system. It aims to check fraudulent and fictitious transactions and abuse of the GST system, while at the same time creating a more transparent enforcement regime for tax-related checks and inspections on the road.

    However, given the fact that e-commerce, especially domestic e-commerce, involves the daily transportation of millions of small parcels of values that are typically less than ₹3,000, the generation of millions of such e-waybills adds a layer of administrative costs. In addition, e-commerce parcels travelling long distances change modes and vehicles several times, including those destined for export. For example, a parcel containing a coffee maker worth ₹2,500 might travel from its manufacturer based in Solapur in Maharashtra to Hyderabad in Telangana by road, from Hyderabad to Delhi by air, from Delhi to a transport hub in Rohtak in Haryana by a large truck, from Rohtak to Hisar in the same state by a smaller truck, and in Hisar, the parcel might be taken from a smaller truck and delivered to the online buyer's door using a tempo. If the same product was meant for export to say Moscow in Russia, it would have travelled from Solapur to Hyderabad by road, from Hyderabad to Delhi by air, and trans-shipped from Delhi to Moscow. Since every change of mode or vehicle requires the e-waybill to be updated, even a small low-value product worth ₹2,500 in our example would need five e-waybill updates for the domestic movement, and two for the export.

Considering the sheer pressure such a huge number of transactions would put on both the industry and the administrator's systems, it was decided to keep out consignments below the threshold of ₹50,000 from the requirement of generating a GST e-waybill.[4] However, if this exemption is removed, it would add a significant cost of compliance and procedural complication for e-commerce.

Even with the exemption allowed for products up to the value of ₹50,000, the fact that e-commerce deliveries require multiple handling and change of modes and vehicles in their journey between sellers' premises and the buyers' doors, means that e-waybill requirements for those e-commerce products that are valued at ₹50, 000 or more are relatively more complicated compared to typical B2B transactions.

Perhaps the biggest challenge for e-commerce related to e-waybills is the fact that several hundred small packages tend to travel together in the same vehicle in every leg of the journey. If tax or any other authority undertaking checks on the road perceives that there is an issue with the e-waybill (or the invoice and associated documentation of packages valued less than ₹50,000 that currently do not require an e-waybill) of just one of these packages, the entire vehicle is held up. Since e-commerce depends on deliveries to buyers within a definite time, not meeting that customer expectation can have serious negative commercial and reputational repercussions. This is especially true for exports. Consider our example again. Assume that there was a problem

---

[4] Rule 137 of GST Rules.

with e-waybill documentation and the truck carrying the coffee maker was held up in the Maharashtra–Telangana border, which caused it to miss its connection from Hyderabad airport to Delhi, and in turn the onward connection to Moscow, this delay would have serious implications on customer expectation who might need the coffee maker as an anniversary gift.

2. Multiple inspections of commercial vehicles: It is not just e-waybill and tax and GST-related compliance; commercial goods carriers on Indian roads are subject to more than 15 different non-tax-related laws and more than 60 notified traffic and motor vehicle-related offenses. Enforcement for these rules, regulations and procedures are with different agencies such as state transport department, police and forest officials. A commercial goods carrier is often stopped multiple times by different enforcement agencies. This adds time and cost. While these challenges are common to all cargo movement by road, e-commerce is especially negatively impacted, given their sensitivity to time-bound delivery.

   Also, as pointed out earlier, if the tax or any other authority has a problem with just one of the hundreds of packages travelling in a goods carrier, the entire vehicle tends to be held up. This problem applies to even international e-commerce packages that travel from hinterland to international airports by road.

3. Airport cargo handling infrastructure: Air cargo infrastructure and handling capability in India is seriously stressed. The major hubs such as Delhi, Mumbai, Bengaluru and Chennai suffer from serious congestion problems, and despite incremental improvements in some of the newer air cargo terminals such as Delhi and Bengaluru, space for management of cargo and efficient handling remain huge problems. In the older air cargo terminals in Chennai and Mumbai, space management and congestion are even greater problems.

Challenges are not only limited to space, but traffic management issues, facilities management and process management have also been flagged as problems (Ministry of Civil Aviation, 2012). Cargo handling and management issues are also prevalent in the second-tier airports that serve as regional hubs such as Guwahati, Jaipur, Indore, Bagdogra,

Varanasi and Lucknow. Rapidly increasing domestic e-commerce volumes are already creating capacity and management constraints in these airports. Given that export consignments use such second-tier regional hubs to connect to the major hubs for their international leg, the capacity constraints in these airports have an impact on the overall export connectivity of e-commerce (ASSOCHAM, 2018).

8.2.3.2. Cross-Border E-Commerce

1. Customs clearance of small parcels (postal and courier): E-commerce has changed the traditional landscape of regulating cross-border trade, especially for customs authorities worldwide. The direct selling version of e-commerce using courier or postal mode is different from traditional B2B cross-border trade in three critical ways:
   a. Average value of each shipment tends to be modest, and most shipments are typically below $150 (or about ₹10,000).
   b. Unlike traditional trade, the recipient of the goods is an unknown entity, that is, an individual consumer, and not a commercially registered business which is easy for regulators to track and seek accountability from.
   c. There is a much higher percentage of 'returns' compared to regular trade.

The sheer increase in the number of such parcels crossing borders using courier/post is creating a huge challenge for customs and other at-the-border regulators. Customs authorities have legitimate concerns about e-commerce using courier or postal channels being abused by unscrupulous parties to undervalue and misdeclare goods to avoid legitimate duties and taxes, or even worse use it to smuggle in banned substances, narcotics and other contraband, counterfeits and weapons.

These challenges have led the World Customs Organization (WCO) director of compliance and facilitation compare cross-border e-commerce with a 'tsunami of small packages' overwhelming the customs infrastructure that has been designed for traditional B2B cross-border trade and not e-commerce (*Air Cargo News*, 2018). Customs organizations around the world are trying to grapple with the huge increase in the number of such typically low-value shipments with limited manpower in their disposal. A more detailed discussion on this aspect, including WCO initiatives, some of the emerging innovations by individual countries and the scope of industry–regulator cooperation, follows in the section 'Regulators Concerns and National Interests'.

Needless to say, managing the customs process for such shipments poses significant logistical and trade facilitation-related challenges. The fact that these shipments are time-sensitive makes these challenges even more acute. Most large economies including India have provided for simplified customs processes for such low-value shipments that use the courier or postal mode which are distinct from regular air or sea freight. Simplified declarations fall under two distinct categories, that is, low-value non-dutiable (LVND) and low-value dutiable (LVD).

LVND, also known as *de minimis*, are essentially shipments below a certain defined threshold value which are not subject to customs duties or other taxes. Some countries exempt only customs duties while imposing all other taxes on such shipments. In some countries, LVND category is limited to only certain types of shipments such as samples or gifts sent from abroad. India has an LVND applicable only for samples and gifts with a threshold value of ₹10,000. The rationale behind having an LVND category is that collecting taxes on shipments of such low value is almost as expensive administratively as the revenue generated, while it adds significant transactions costs and inefficiency to the customs clearance process and diverts scarce human and institutional resources of customs administrations from more critical areas of concern.

LVD also represent shipments below a certain defined threshold value which while being subject to all duties and taxes use a much more simplified customs declaration and clearance process and are typically cleared much faster. The LVD category has become a critical part of the solution for cross-border direct selling e-commerce. The levels of facilitation available under the LVD category in any country are the defining factor of the extent of ease of doing business available to cross-border e-commerce.

Postal networks have emerged as extremely important channels of cross-border e-commerce. Postal operators in many countries have made e-commerce the central focus of their growth and sustainability in light of rapidly falling volumes of letter and other traditional postal products. E-commerce typically uses letter post or Express Mail Service (EMS)s postal products.[5] Letter post and postal EMS have much lesser declaration and customs clearance requirements even when compared to courier LVD and LVND categories and have become a preferred medium for the cross-border trade in low-value items (often valued at less than $2–3 per unit). The low cost of using letter and the relatively less rigorous customs scrutiny represents a challenge for the importing country (and an opportunity for exporters), which represent serious implications for net e-commerce importing countries like India. A more detailed discussion on this topic follows in Section 4.

8.3. Operational and Policy Challenges for Indian E-Commerce Exporters Using Courier and Postal Mode

Commercial exports were not allowed through courier mode in India. Strong lobbying from the industry eventually led to changes, and commercial exports up to the value of ₹25,000 were allowed in November 2016; further liberalization took place in March 2018, increasing the allowed value per shipment for export through courier to ₹500, 000.[6] The reason for these restrictions having been in place was that the courier customs process was managed manually, that is, submission of physical paper documents and their manual scrutiny. This means that there is a significant risk of fraudulent practices. The

---

[5] Letter post carrying goods are defined by the Universal Postal Union as small packets carrying goods of up to 2 kg in weight; they typically have no track-and-trace mechanism. EMS is the time-definite product offered by postal operators and recognized as a part of the Universal Postal Union network (thereby receiving the benefit of postal clearances). EMS products have a weight limits of up to 30 kg (some countries limit it at 20 kg).

[6] Notification No. 142/2016-Customs (N.T.) introduced Courier Shipping Bill (CSB) V, which allowed for commercial exports up to a value of ₹25,000. Notification No. 68/2018-Customs (N.T.) increased that limit to ₹500,000.

key concerns were related to fraudulent claims on export incentives and fraudulent invoicing for money laundering and 'hawala' transactions.

Unlike an electronic system that can develop data-based robust risk management, manual processes are limited in scope in being able to identify and flag issues of non-compliance and fraudulent abuse. Another concern of the customs administration was that if such commercial export shipments are allowed through courier mode, their volumes would swamp the already severely understaffed courier terminals in major airports such as Delhi, Mumbai, Bengaluru and Chennai, not to mention put a strain on the infrastructure and space available to process in-bound and out-bound trade.

While these concerns were legitimate to an extent, the restrictions created an impediment to the growth of direct selling exports, which is especially lucrative for SMEs, precisely at the time when global cross-border direct selling started to see a huge upswing. In the period between 2010 and 2016, exporters in countries such as China and Vietnam were expanding their footprints and establishing their credibility in key buyers' markets such as the USA, Canada, Japan and EU.

These crucial lost years meant that many interested entrepreneurs simply gave up trying to crack the direct selling e-commerce market when the market was in growth phase, and lost out in terms of developing the economies of scale, the network of contacts and credibility with buyers.[7] While direct selling cross-border e-commerce exports from India has since been growing much faster, it has to make up for a lot of lost ground, and its numbers are nowhere close to relatively more successful entrepreneurs from China and Southeast Asian countries like Vietnam.

The fact that these restrictions were lifted in 2016 with the same manual regime in place (courier clearances continue to be in manual

---

[7] Based on the author's conversations with several entrepreneurs who had tried to develop cross-border direct selling models, and discussions that took place between groups of such exporters and customs administrations in forums such as the Customs Consultative Group (CCG).

mode for exports; an electronic clearance system, the Express Cargo Clearance System (ECCS) is in use only for imports, that too limited to the cities of Delhi, Mumbai, Bengaluru and Chennai) goes on to underline that effective solutions could have been proactively found even earlier, despite the policy and infrastructural concerns, and this experience could serve as a cautionary tale for policymakers in terms of needing to adapt much quickly to changing technology and associated transactional and business models.

This problem was further exacerbated by the fact that India Post was not adequately equipped to provide comprehensive end-to-end solutions to e-commerce exporters from India using the postal mode. One of the most interesting aspects of China's success in e-commerce exports has been the deep and enduring partnership that China Post has developed with e-commerce exporters from that country, and has leveraged the international postal network to make effectively turn China Post into a reliable and cost-effective conduit for even extremely modestly priced products (Tong, 2016)[8] (as will be discussed in greater detail in Section 4).

Unable to export using courier, and India Post services not being fully adequate for such business, the growth of cross-border direct selling suffered in India between 2010 and 2016. With the impediments gone, direct selling e-commerce exports from India have seen good growth between 2016 and 2018.

Another critical challenge for e-commerce exports is returns. Depending on the product category, returns tend to be in the range of 20–40 per cent of total goods shipped out by e-commerce retailers. While these numbers typically represent domestic transactions and cross-border e-commerce would have typically lesser number of returns, they are still substantive in percentage terms. However, returns impact both direct selling and fulfilment models of e-commerce, and the complications of returns (including managing large amount of unsold inventory in foreign warehouses) are relatively more acute in

---

[8] Alibaba CN post press release. See https://www.ems.post/en/news-events/news/china-e-commerce-growth. Also see https://www.ecomcrew.com/why-china-post-and-usps-are-killing-your-private-labeling-business/

the fulfilment model, and therefore a more detailed discussion on this topic follows in the next section on challenges of the fulfilment model of e-commerce using general freight as a mode of transmission.

8.4. Operational and Policy Challenges for Indian E-Commerce Exporters Using Freight

As was pointed out, general ocean and air freight is the dominant mode of cross-border transmission for the 'fulfilment' model of e-commerce exports. While the general challenges of trade facilitation, including infrastructure and regulatory issues that add delays and transaction costs to Indian exporters in general, also impact such exports that use regular freight services, these challenges, policy measures for their redress and recent improvements in the overall ecosystem of cross-border trade in India have been discussed in several different publications and are not the focus of this chapter, not being specific to e-commerce. This section would instead focus on certain regulatory issues that plague e-commerce exports using the fulfilment model being exporter using general freight (i.e., ocean and air freight).

8.4.1. Management of Returns and Unsold Inventory

When e-commerce exporters use the fulfilment model, products are shipped out in anticipation of an expected demand for such products in that market. E-commerce exporters are therefore taking a risk that inventory might remain unsold due to a range of issues including change of consumer preferences, competition or purely error in predicting demand patterns. However, like any retail end of business, e-commerce exporters would typically prefer to have a little unsold inventory rather than loose custom by running out of products and not being able to meet customer demand. Thus, it makes business sense to have more stock sent into the warehouses close to the market so as to avoid a stockout scenario.

But such unsold inventory can add significant transaction cost on the e-commerce exporter, since it is both difficult and expensive to have these products returned. It is expensive, since unsold inventory would typically represent a much lower quantity of goods, and therefore not having the economies of scale of the original outbound consignment, the logistics costs per unit for having the goods returned would typically go up. The fact that another round of transportation and other logistics costs are being added in itself can make this exercise unfeasible, especially if the margin on such products is low to start with. This challenge is further exacerbated if these products are volumetric.

Even if the transport and logistics costs in themselves are manageable, the customs processes related to returning products that have been exported to the origin (i.e., their re-entry back to India) are extremely complicated. Besides another addition in terms of costs in the form of customs brokerage and other associated agency costs, the customs requirement for having clear documentary evidence to prove that the returned product is exactly the same one that was shipped out is extremely difficult to meet. While some products such as mobile phones, laptops and other such electronic accessories have unique identifiers (e.g., IMEI number for mobile phones), this is not true for a host of other products.

In fact, products that are typically exported via e-commerce from India such as shoes, toys, apparel, accessories, fashion jewellery and handicrafts do not have unique identifiers, and proving that they are exactly the same product that was shipped out is next to impossible in most cases. Suggestions of having an end-to-end track and trace mechanism using some form of electronic chip or barcode is unfeasible besides being expensive and would, in many cases, also be subject to manipulation. Besides, enforcing such a mechanism (i.e., by scanning barcodes or chips and confirming authenticity of such products) would in itself be expensive and administratively burdensome, given the sheer number of individual items that form the part of such return shipments (see Box 8.1 for an illustrative example).

Thus, any return to origin (i.e., India) for such exports typically involves the payment of import duty on these items, though they do not represent a commercial import but a mere return to the original owner of goods. This puts a huge transaction cost on return of goods and makes the process completely unfeasible.

Box 8.1 Problem of Returns in Cross Border E-Commerce

As an illustrative example, imagine an e-commerce exporter using the fulfilment model is sending out 4,000 leather jackets and 1,500 ladies' boots to Germany from India in anticipation of sale during Christmas season. However, at the end of the season, he has an unsold inventory of 1,000 jackets and 300 boots. Assuming he has put a unique barcode in each of these units, and he had submitted this data in some form when the goods were exported, when these items re-enter India, they would have to be scanned and matched against the database submitted at the time of export. Since even a random credible sample would mean scanning 10–15 per cent of the items, this would mean customs officers scanning 100–150 jackets and 30–45 boots individually. And this would represent the return shipment of just one exporter.

Exporters are thus left with no other option but to liquidate the goods, that is, sell or dispose the goods at whatever price they get. This adds another layer of regulatory challenges related to invoicing, a discussion on which follows.

8.4.2. Invoicing and Inward Remittances

Existing custom and foreign exchange regulations administered by RBI require that the buyer's name and exact amount of the sale transaction be mentioned in the invoice. This information is submitted to RBI and is used for correspondence at the time of remittances received by the exporter from the sale of goods abroad. Since neither the buyer nor the final price is known at the time of export from India in the fulfilment model, this becomes a challenge.

The final selling price of the good in the fulfilment model is very dynamic and would have to take into account seasonal and other factors related to changes in price, warehouse and last-mile-related expenditure in the export market and, as discussed in the previous section, the need to get rid of excess stock at highly reduced prices.

Some flexibility is provided; that is, the name of the final buyer can be changed, provided there is default by the original buyer and the reduction in the sale price is not more than 25 per cent of the price declared in the original invoice. Customs also allows that if the final sale value is not ascertainable at the time of export, an expected value can put in the invoice under a written affirmation by the exporter to the realization of full sale of these consignments within a specific date.

The existence of these somewhat rigid conditionalities and the administrative process required for compliance with customs, and RBI adds layers of transaction costs to fulfilment exports. In the case of invoice value, having more than 25 per cent variation in total consignment value (due to price changes, discounts, need for liquidation and so on) is a very real possibility. Under such circumstances, that is, when there is more than 25 per cent variation between original expected price declared at the time of export and actual remittances, permission is required from Authorized Dealer Category 1 (AD1) Banks, which adds another layer of processes and transaction costs.

Furthermore, there is a very real chance that the exporter would not be able to meet the conditions of their affirmation to customs of realization of sale by a certain period and expected price, which results in more administrative processes and hurdles. These regulations end up discouraging many potential exporters from entering the cross-border e-commerce opportunity. Many countries such as UK, China, the USA and Singapore, to name just a few, recognize the fulfilment model of exporting consignments to another country and the final sale being affected there and have simplified rules that help facilitate such exports; India needs to explore such solutions proactively.

8.5. The Regulatory and Compliance Challenge of E-Commerce

Just as e-commerce exports represent an opportunity, the huge increase in the imports of such items is representing a huge policy challenge, at both strategic and operational on-the-ground levels. The strategic level challenges are related to the fact that increasing volumes of trade in such personalized small packages allow traders to fly under the radar and abuse the system through selling items at less than their cost (effectively dumping), or that of relatively poor quality and thereby trying to get around quality and product standards. Another challenge is that many countries provide some relief in tax (both customs and local indirect taxes) for individual (as opposed to commercial) consumption or for gifts being sent across the border. These are used as loopholes for traders to get away with not paying customs duties and taxes, unfairly impacting local businesses which are subject to these taxes.

Since certain countries, mainly China but also a few other East and Southeast Asian economies, have developed a very large export-oriented manufacturing base, especially for relatively modestly priced mass produced consumer goods during the global economy boom years in the first decade of this century, there is a tendency to leverage this capacity for exporting through e-commerce. This flood of exports from China and a few other countries is therefore a matter of concern for policymakers at the strategic level. But these strategic-level concerns have a direct link to logistics chain and associated regulation in countries' abilities to respond to this challenge and manage it. In this section, a few of these issues would be discussed briefly since they have a direct bearing on the design of logistics supply chain and enforcement of regulations around them, in the present and for the future.

8.5.1. Postal Channel-related Challenges

Unlike in the case of general freight or even courier services, the declaration format for postal products is extremely simplified. The typical customs declaration format used for letter post parcels and EMS is the CN22 document (Figure 8.3). CN22 only requires self-declaration of quantity, description of items and value of the good. If it is a commercial item, then the consignor is required to provide the HS code of goods in the parcel, only if they know. In other words, providing the HS code is not mandatory. It is also pertinent that the consignor or sender can self-declare the items as a gift. Since CN22 can be used as the standard declaration format for goods of value up to SDR300 or about \$410 (close to ₹28,000), this in principle covers a vast majority of e-commerce shipments, including the use of the postal route for

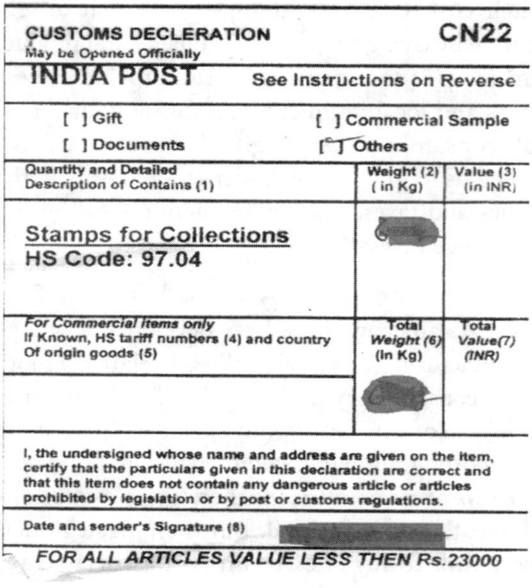

Figure 8.3 *Standard CN22 Document*
Source:

commercial transactions. It is also pertinent to note that the indication of country of origin is not a mandatory declaration.

Given the sheer volume of number of consignments traded across borders today, it is impossible to go through every single declaration individually by officers. It is for this reason that customs administrations are increasingly dependent on risk management systems that use data filed in advance in customs declarations to apply risk-weighted formulas and use this information to focus on a select subset of consignments that represent the most risk, whether from a revenue or other angles. While this advance data is available in general freight and courier environments, it is not in the postal ecosystem.

Given this new 'tsunami' of traded goods using small parcels, a large chunk of which uses postal channels, this is a matter of huge concern to regulators. The HS code classification, country of origin and value (backed by a proper invoice) are key elements of the risk management system. The risk is not simply of revenue loss and loss of competitiveness for domestic industry due to abuse of the trading system using postal channels. The HS code allows risk screening for sensitive products that might require further tests to ascertain their quality and safety for consumption, for example, food items, pharmaceuticals or health supplements, even toys or small electronic gadgets.

The country of origin is an important data element that seeks to establish whether exports from a country of origin are being channelled through another in order to take advantage of regulatory flexibilities or lower duties and taxes due to trade agreements. It also helps identify origin of specific risks, for example, likelihood of certain types of illicit trade and smuggling of products.

Formal historical record keeping of these combination of data elements related to HS code, origin, and value and information gleaned from commercial invoices used for such trade, and their formal historical record keeping, allows better management of all types of such risks, including increasing new areas of concerns related to abuse of intellectual property.

The postal channel remains institutionally weak, given the fact that it does not require consignors to provide quality data in these important counts. Even in the case of LVND category of courier with simplified declarations, the country of origin and HS code are always formally declared in the customs documents and are needed to be backed by a formal invoice. Furthermore, Universal Postal Union (UPU) rules do not make postal operators responsible for the declaration, unlike in the case of freight for importer where their agents are responsible or in the case of courier where the courier company is accountable.[9]

Another major area of concern for postal products is that postal operators are now trying to catch up institutionally and in terms of developing IT-enabled systems to support advance sharing of data with customs. Currently, there is no mandatory requirement for postal

---

[9] UPU Convention Article 23, as defined in WCO–UPU (2018, p. 11).

Box 8.2 Terminal Dues: Unlevel Playing Field in Logistics

Several countries, especially developed countries, have long complained about the issue of 'terminal dues'. Terminal dues is the payment made by the sending country postal operator to the receiving country postal operator for the use of the domestic network in receiving country. As per a 1969 UPU agreement, developing countries charge a relatively high terminal due, while developing countries charge a relatively low one. For example, postal packages with exported goods from China to the USA have to pay much lesser for the hinterland costs in the USA borne by USA Postal Service than the other way round. In fact, in many cases, the cost of domestic mail in the USA is more expensive than the international mailing charges paid from China to the same destination in the USA. This is true vis-à-vis many developed countries. Until the time the postal exchange between developed and developing countries limited in scope, and did not represent a channel for trade, this special and differential treatment was acceptable. However, since the e-commerce boom starting around 2010, the sheer volume of small packages originating from developing countries, especially China, has put a stress on this system. Developed countries felt that this 'unfair' logistics eco-system whereby exporting countries like China were being essentially subsidized by the postal operators in developed countries to access their markets had to end. Strong lobbying action from the USA, including a threat to leave the UPU, has led to renegotiations on the rates, and developed countries will now start setting higher rates that reflect actual costs of shipping on international packages to their countries.

---

operators in the country of origin to share even the minimal data in the customs declaration (i.e., CN22 or CN23) with the destination country.[10]

While there is a requirement effective 2018 that even small packets containing goods mandatorily have barcoding (based on the UPU standard 13-digit S10 identifier) to provide information to customs administrations, the only information that is contained in S10 of

---

[10] Regulation 20-001 2.2, as defined in WCO–UPU (2018, p. 14).

relevance to customs is the country of origin of the packet (as opposed to the good) and whether it is a letter post containing goods, EMS or other postal product, and does not address the key data points required for establishing a robust risk management system.

8.6. Regulators' Concerns and National Interests: Challenge of Facilitating Trade Without Compromising Compliance

While this 'tsunami' of postal and courier services raises legitimate concerns for customs and other border regulators, it represents a genuine new model of trade, one which democratizes transactional relationships, allowing even small niche producers and sellers reach consumers globally. Thus, there is a need to provide efficient logistics channels and effective trade facilitation to this trade in small packages using courier and post (the fulfilment model using general freight channels would expectedly be the beneficiary of the WTO Trade Facilitation Agreement, and the regulators concerns around that trade are far more generic and less critical).

It is for this reason that WCO, in partnership with UPU, and other industry partners have been trying to evolve rules and models that, while facilitating such trade, do not compromise on the legitimate at the border regulations (WCO, 2018a). India is currently at the forefront, given that it had assumed the Asia Pacific Regional Vice-Chair in July 2016, and led the way by organizing the WCO Regional Seminar on the Cross-Border E-Commerce Framework of Standards.

It requires a technology-based solution that allows customs authorities to verify the authenticity of a transaction and related details, and implement a risk management strategy that prevents the abuse of the e-commerce route to abuse revenue-related obligations and compliance with other laws and regulations. As Waters (2017) demonstrates, verification systems using credible digitized information that can be securely shared are the key to logistical security even for the most sensitive of environments such as military supply chains in conflict zones.[11] While thousands of small merchants sell across borders using e-commerce platforms, a bulk of such transactions are done through large global e-commerce platforms such as Amazon, eBay, Alibaba, Rakuten, Lazada and MercadoLibre.

These are credible companies that trade globally. An online transaction on their portals, with e-payment therefore represents a credible documentation of four facts:

1. The actual payment made for the product in dollars, which for customs clearance purposes represents the invoice value (addressing the issues related to revenue loss due to under-invoicing and protecting domestic industry)
2. The type of product that was sold, that is, the product description of classification (addressing issues related to proper application of product-specific rules of standards and safety, and the right applicable duty to protect domestic retail services and industry)
3. This was a legitimate 'retail' sale, that is, an individual buyer made a retail transaction from an individual seller in an e-retail channel. In other words, a genuine B2C transaction, not wholesale commercial B2B transactions masquerading as B2C (to ensure that there is minimum misuse of the e-commerce channel and any duty flexibilities available for low-value shipments meant for personal consumption or gifts)
4. The details of the seller (merchant) who is selling through the platform (to help achieve some level of accountability for goods sold with a specific entity)

Providing customs the transaction identification number (TID) of each transaction (along with the four elements of data described above) creates the confidence that if there is need, then customs could validate this information and ensure that only genuine B2C transactions

---

[11] Immutable digital information shared within a secure, access-controlled ecosystem is the essential definition of a blockchain. But the solution being discussed in this section is much more basic compared to a multiple-user system with multidirectional flow of information, which would be characteristic of logistics-related blockchains being developed.

are taking place and there is control on regulatory and compliance concerns such as under-invoicing and misdeclaration of product type.

An important policy question that would arise is why such large e-commerce companies would agree to share sensitive data with customs and regulators. The way around this challenge is to provide these companies credible assurance to protect their data with the incentive that their packages would get some level of priority treatment in customs clearance as a reward for their participation in a data-sharing programme.

Further validation about the transaction value of the goods can be provided by the payment portals that actually handle the cross-border payment for the goods moving across borders. About 20–25 large payment gateways dominate cross-border e-commerce payments. These include prominent names such as Visa, Mastercard, PayPal, Alipay, PayU, Amazon Pay and Paytm, to name just a few. One could explore developing regulatory obligations emanating from the central banks (e.g., RBI in the Indian case) for sharing the payment confirmation details of transactions.

Just like a few e-commerce platforms and payment portals dominate their respective markets, international express shipments (i.e., courier) are managed by a very few large global operators. These include the 'so-called' international integrators such as DHL Express, FedEx, and UPS and larger regional operators such as Aramex, SF Express, DPD group and Hermes. All such large operators maintain comprehensive operating systems with rich, real-time data with end-to-end tracking of the shipment. If regulators are granted access to specific elements of data, with risk filter defined in advance, it would help pinpoint non-compliant activity and check them.

For example, risk filter could frequent use of a single type of know-your-customer document (i.e., a government-approved ID required to clear individual B2C shipments to identify the consumer in the importing country) would indicate that individual e-commerce route might be being used for commercial purposes. Similarly, a regular recipient of 'gifts' at a particular address would also indicate in that direction. Like in the case of e-commerce portals and payment platforms, express delivery companies would also need assurance of data protection. Similarly, having an incentive, for example, faster than average customs clearance for those express delivery companies that enter into a partnership with customs, would also ensure greater levels of participation and commitment. As a matter of fact, large aggregator express delivery companies such as DHL, FedEx and UPS enjoy higher levels of facilitation in some jurisdictions (e.g., the US, Canada and UK) precisely because they have entered into a formal agreement that allows customs authorities selective access to the data in their operating systems (with assurance of data security and privacy as granted by the national laws of these countries).[12]

Such four-layer confirmation of data through integration of information flows among the key stakeholders that make cross-border transactions possible, that is, the e-commerce platforms, payment portals and express delivery companies that manage transport and customs processes, and customs and other regulators, could create a holistic risk management mechanism that could effectively regulate the exponential growth of e-commerce-related small packages without impeding trade or having to deploy in enormous manpower and other resources to ensure compliance. Figure 8.4 provides a basic working model of this solution.

8.7. Conclusion

E-commerce represents a new, facilitated ecosystem of transacting business online, breaking down many of the traditional barriers of space, geography, information and optimal transaction size required, thereby democratizing the cross-border transaction space. But while there is some elimination of barriers in terms of information and intermediaries, the actual act of physically transporting the goods is still subject to the constraints of regulatory and infrastructural

---

[12] The Canadian Courier Low Value Shipment (CLVS) Program offers a great example of 'best practice' of such cooperative framework between customs authorities and express (courier) operators which lead to much higher levels of facilitation while addressing regulator concerns. For more details, see https://www.cbsa-asfc.gc.ca/publications/dm-md/d17/d17-4-0-eng.html

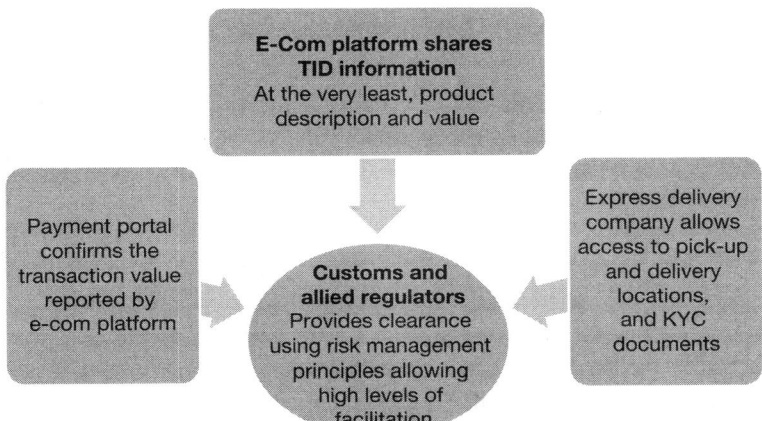

Figure 8.4 *Illustrative Representation of Multi-Stakeholder Supported Comprehensive Compliance Assurance Framework for Small Parcel Shipments in E-Commerce*

Source: Based on authors presentation to WCO Asia/Pacific Regional High-Level Seminar of Cross-Border E-Commerce Framework of Standards, 17 July 2018, New Delhi.

challenges of the traditional cross-border trade in goods. The growth of e-commerce adds other dimensions to the existing challenges of the physical movement of goods across borders represented by the exponential growth of small parcels where the recipient of these goods is an individual and not a business.

The fact that traditional cross-border trade infrastructure and regulatory institutions were designed to deal with B2B trade where individual consignments are typically multi-unit and large means that the direct selling model of e-commerce with millions of small packages with limited units of goods in each consignment, and the importer on record being an individual (as opposed to a business with registration and history with tax and other authorities), requires a response from both logistics and regulatory communities. The Working Group on E-commerce set up in WCO and the internal discussions in UPU on a number of issues including preferential terminal dues available under existing arrangements represent some of the responses that have emerged so far.

This chapter has presented a very broad perspective on the scale of opportunity of logistics of e-commerce and its rapid growth, chosen to focus much more on the specific models of e-commerce, preferred logistics solutions associated with these models, and infrastructure and regulatory challenges that are unique to these models, and proposed some policy-related solutions. The need to focus on different models and associated logistics solutions is critical, since innovations in big data would also the way cross-border e-commerce is conducted, and therefore the logistics modes and solutions being used. For example, as predicting consumer behaviour becomes more robust using big data tools, it would be easier to know in advance how much inventory is required in which market. This in turn would enable e-commerce traders to move their goods closer to the buyer in advance of the transaction. Thus, the need to ship small packages through courier or EMS would be substantially replaced by the use of general freight (air or ocean) and warehousing in the export market.

The essential takeaway from this chapter remains that there are several operational, regulatory and strategic issues that have emerged from the growth of e-commerce. The operational and regulatory issues discussed in this chapter while being India specific are not dissimilar to other developing countries, and these low-hanging policy issues need to be addressed quickly in order to develop e-commerce exports. The strategic issues are overarching and are common across countries. Minimizing the threat from a huge increase in underregulated trade in small packages is important in order to safeguard a level playing field for Indian manufacturers and retailers, and it is important to find ways to partner and work with all major stakeholders in the e-commerce ecosystem including payment gateways and logistics companies, especially courier and postal operators, to achieve this goal.

References

Air Cargo News. (2018, 15 March). Call for data-sharing to speed up e-commerce. Retrieved from https://www.aircargonews.net/airlines/iata/call-for-data-sharing-to-speed-up-e-commerce/

AliResearch–Accenture. (2015, June). *Global cross border e-commerce market 2020.*

Asian Development Bank. (2018). *Embracing the e-commerce revolution in Asia and the Pacific* (Asian Development Bank and United Nations Economic and Social Commission for Asia and the Pacific report). Retrieved from https://www.adb.org/sites/default/files/publication/430401/embracing-e-commerce-revolution.pdf

ASSOCHAM. (2018). *Civil aviation and cargo: A knowledge report* (p. 41). ASSOCHAM and ACTUS Advisors. Retrieved from http://www.auctusadvisors.in/news/Assocham%2011th%20Conf%20-%20Civil%20Aviation%20&%20Air%20Cargo%20-%20Auctus%20Knowledge%20Paper%20%5B10-08-2018%5D.pdf

Bourlakis, M., Denyse, J., & Ali, I. (2018). *The next industrial revolution: How e-commerce is transforming B2B* (Deutsche Post DHL white paper). Retrieved from https://www.logistics.dhl/content/dam/dhl/local/global/core/documents/pdf/g0-core-whitepaper-dhl-b2be-commerce-en.pdf

Colton, D., Roth, M., & Bearden, W. (2010). Drivers of international e-tail performance: The complexities of orientations and resources. *Journal of International Marketing, 18*(1), 1–22.

DHL. (2017). *The 21st century spice trade: A guide to the cross-border e-commerce opportunity* (Deutsche Post DHL white paper). Retrieved from https://www.dhl.com/content/dam/downloads/g0/press/publication/g0_dhl_express_cross_border_ecommerce_21st_century_spice_trade.pdf

Express Industry Council of India (EICI). (2018). *Indian express industry – 2018: A multi-modal play in building the ecosystem* (Deloitte report prepared for EICI). Retrieved from https://www.eiciindia.org/images/Indian_Express_Industry_2018.pdf

Global Express Association (GEA). (2018, March). *Overview of de minimis value regimes open to express shipments world wide* (GEA policy brief. Retrieved from https://global-express.org/assets/files/Customs%20Committee/de-minimis/GEA%20overview%20on%20de%20minimis_28%20March%202018.pdf

He, Y., Li, J., Wu, X., & Jiang, J. (2011). Impact of e-commerce on international trade: Based on an iceberg cost model. *International Journal of Trade, Economics and Finance, 2*(3), 175–178.

Hinojosa, A. (2018). E-commerce: What's in a name? World Customs Organization. Retrieved from http://www.wcoomd.org/-/media/wco/public/global/pdf/topics/facilitation/activities-and-programmes/ecommerce/experts-corner/ecommerce_whats_in_a_name.pdf?db=web

IATA. (2019a). *Air cargo and e-commerce enabling global trade* (International Air Transport Association white paper). Retrieved from https://www.iata.org/contentassets/4d3961c878894c8a8725278607d8ad52/stb-cargo-white-paper-e-commerce.pdf

IATA. (2019b). *The cargo facility of the future* (International Air Transport Association white paper). Retrieved from https://www.iata.org/contentassets/95ea6854c763444d9a6f46004e46c374/stb-cargo-white-paper-cargo-facility-future.pdf

KPMG. (2018, July). *Indian brands going global: A USD 39 billion opportunity* (a KPMG and Google study). Retrieved from https://assets.kpmg/content/dam/kpmg/in/pdf/2018/07/Opportunities-Indian-brands-global-markets.pdf

Lewis, I. (2001). Logistics and electronic commerce: An interorganizational systems perspective. *Transportation Journal, 40*(4), 5–13.

Lieb, R., & Lieb, K. (2016). 3PL CEO perspectives on the current status and future prospects of the third-party logistics industry in North America: The 2014 survey. *Transportation Journal, 55*(1), 78–92.

Ministry of Civil Aviation, Government of India. (2012). *Air cargo logistics in India* (a Working Group report, pp. 38–51). Retrieved from https://www.civilaviation.gov.in/sites/default/files/Committee%20reports%207.pdf

Mukherjee, A., & Kapoor, A. (2018, March). *Trade rules in e-commerce: WTO and India* (Indian Council for Research on International Economic Relations Working Paper No. 354). Retrieved from http://icrier.org/pdf/Working_Paper_354.pdf

Rose, W., Bell, J., Autry, C., & Cherry, C. (2017). Urban logistics: Establishing key concepts and building a conceptual framework for future research. *Transportation Journal, 56*(4), 357–394.

Shong-Iee, I. (2007). The emerging global direct distribution business model: Industry and research opportunities. *Transportation Journal, 46*(4), 58–65.

Tong, F. (2016, 19 January). Parcel shipping from China grows 70% in 2015 as e-commerce soars. Retrieved from https://www.digitalcommerce360.com/2016/01/19/parcel-shipping-china-grows-70-2015-e-commerce-soars/

UPU. (2017). *Report of Electronic Advance Data roadmap steering committee*, Postal Operations Council, Committee 1, Universal Postal Union (UPU) Document No. POC C 1 2017.2–Doc 6b. Retrieved from http://www.upu.int/uploads/tx_sbdownloader/electronicAdvanceDataRoadmapEn.pdf

Waters, T. (2017). Multifactor authentication: A new chain of custody option for military logistics. *The Cyber Defense Review, 2*(3), 139–148.

WCO. (2017, March). *WCO study report on cross-border e-commerce*. Retrieved from http://www.wcoomd.org/-/media/wco/public/global/pdf/topics/facilitation/activities-and-programmes/ecommerce/wco-study-report-on-e_commerce.pdf?la=en

WCO. (2018a, April). *Summary report of the third meeting of the Working Group on E-Commerce* (WCO Document No. EM0026E1). Retrieved from https://www.ifcba.org/sites/default/files/ctd_files/em0026e%20-%20Summary%20Report.pdf

WCO. (2018b, June). *WCO cross-border e-commerce framework of standards*. Retrieved from http://www.wcoomd.org/-/media/wco/public/global/pdf/topics/facilitation/activities-and-programmes/ecommerce/wco-framework-of-standards-on-crossborder-ecommerce_en.pdf?la=en

WCO–UPU. (2018, April). *WCO–UPU postal customs guide* (joint WCO and UPU policy tool). Retrieved from http://www.upu.int/uploads/tx_sbdownloader/ guideWcoUPUCustomsEn.pdf

Yang, Y., Hui Y., Leung, L., & Chen, G. (2010). An analytic network process approach to the selection of logistics service providers for air cargo. *The Journal of the Operational Research Society, 61*(9), 1365–1376.

Yousefi, A. (2015). *The impact of cross-border e-commerce on international trade.* Paper presented at the 16th International Academic Conference, Amsterdam, 12 May.

CHAPTER 9

Changing Payment Landscape in India

Sayal Gupta and Sourav Das

9.1. Introduction

This chapter deals with the transformation in the payment domain of the country and its impact on the various e-commerce domains such as multi-brand retail, hotel and travel booking, over-the-top (OTT) services' subscriptions, etc. In the chapter, we will also discuss the level of sensitivity among the millennials about the data privacy and its utilization by the applications they use in their daily lives. The data used in this chapter was procured from diverse section of the society, but major contributors or respondents were millennials—aging between 18 and 25 years—in order to achieve the accurate result for the objective we've determined in this study.

During the last five years (i.e., post-2014 elections) many things in the Indian payment system's domain have changed that drove us from the historical and conventional mode of payment to the modern and technologically advanced modes. Also, we would understand the various types of e-commerce logistics that are present in the contemporary era that ensure the last mile delivery. Help of technology such as artificial intelligence and internet of things (IoT) also played an important role in ensuring the last mile delivery to the customers.

9.2. E-Commerce

E-commerce means buying and selling of goods and services including digital products over digital and electronic network (Ministry of Commerce and Industry, 2018).

This definition displays the overall revolution in the buying and selling domain, where goods and services are availed just over a click on the Internet by millions and billions of people the world over every day. And majority of this transition is experienced from India, but it could not have been possible without major driving engines to catapult this growth trend. These engines are as follows:

1. Increased use and decreased prices of smartphones in the country
2. Reduced data tariff plans after the entry of Reliance Jio in the telecom industry
3. Increase in the use of digital marketing tools by the companies to boost their sales

According to the report published in the year 2018 (Jain, Sanghi, & Bawabkule, 2018, 8–9), smartphones prices in India saw a drop from an average of $250–260 in the year 2011 to $120–130 in the year 2017, which depicts that, over a period of 6 years (less than a decade), the average price of smartphones in India declines to the half. This increased the number of smartphone users in the country from 68 million in the year 2013 to a staggering 320 million in the year 2017 which is almost 5 times increase within merely 4 years. Along with this, the report suggests that annualized realized data tariffs per GB of data as a percentage of Gross National Income (GNI) per capita reduced from 2.6 in the year 2015 to 0.5–0.9 in the year 2018, which is around 73 per cent drop over a period of 3 years only (during this time, Reliance Jio made its entry to the Indian Telecom Sector). Apart from this, the number of Internet users in the country soared from

239 million in the year 2013 to 430 million in the year 2017 which is 1.8 times increase over a period of 4 years.

9.3. Background

Soon after the demonetization of higher currency notes was announced by the Prime Minister of India on 8 November 2016, a new era of digital payments begun in the country. Demonetization complimented the government-run Pradhan Mantri Jan Dhan Yojana[1] that aimed to open bank accounts for Antyodaya and issue RuPay cards to the new account holders. Later, Bharat Interface for Money UPI or BHIM UPI was also added as a new payment interface by the National Payments Corporation of India (NPCI).

This chapter will acquaint you with the current scenario of payment transformation in India after almost three years of the demonetization in the country.

9.4. Mode of Payments

In a cash-dominated democracy, a size big as India, overnight revolution of digitization arrived in the winters of 2016, changing the way of payment in country forever. From a cash-dominated mode of payment, we started looking for other modes, as the cash in circulation was limited and population to consume it was huge. Our study has identified the usage of following mode of payments along with the frequency of their usage by the respondents:

1. NEFT/RTGS
2. Debit cards
3. Credit cards
4. Net banking
5. Unified Payments Interface (UPI)

---

[1] An initiative by the Government of India to provide basic banking facilities to every household in the country.

6. Mobile wallets
7. PayPal

NEFT/RTGS, debit cards, credit cards and net banking were the modes people acquainted with for a long time now with the introduction of technology into the Indian banking system, but UPI and mobile wallets were the terminologies with which people were still not pretty much familiar; however, PayPal remains a not-to-be-chosen option by the respondents.

As per our study, statistically, UPI and mobile wallets were chosen by the majority of our respondents as their daily mode of payment while they are transacting online. While respondents prefer to transact with cards (credit and debit) on weekly basis. However, our study depicts that the old modes such as NEFT/RTGS, net banking, etc., have become more obsolete among the respondents with the entry of new-age modes mentioned above, as they are transacting through them only half-yearly or yearly basis.

As the respondents chose cards to transact with only on the weekly basis, it is important to know what card they are using and why? For this we gave them the following options:

1. Visa
2. MasterCard
3. RuPay
4. American Express
5. Diners Club
6. Discover
7. Citi

Even after strong support from the Government of India which even led to the litigation by MasterCard, RuPay is not the first choice of the respondents. As per our analysis to the survey, 47.7 per cent of the respondents chose Visa as their preferred card type followed by 35.5 per cent for MasterCard and RuPay is toiling behind with only 15.5 per cent while others could share the rest piece of cake.

Before, moving onto the portion where we will identify the reasons of respondents for choosing Visa and MasterCard over RuPay, let us briefly know about this initiative of the Government of India.

9.4.1. RuPay Card

Although introduced in 2013, these cards got their due only after the Pradhan Mantri Jan Dhan Yojana was launched, the scheme aimed at penetrating banking facility to the poorest of the household in the country, and, along with bank accounts, the account holders were issued the RuPay cards. NPCI stated the following advantages of these cards:

1. Lower cost and affordability
2. Customized product offering
3. Protection of information of Indian consumers
4. Provide electronic product options to untapped/unexplored consumer segment
5. Inter-operability between payment channels and products

Almost all the scheduled commercial banks in India are issuing these cards to the applicants, along with 251 regional rural banks and co-operative banks that are live on e-commerce, 11 banks—Bank of Baroda, Bank of India, Citibank, HDFC Bank, ICICI Bank, IDBI Bank, IndusInd Bank, Kotak Mahindra Bank, Punjab National Bank, State Bank of India and Union Bank of India—listed as e-commerce acquiring entities by NPCI.

This level of penetration and various benefits like cashback offers, insurance cover, exclusive merchant offers, national and international lounge access programmes, etc., are the reason due to the which the transactions through RuPay cards on e-commerce raised to 292.84 million, valuing around ₹254.21 billion between April 2018 to December 2018.

With the data such impressive, it's quite ironical to find RuPay lagging behind the leaders of the industry, but we also tried to find out the reasons behind this lag, which are listed as follows:

1. *Offers, discounts and cashbacks.* Both MasterCard and Visa provide numerous discounts on the food chains, travel partners, OTT portals, etc., which is yet to be realized by RuPay.
2. *Easy availability.* We normally witness the acceptance of VISA or MasterCard in the market. However, now the service providers have started accommodating RuPay along with these two, but people's perception has not changed much. Also, the trends steadily are in favour of RuPay, as no or minimal charges are levied on the contrary to Visa and Mastercard.
3. *International acceptance.* With RuPay being launched in the UAE recently by the Prime Minister Narendra Modi, it is steadily enhancing its presence worldwide. While the President of India, the Vice President of India and the Prime Minister of India usually shop with RuPay card internationally to promote it, it is still far to compete with the two leaders in the industry that have sheer prominence and dominance in countries across the globe.
4. *In-built features (like Tap & Go).* While Visa and MasterCard touching new-age technologies such as WaveTech, Tap & Go, no pin below ₹2,000 transaction, etc., RuPay is still going with the conventional way of payment through cards. Even RuPay cards with chip were a rare find and are steadily increasing in numbers now. But to compete with the leaders, it has to bring more robust shift technologically.
5. *EMI on debit cards.* E-commerce giants such as Flipkart and Amazon India partnered with banks such as HDFC Bank, ICICI Bank, etc., for providing EMI on their debit cards so that they can avail no cost EMIs. Here also, the cards powered by Visa and Mastercard are accepted pre-dominantly than RuPay. Hence, it would be advantageous if the e-commerce portals start accepting EMIs on RuPay debit cards as well.

One of the interesting finding was that 9 per cent of the respondents claimed that they never got a choice except RuPay from the issuer or the bank. These may be the accounts with the zero or minimum balance amounts in public sector banks that issue RuPay cards along with insurance cover. While talking about the insurance cover, we also found that only 3.2 per cent chose their card brand for availing the benefit of insurance cover, clearly suggesting that the insurance cover is not prime motive to avail debit cards among the millennials.

Now that we're done with cards, let us move on to the most prominent and most desirable mode of payment today, that is, UPI. UPI was launched just before the demonetization in the form of BHIM UPI, but its true potential is yet to be realized. Let us read a few facts about UPI before heading towards the analysis of our study.

9.4.2. Bharat Interface for Money UPI/BHIM UPI

What is UPI? UPI is the technology/system that integrates/powers multiple bank accounts into a single mobile application.

It is unique in context, apart from integrating multiple bank accounts to single application, as it is secured with single click two-factor authentication and use of virtual ID assisted with regulatory guidelines of NPCI.

As per the data published by Reserve Bank of India, the UPI transactions soars from 0.3 million valuing around ₹0.9 billion in November 2016 (just after demonetization) to an astounding 620.17 million valuing ₹1.026 trillion by December 2018.[2]

Data further suggests that out of the mentioned number of transactions in December 2018, 602.99 million transactions valuing ₹949.85 billion were done from the applications such as Paytm, PhonePe, Google Pay (formerly known as Tez), etc. Such numbers were highly achievable because of the promotional offers, cashback, scratch and win, referral and rewards (RnR) programmes introduced by these portals. This further depicts the penetration of the e-commerce websites in this domain is quite visible. Also, from a report published in *The Economic Times*, it is suggested that majority of such transactions are done on the e-commerce portals such as Flipkart and Amazon (Bhakta, 2018).

To find out the reality of UPI transactions after almost three years of demonetization, we asked the respondents about their preferred UPI

[2] https://www.npci.org.in/product-statistics/upi-product-statistics

portal. Their response was astonishing with around 51 per cent of the respondents chose Google Pay followed by Paytm and PhonePe, with figures around 18 per cent for both. The government-backed BHIM UPI was preferred by 9 per cent of the respondents just above Amazon Pay which was preferred by only 3.2 per cent of the respondents. Again, we studied deep about the reasons and found that the user interface (ease of use) was the key reason for the respondents to choose their preferred UPI service: around 63 per cent of the respondents chose user interface, followed by offers and cashbacks (32%) and around data usage (2%), and privacy policy and aggressive advertisement (2%).

Here, a noteworthy thing was that the respondents were least concerned about the data usage and privacy policy by the application they chose. As majority of the respondents in our survey have chosen Google Pay as their most preferred portal for UPI transactions, the issue of data localization, considering the fact that Google is an American MNC, prevails. The behavioural pattern of Indian consumers suggests that user interface and offers and cashbacks are more important to them than the data, which also includes the bank details, to be used by the service provider. After the Facebook–Cambridge Analytica data scandal, data localization has become an issue in many of the countries worldwide and the citizenry is getting aware of the data usage and privacy policy of the applications, but here the results are contrary to that fact.

Also, another inference from the analysis is that aggressive marketing fails to woo the Indian consumer until and unless the user experience is worthy, or they are getting any monetary benefit in the form of cashbacks or discounts from the service provider. This is the reason why UPI companies such as Google, Paytm, PhonePe, etc., invests their capital for alliances with various services. For example, Google Pay ventured for payments with RedBus and Goibibo, the two leaders in travel domain, FreshMenu and Foodpanda in the food app domain, and Zerodha in finance domain. Likewise, Paytm ventured for payment with various municipal corporations of Indian cities along with their ventures with DISCOMS and water boards. Similarly, PhonePe is enhancing their ventures with cab aggregators like Ola, food caterers like Faasos, FreshMenu, Behrouz, OvenStory, CakeZone, etc., along with their popular partnership with Delhi Metro Rail Corporation and IRCTC.

9.4.3. Cash on Delivery (COD)/Pay on Delivery (POD)[3]

But even after so much transformation, majority of Indians still prefer COD or POD as their preferred mode of payment due to multiple reasons.

Familiarity. Indians are more comfortable with cash payments than digital, especially in rural and semi-urban regions. In November 2016, the Indian government reduced the number of banknotes— currency—in circulation. This has cut down on ATM withdrawals. But the average withdrawal amount is now higher. The demand for cash reached its tipping point in April 2018 when ATMs in several states ran out of currency, putting further pressure on the Reserve Bank of India, the country's central bank, to print more bills.

Lack of infrastructure. The lack of a digital payment infrastructure is why many Indians are reluctant to go cashless. Most digital payment gateways require a smartphone and data connection. While cell phone penetration in India will likely be 85–90 per cent by 2020 (up from the current levels of 65–75%), most observers predict that only half of smartphone owners will subscribe to network data service by 2020.

Thus, many consumers shop online using outdated smartphones where the only payment option is COD.

Lack of trust. It is likely the most common reason for not using digital payments. Most Indian shoppers are wary of perceived security risks. They are unaware of common security measures that protect online transactions. Banks may provide them with a debit card or similar, but the process to use it is often confusing and intimidating.

Further, reports of increasing incidents of online fraud and data breaches heighten consumer worries. Thus, the easiest way to avoid

---

[3] This section is based on Manish Dudharejia's (2018) article.

this kind of fraud is COD—making the payment after an item is delivered and inspected.

Absence of cyber laws. India lacks cyber laws to protect consumers from losing money or sensitive information during digital transactions. Although the new Consumer Protection Bill, 2018 is an improvement over its predecessor—the Consumer Protection Act, 1986—it does not adequately address online payment and ecommerce frauds, according to many legal observers.

Other laws such as the Banking Regulations Act and the Banking Ombudsman Scheme apply in part to online transactions, but the legal and technical roadblocks can make it almost impossible to prosecute fraudsters.

Moreover, none of the anti-fraud rules regulate e-wallets. The Reserve Bank of India's recent plan for digital wallet companies to comply with the extensive know your customer (KYC) norms can make it easier to track digital payments. Nonetheless, India needs a comprehensive legal framework to regulate its digital payments and ecommerce market.

Although the online portals and services come with advanced securities, but the aforementioned apprehensions still persist so much so that 50 per cent of the total transactions done through online e-commerce portals are still COD/POD.

9.5. What and Where People Shop Online?

After the payment modes, the question arises in mind that where we make these payments and what do we purchase using these modes of payments. Table 9.1 will provide a better picture of the same.

As per Table 9.2, the train, bus or flight booking is identified as the most preferred while transacting online by the respondents, due to the fact that India is a travel loving country, here keeping the user behaviour in mind travel apps like ixigo, MakeMyTrip, Paytm, etc, are updating their user interface to be user friendly. Ixigo even waived off the charges on train bookings in order to increase rail ticket bookings

Table 9.1 *Transaction Categories of the Respondents*

S. No.	Category	Percentage of Responses
1.	Grocery	52.3
2.	Electronics	61.9
3.	IT and accessories	35.5
4.	Job and non-job applications	46
5.	Fruits and vegetables	28.4
6.	Train, bus or flight tickets	72.3
7.	Insurance and banking Services	41.3
8.	OTT services (like Netflix, Amazon Prime)	62.6
9.	Food aggregators	70.3
10.	Hotel or room booking	47.7
11.	Movie or show booking	58.1

along with the user-friendly patch with IRCTC portal while booking. As per the report published in *The Financial Express* (Soni, 2019), ixigo became the sixth most downloaded travel app in the world.

We will further identify the portals used by the respondents to shop online (see Table 9.2).

Leading apps that can be clearly identified are Amazon, Paytm, Flipkart and Myntra, followed by a decent share by Big Basket and Grofers. The top three apps cater to multiple categories of consumer goods including electronics and IT products and now even groceries; hence, we can infer that the respondents prefer a portal that is one-stop shop for them. However, the tailored portals such as Myntra for clothing, Big Basket for fruits and vegetables and Grofers for groceries have a decent share.

However, we must not overlook the percentage share of Alibaba (3.9%) which is among the least used apps by the respondents. With the majority of its customers being in China, it is now eyeing the second-largest market, that is, India. This is the reason why Alibaba has invested in 30.15 per cent stake in an Indian unicorn

Table 9.2 Portals Used by Respondents

S. No.	Applications	Percentage of Respondents
1.	Paytm	66.5
2.	Big Basket	29.0
3.	Grofers	11.0
4.	Amazon	83.2
5.	Flipkart	61.3
6.	Alibaba	3.9
7.	Myntra	46.0
8.	Urban Clap	5.8
9.	First Cry	1.9

Paytm. Also, as per the recent news reports, Alibaba is launching a movie ticket portal UCWeb in competition to Paytm and Book My Show. Currently, as per the statistics, only around 3 per cent Indians shop on Alibaba; hence, the stake invested by Alibaba in Paytm and UCWeb will enable the Chinese unicorn to penetrate into the Indian market.

9.5.1. Food Aggregators Scenario in India

Food aggregators transformed the Indian way of eating. The revolution started with Zomato when it became the first company to show menu to the consumers online on their app that helped most middle-class people to avoid extravagant and fancy restaurants for family outing and choose a decent and pocket-friendly restaurant. But as the tech transformation came into picture, it formed a strategic tie-up with the restaurants to deliver food to consumer's doorstep. Soon, Swiggy came into picture when they provided their own delivery executives to the restaurants for delivering food to the end-consumers in order to plug the bottleneck of unavailability of delivery executive at the restaurant's end, which resulted in high cancellation of orders at Zomato.

Now, all food aggregating apps have their own team of delivery executives managed under area manager of the particular area or the region. As per our study, 84 per cent of the respondents chose Zomato as their preferred app to order food whereas Swiggy is not too far behind (75.5%), followed by Uber Eats (49%) and Domino's (30.3%). The share of Domino's is exemplary even though it delivers its own food as compare to other three leading apps that delivers food from multiple brands, chains and restaurants. In the same segment, although one of the oldest food delivery app, Foodpanda is lagging behind with only 11 per cent of the respondents opting for it as their preferred app to order food. When talk about the single brand food delivery, Pizza Hut is not as convincing as Domino's where only 9.7 per cent of the respondents chose it to be a preferred app. Whereas, apps such as Faasos and Dineout were used by only 11 per cent and 0.6 per cent respondents respectively.

9.5.2. Cab Aggregators

Indian ecosystem changed dynamically from booking a cab for picking or dropping someone from airport to booking a cab for any occasion like birthday, farewell or without any occasion like no mood to walk or to use public transport. This revolution came due to the arrival of cab aggregators like Ola and Uber in India. Earlier we could only remember queues of Meru Cabs at train terminals or airports, but now it's much more sophisticated to book cab with an app.

Majority of the respondents as per our study chose Uber and Ola over Meru or Easy Cabs which are reduced to a marginally low share. However, the interesting outcome of the study was that respondents chose Zoomcar and Revv more than Meru or Easy Cabs. Although the former ones are self-driving car services and not the cab aggregators, a significant higher percentage of vote in their favour shows the changing thinking pattern of Indian consumers and their concern about privacy.

Although the noteworthy aspect is that people only choose Zoomcar or Revv for long drives and holidaying rather than daily commuting. But, a change their strategies has been noticed with the launch of initiatives like ZAP subscription by Zoomcar where you have to pay subscription fees while you're using the car and you can put it on hire when you're not using it, to change the ecosystem of driving.

Recently, at the annual convention of the Society of Indian Automobile Manufacturers (SIAM), Uday Kotak, Managing Director of Kotak Mahindra Bank, said, 'People prefer cabs over purchasing their own car'. Not to forget that Indian automobile sector is currently facing slump. Here, the arrangements like ZAP subscription will also affect the purchasing intent of the Indian Consumers.

9.5.3. OTT Service Providers

India has come a long way from CRT television and antenna sets to the era of OTT subscriptions. Now, Indian consumers prefer to sit back at home and watch their favourite movies, shows and documentaries on OTT service providers like Netflix, Amazon Prime, Hotstar, etc., among others.

As per our study, around 82 per cent chose Netflix and 75 per cent chose Amazon Prime Video as their preferred OTT service, followed by Hotstar (45.2%) and ALT Balaji, Jio Cinema and Voot (13.5% each), while the latest entrants to the segment such as Vodafone Play, Eros Now, Viu, HOOQ and SonyLIV are still to make their presence felt in this domain.

We studied a little deeper about the reason of the respondents to choose their respective OTT service providers and 71.6 per cent of the respondents sighted content to be the reason for their choice. We all know that Netflix and Amazon Prime provides niche content from India and abroad to its viewers, hence they are the major shareholders of the viewers subscription. On the other hand, Hotstar lags behind as it promotes the app primarily on sports content powered by Star Sports Network, resulting in maximum footfall during sports season like ICC World Cup, Wimbledon, FIFA World Cup, Indian Premier League, etc., but not the rest of the time. However, Hotstar gained success with the 'Game of Thrones' and 'Chernobyl', while latter was even rated as the most viewed series online till now. This manifests that the content matters to the viewers, more niche the content more eyeball it will capture. Not to forget that Netflix gained accolades for their series 'Sacred Games', 'Delhi Crime' and 'Money Heist' whereas Amazon Prime Video is penetrating Indian audience with their series like 'Mirzapur' along with the promotion of content in Dravidian languages (Telugu, Tamil, Kannada and Malayalam).

However, portals such as Jio Cinema, SonyLIV, Zee5 push the content which they display on TV ignoring other niche content. They probably wanted to give more options to the Indian consumers but, on the contrary, ended up getting them confused and cluttered along with their user interface which seems to be inferior to that of Netflix, Amazon Prime Video and Hotstar.

Netflix minimum plan is of ₹199 per month, Amazon Prime Video bills you either ₹129 per month or ₹999 per annum, whereas portals such as Zee5, Vodafone Play, SonyLIV, Jio Cinema, etc., provide the subscription at a lower price; people still prefer the former ones, not the latter ones. As per our study, only 20 per cent chose subscription cost as a constraint to choose the OTT service. Which is on the contrary to the notion that Indians are much concerned about the pocket than the content.

Further in our study, we found that none of the respondents chose OTT service while keeping data usage and privacy policy in mind or in consideration. Here also we face an issue of data localization, as majority of OTT service providers are not Indian; hence, the behavioural data recorded in the apps can be manipulated by the owning companies, but, as the matter of fact, users are not aware of it as of now.

9.6. Data Usage and Privacy Policy

The Constitution of India guarantees every citizen a fundamental right to privacy as per the judgement read by Supreme Court of India, but even then India doesn't have a specific law or act dealing with data protection or data localization whereas its neighbour China has a stringent data protection law of inter-border or international transfer of data originally mined within the territorial limits of People's

Republic of China. Most of the developed nations in the world have sensed the need of data protection laws and framed their respective laws such as GDPR in European Union, Federal Trade Commission Act of the USA or Israel's Privacy Protection Regulations (Data Security). On the other hand, one of the fastest growing major economy is without any stringent data protection laws as we still bank upon the Information Technology Act, 2000 and are not updating to the modern day threats associated with data generated within the territorial limits of the Republic of India. But the onus is not only on the government; it is much closely related to the people's approach towards their own data privacy rights and it is quite clear from our study as well.

KYC is a medium where payment portals and aggregators fetch the details of the users such as Aadhaar number, PAN, etc., giving them benefit to transfer money directly to the bank account or enabling extra in-app features which aren't available for non-KYC users. In our study, we asked respondents about their comfort to provide their KYC details to these portals and aggregators. Around 67.8 per cent of the respondents were moderately to highly comfortable and rest 32.2 per cent were least comfortable to share their KYC details. Almost half of the respondents are in the favour of providing their KYC details or personal details to the payment portals which may or may not use the same for their personal benefit or just use for the purpose of analytics.

Twist in the tale arrived when we further asked the respondents to tell how frequent they read the privacy policy and data usage policy of the app before clicking 'I agree'. Only 15.5 per cent of the respondents suggested that they read it almost every time while the rest just click on it and move ahead. Here, we can find the pattern with above scenario of providing KYC details to the portals and aggregators: We do not bother ourselves to read the privacy policy and data usage policy and often provide KYC details to these portals just for the sake of availing extra benefits, prime perks of the app, for receiving money directly to the account, and so on. The reason could be anything, but, if some extra benefits offered, we tend to go for availing them even without reading the privacy policy and data usage policy by the apps.

But we are learning with the changing times and also from the data privacy scandals in the West. In response to our other question to the respondents, data privacy was the third most important feature after ease of transaction and payment security.

9.7. Conclusion

India remains the fastest growing major economy of the world, and, having the highest demographic dividend, it is potentially a bright spot for the globe in the contemporary business environment. India's success in its GDP growth is often calculated by its enriched service sector, but e-commerce is gradually stepping its way as one of the major contributors to the GDP.

Till now, e-commerce industry contributed around 2.2–2.5 percent of GDP of India, owing to the COVID-19 crisis this number is expected to be hampered. Payments are the engine of this growth. Indian payment system changed drastically over the period of last 3–4 years, or post-demonetization to be precise, benefitting the Indian e-commerce by and large. Nonetheless, it has integrated ordinary citizens of India to the mainstream.

Finally, in our conclusion, we would suggest that the people of India should realize the data privacy and protection. However the government should enact stringent laws for data protection and localization, precedent is the similar laws enacted in the Western countries and China as well.

References

Bhakta, P. (2018). UPI registers 25% increase in transaction amounts settled. *The Economic Times*, 2 November. https://economictimes.indiatimes.com/small-biz/startups/newsbuzz/upi-registers–25-increase-in-transaction-amounts-settled/articleshow/66470013.cms

Dudharejia, M. (2018). Cash on delivery dominates Indian ecommerce. *Practical Ecommerce*. https://www.practicalecommerce.com/cash-delivery-dominates-indian-ecommerce

Jain, N., Sanghi, K., & Bawabkule, N. (2018). *Digital Consumer Spending in India: A $100 Bn Opportunity*. Boston Consulting Group and Google.

Ministry of Commerce and Industry. (2018). Review of the policy on foreign direct investment (FDI) in e-commerce. Press Note 2 by Department of Industrial Policy and Promotion. https://dipp.gov.in/sites/default/files/pn2_2018.pdf

Soni, S. (2019). Ixigo becomes world's 6th most downloaded travel app; 3rd in India ahead of MakeMyTrip, IRCTC in train booking. *The Financial Express*. https://www.financialexpress.com/industry/sme/ixigo-becomes-3rd-most-downloaded-travel-app-ahead-of-irctc-makemytrip-goibibo-redbus-oyo-etc/1530444/

CHAPTER 10

Legal Issues in E-Commerce
Role and Liability of an Intermediary

Komal Kapoor

Today markets have changed their faces. Physical markets are now becoming obsolete as the consumers are shifted to the digital screen marketplace. Initially, Internet was used as a tool for communication between people. With the passage of time, people realized the remarkable capacity of the Internet to interact and create unlimited new opportunities. E-commerce, also called e-commerce, is increasing around the globe. E-commerce mostly consists of e-business transactions related to the purchase and delivery of goods and services. E-commerce includes retail trade between business and consumers (B2C) as well as business-to-business (B2B) trade. Businesses use the Internet, extranets or electronic data interchange (EDI) in carrying out e-commerce. E-commerce is now being used in all types of business, including manufacturing companies, retail stores and service firms. It has made business processes more reliable and efficient. Consequently, e-commerce is now essential for businesses to be able to compete in the global marketplace. It has made an incredible journey from the financial industry to the dot.com 'bomb'. But, as nothing comes without drawbacks, even e-commerce has its own drawbacks: Cybercrime is one of biggest problem for the e-commerce trade which includes millions of rupees frauds, personal data theft, etc. Cybercrimes are the hurdles in the road of success of online business. This chapter will examine the origin of e-commerce and describe retail trade on the Internet, process of e-commerce, legal position of e-contracting, e-payment systems in India, the role and liability of intermediaries in e-commerce, the legal issues that relate to e-commerce and the legal safeguards that are available in India.

10.1. Introduction

E-commerce business, in common parlance known as e-commerce, has shown unprecedented growth in the recent past globally. Smith (2008) traces the origin of electronic or e-trading; however, the invention of Internet and with it the development of World Wide Web not only gave a threshold push to the e-commerce business to establish itself as a successful business model but also gained popularity among people owing to its unique approach. At the helm of e-commerce rests the use and access of the Internet which is the source through which various financial and other business transactions are carried out. Internet also gives option to carry out multifarious business activity such as market research, information management, product selection, ordering, payment, to name a few. As per Fianyi (2015), the core concept of e-commerce primarily revolves around transactions that are conducted over Internet and which are mainly concerned with the delivery of goods and services in the notional environment. Further, it also includes the transactions related with online money transfer.

The e-commerce concerns with the business model that deals with trading among B2C and B2B which is carried out by making use of the Internet, extranet and EDI.

At the dawn of the 2000 millennia, the world entered the Fourth Industrial Revolution which was premised on the touchstone of information technology (IT). India, post its opening up of market with the economic policy of globalization, privatization and liberalization was exposed to this new phenomenon which was unparalleled in the human history (Bidgoli, 2002). Resultantly, the number of business models that were based solely on the Internet saw an exponential growth in the next two decades, that is, 2000–2018. In this flow, with more penetration of Internet into interiors of India, coupled with reduction in data rates to access Internet, most sellers who were transacting their business of purchase and sale through physical medium began offering their products and services over the online world. It can also be noted that by adopting the captioned model, online selling and purchasing have become very famous among the Internet users since a notional display shop is formed which categorically displays the products that are sold. It can be said that the watershed moment of Indian e-commerce industry was in and around the mid 2000 wherein the electronic industry, facilitated by government policy to create an ecosystem of IT, was at boom.

This development in the online arena not only provided cost benefits to the sellers but it also offers benefits to the customers in the nature of discounts and free deliveries, etc.

Unni (2002) states that what is to be emphasized herein is that in presenting the gamut of products, e-commerce is being increasingly used at an unprecedented rate in other types of businesses such as manufacturing, retail and services. It won't be out of place to mention that e-commerce has created a sense of reliability and efficiency in the business processes so as to enable them to cater to customer demands in a much more effective manner. Hence, before moving forward, it is imperative to first understand the concept of e-commerce.

10.2. 'E-Commerce': Understanding the Concept

As per Kamath (2017), neither it is feasible nor is it possible to give or attempt to give an exhaustive definition of the term 'e-commerce' since the complexities of its working are still being understood. Further, there exist too many intermingling forces that are at work at the same time while transacting business through this medium. Generally, it has been understood that the mechanism of undertaking business transactions via e-medium is unconventional and is different from the brick and mortar stores. E-commerce not only covers within its domain the purchase and sale of goods or offering or rendering services via electronic platform but also extends itself to other accidental and incidental functions connected with the transactions such as the following:

- Onsite delivery of goods and services
- Facilitation of payments
- Maintaining stock to ensure supply chain
- Service management

Dewanjee and Vyas (2016) enlist the some differences between electronic trade and traditional commerce that are presented in Figure 10.1.

It is common knowledge that historically as well as traditionally the businesses were carried out through brick and mortar establishments; moreover, before the explosion of e-commerce activities, it was an inherent belief that businesses can only be carried out through the traditional business structure that existed. With the advent of e-commerce business model at the dawn of the information age, the erstwhile business practices, beliefs, etc., are now being viewed by some as relics of the past. The inception of e-commerce business has totally transformed and lay redundant the business principles, practices, etc., which were traditionally followed in the business sphere. What e-commerce business model has done is that it has empowered the consumers. The following business models are facilitated by e-commerce (Dewanjee & Vyas, 2016):

1. *Business-to-business or B2B.* B2B e-commerce comprises of business methods which includes distribution and procurement of goods and services between companies and not between companies and individual consumer. E-commerce has helped businesses to create, build and expand their relationships with other businesses. One fine example of B2B business in India is an online e-commerce company is IndiaMART (www.indiamart.com). This acts as a platform providing opportunities to businesses to find other competitive business entities (Dewanjee & Vyas, 2016).

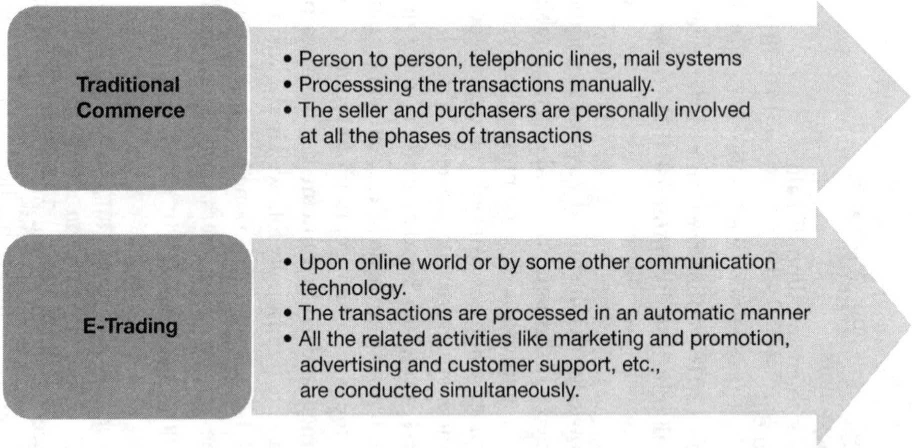

Traditional Commerce

- Person to person, telephonic lines, mail systems
- Processing the transactions manually.
- The seller and purchasers are personally involved at all the phases of transactions

E-Trading

- Upon online world or by some other communication technology.
- The transactions are processed in an automatic manner
- All the related activities like marketing and promotion, advertising and customer support, etc., are conducted simultaneously.

Figure 10.1 Traditional Commerce and E-trading: Distinction

2. *Business-to-consumer or B2C.* Traditionally, as well, the most common form of business transaction has been between businesses and consumers. This is not a new form of business. To add fuel to such transactions, the electronic medium has minimized the distance between the consumers and businesses and has helped such B2C business transactions to gain further momentum.

The differentiation between traditional B2C business mode and an e-commerce facilitated model can be fruitfully understood on an insightful perusal of a flow charts (Figure 10.2).

3. *Customer-to-customer or C2C.* The historical dealings between customer and customers were generally known as barter system where one customer who had access of something gets that exchanged with another customer who was in need of that product. The consideration that was involved in it was not money but a product itself. However, the present scenario of C2C business is quite different from the traditional C2C transactions. Now there are several online platforms where customers can list their products and offer them for sale to other customers. A counter customer who finds that product attractive or of his use may purchase the same by making the payment and by taking the delivery of the product. For instance, online classified sites such as Quikr and OLX are

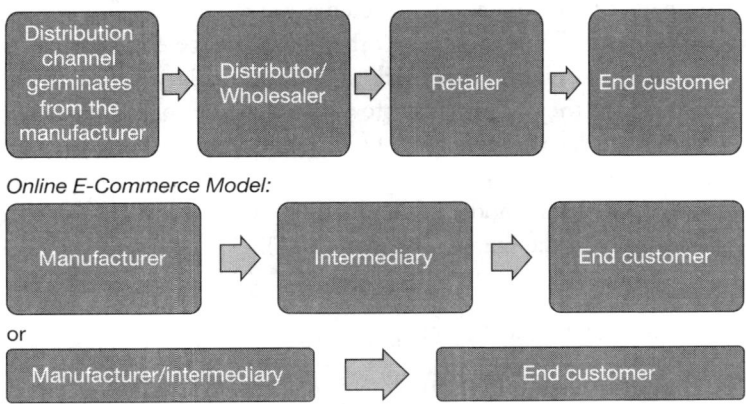

Figure 10.2 *System Participants in Traditional Commerce and E-commerce Model*

some well-known portals where customers can transact inter se (Dewanjee & Vyas, 2016). Looked from the lens of a consumer, it is a revolution in itself as it exterminate the harassment which a customer goes through with respect to establishing communication with other consumers to a large extent, specifically those who are well versed with the use of electronic gadgets.

4. *Customer-to-business or C2B.* As compared with the above-stated business models, C2B transactions are relatively newer, since it is almost reverse of the traditional commercial models. In this type of model, the consumers offer their services to the businesses against consideration. Some services that are covered in this type of business is offering of product development idea, creation of logos, ideas of attractive advertising, etc. (Nemat, 2011).

5. *Business-to-business-to-consumer or B2B2C.* This model is a modified version as compared to the B2C e-commerce model, since one more business entity gets involved in this type of transaction. This new business entity is the intermediary that provides the platform which facilitates seller to display their product and buyers to choose among the variety of goods available on the portal. The only function of this intermediary is to provide a technology platform to facilitate the same and purchase of goods and services amongst the sellers and the buyers. Some leading e-commerce companies that work as an intermediary are Paytm Mall, Flipkart, Amazon, etc. There are some other e-commerce entities such as Snapdeal and Jabong that work as an intermediary as well as the sellers since they follow inventory-based model of e-commerce. Needless to say that this model has grown tremendously over the years. This growth is visible from the fact that many companies have adopted this model of conducting business and are working successfully in the market (Nemat, 2011).

10.3. Electronic Contract

With the advancement in technology and access to Internet, not even the domain of law remained untouched. The prime example wherein Internet or electronic mode became relevant in law is with respect to parties entering into 'e-contract'. As per Unni (2002), e-contract is a contract that is entered into and created in the course of e-commerce between two persons connected via electronic means including but not limited to emails, computer systems. Since e-contracts are nothing but functionally equivalent to traditional contracts, the principles that govern the traditional contracts are also equally applicable to e-contracts. Traditional contract principles and remedies also apply to e-contracts.

10.3.1. Formation of an E-Contract

Kamantauskas (2014) states that clickwrap, browse wrap and shrink wrap contracts are common forms of e-contracts. One common thing that is prevalent in all the three forms of contract is that the terms and conditions of the contract are provided to the other contracting party not in a traditional hard copy but by electronic means. The affirmative acceptance of the contracting party is recorded by means of clicking on 'I accept' tab in clickwrap contract. Further, the contracting party is provided with the opportunity to read the terms and conditions before proceeding with accepting the same. On the other hand, in case of browse wrap contracts, specific agreement with respect to terms and conditions is not required. Mere surfing on the website entails a presumption of accepting the terms of its use. As per Wittmann and Vancouver (2007), shrink wrap agreements, on the other hand, are somewhat irrelevant to the e-commerce transactions but are relevant in relation to the kind of product with which it is associated. The main difference between the shrink wrap as compared to browse wrap and clickwrap is that the customer can read the terms of agreement only after opening the box, such as a software license agreement, etc.

10.3.1.1. Online Contracts: Its Validity

For initiating any transaction, be it an e-commerce transaction or a paper-based transaction, valid contract is a must. In India, every contract, be it an e-contract or any traditional contract, it is governed by the Indian Contract Act, 1872. The Act inter alia codifies the law on the point and Section 10 read with Section 2(h) of the Act set forth the necessitous pre-requisites that ought to exist for the formulation of a valid legal contract in India. An insightful perusal of the above said provisions would reveal the following principle:

1. Free consent
2. Lawful consideration
3. Competency to contract
4. Lawful object
5. Not declared void under the Contract Act (Section 24–30)

The only thing that is to be researched upon and analysed is that to what extent the contractual principles of the Indian Contract Act applies to e-contracts. As per Kalia, Arora, and Law (2017), it is to be noted that the Information Technology (IT) Act, 2000 recognizes the validity of e-contracts. Hence, unless any express prohibition is imposed by any specific statute upon the status of e-contracts such as clickwrap, browse wrap and shrink wrap, the IT Act, 2000 fortifies their validity if they fulfil the requirements as enumerated in the Indian Contract Act, 1872.

The fact of the matter is that there is almost no scope of negotiation or deliberations in e-contracts since they are mostly standard term contracts which are applicable on every one who enters into the website of a third party. The relevant question that now arises is that whether these standard forms of contracts are unconscionable and onerous.

10.3.1.2. Position of E-Contracts in India: On Whether Standard Form Online Contracts Are Unconscionable

As per Kumar (2017), in India, laws as to e-commerce are dispersed into various statutes, rules and regulations. The purview of the IT Act, 2000 legally recognizes all correspondence by electronic mail, information in an electronic form with electronic signature. However, in India, the law is not settled on the question that whether the standard forms of online agreements are onerous and unconscionable. Courts in India have however dealt with the cases where standard terms of contract and other terms of contracts were negotiated between the parties where one party is in a dominant position. Indian Contract Act provides various provisions that deal with unconscionable and onerous contracts. (Kumar, 2017). The Contract Act mandates that the contracts where consideration and object are opposed to public policy or where the agreement is executed without free consent of party, such agreements would be considered as unconscionable. The Indian courts have also placed the burden upon the person in dominant position to prove that the contract was entered into without any dominance and with free consent.

Section 16(3) of the Indian Contract Act, 1872 categorically states that where a person to contract is in a dominant position so as dominates the will of the other and enters into the contract with him and prima facie the agreement appears to be unconscionable, then the burden of proving the fact that such contract entered into with free consent will be upon the person in dominant position.

In the case of LIC India vs Consumer Education & Research Center, Hon'ble Supreme Court of India observed while interpreting an insurance policy granted by Life Insurance Corporation of India that the clauses in the policy that restrict the benefit of the policy only to those people who are employed with government as opposed to public policy and ultra vires to Section 14 of the Constitution of India. The Court noted,

> In dotted line contracts there would be no occasion for a weaker party to bargain as to assume to have equal bargaining power. He has either to accept or leave the service or goods in terms of the dotted line contract. His option would be either to accept the unreasonable or unfair terms or forgo the service forever.

In view of the above-stated provisions and legal position, it is pertinent to create thoroughly vetted contracts that provide adequate opportunities to the other party to familiarize themselves with the terms thereof.

10.4. Role of Intermediary in E-Commerce

The term 'intermediary' is defined under Section 2(w) of the IT Act, 2000 as

[A]ny person who on behalf of another person receives, stores or transmits that record or provides any service with respect to that record and includes telecom service providers, network service providers, internet service providers, web hosting service providers, search engines, online payment sites, online-auction sites, online market places and cyber cafes.

10.4.1. Is an Intermediary Liable for Third Party Actions?

The most relevant question in this is whether online marketplaces and e-commerce companies that merely provide a platform for facilitation of sale and purchase of goods and services are liable for the acts of third parties who sell and list their products to customers. Another relevant question in this field is that whether 'intermediary' would be liable for the acts of third parties that utilize the platform for carrying out illegal activities.

The pertinent answer to these questions are enumerated under the provisions of Section 79 of the IT Act, 2000 which is a safe harbour provision that exempts the intermediaries from liability with respect to the information and data hosted by it on behalf of third parties. However, there are certain requirements that are required to be fulfilled before seeking benefit of safe harbour provision.

1. The role of the intermediary is not more than that of providing access to technical computer system which facilitates display of information by third parties; or
2. The intermediary cannot in itself choose the initiator or recipient of information. Further intermediary has no power to alter the information which is transmitted from source to recipient via the IT platform of the intermediary; and
3. Due diligence as enumerated in various guidelines issued by central government or provisions of law is strictly adhered to by the intermediary.

As per the IT Act, 2000, the protection under section 79 is not granted in cases where

[U]pon receiving actual knowledge, or on being notified by the appropriate Government or its agency that any information, data or communication link residing in or connected to a computer resource controlled by the intermediary is being used to commit the unlawful act, the intermediary fails to expeditiously remove or disable access to that material on that resource without vitiating the evidence in any manner.

The central government in exercise of the powers conferred upon them by IT Act, 2000, in April 2011 notified Information Technology (Intermediary Guidelines) Rules, 2011. As per the guidelines, the intermediary is required to observe due diligence:

- 'The intermediary must publish the rules and regulations, privacy policy and user agreement for access or usage of the intermediary's computer resource by any person. Such rules and regulations must inform the users of computer resource not to host, display, upload, modify, publish, transmit, update or share certain prescribed categories of prohibited information'.
- 'The intermediary must not knowingly host or publish, any prohibited information and must disable the same within 36 hours of knowledge about the same, and where applicable work with the user or owner of the information to disable such information'.

As stated above, an e-commerce company that provides a platform and facilitates the sale and purchase of goods and services can claim protection under section 79 only in cases where the e-commerce entities observe due diligence as provided above.

There is a practical difficulty in observing the due diligence guidelines is that the e-commerce entity is required to take down/ block the infringing and illegal content from the portal on its own judgement and upon receipt of notification from either the effected person or from appropriate authority of the government.

These guidelines hence became a matter of debate within the industries due to the following two reasons:

- This provision of taking down of content by judgement or notification provides the intermediary a discretion with respect to the removal of the listing from the portal which further provides pick and choose option on whims and fancies.
- Debate arose as to whether within the time period of 36 hours the intermediary is required to take down all related listings or only the ones which have been notified to it by the affected person or the authority of the government.

In the leading judgement of Shreya Singhal vs. Union of India, 2015, the constitutional validity of Section 79 of the IT Act was challenged before the Supreme Court on the ground of it being ultra vires of the Constitution.

The major contention before the court was that the guidelines and provisions of Section 79 of the Act are violative of Article 19(2) since they provide discretion to the intermediaries to decide upon whether an 'unlawful act' is being committed or not.

The Supreme Court in its judgement, held that

[T]he provisions regarding the issue of 'knowledge' of the intermediary, and the consequent actions to be taken by the intermediary, i.e. Section 79(3)(b) of the IT Act, and Rule 3(4) of the Intermediary Rules are to be read down to mean that the intermediary must receive a court order/notification from a government agency requiring the intermediary to remove specific information.

Further, the Supreme Court has also stated,

[A]ny such court order or notification must necessarily fall within the ambit of the restrictions under Article 19(2)—therefore providing that any order for removal of content that is considered 'illegal' must fall within the reasonable restrictions provided for under Article 19(2) of the Constitution of India i.e. such removal must be in the interests of the sovereignty and integrity of India, the security of the State, friendly relations with foreign States, public order, decency or morality or in relation to contempt of court, defamation or incitement to an offence.

The captioned judgement has provided some clarity by interpreting the provision of Sector 79 of the Act. Clarity has been provided to the provision that the product can only be removed by the intermediary upon the receipt of specific notice from the government agency.

10.5. E-Commerce Transaction: The Process

E-commerce is famously understood to mean conducting business over the Internet. Model of e-commerce facilitates buying and selling of products and services by providing an online platform over the Internet over notional environment. The e-commerce transaction is not only confined to buying and selling of the product but also includes within its domain money exchange. Therefore, it is necessitated that, in furtherance of the trading activity online, a safe and reliable medium of online money exchange exists.

An e-commerce company in general parlance is the provider of online marketplace service, wherein branded and other merchandises are displayed for sale online by the various registered merchants/sellers for sale of their products and for the purchasers who can purchase the same. The above said contract of sale which is entered into by the merchant/seller and the prospective buyer/purchaser is subject to the marketplace terms as well as terms and conditions in general as enumerated by the company that provides the online marketplace platform to facilitate the transaction among them. Therefore, there exist three contracts that are independent of each other between the parties involved in the culmination of the entire transaction.

Contract 1. Between online marketplace platform e-commerce company and the merchant/seller. In the first contract it is agreed between the two that the merchant/seller will display the product which they intend to sell on the online platform offered by the e-commerce company.

Contract 2. Between online marketplace platform e-commerce company and the buyer/purchaser. In this contract, it is agreed through terms and conditions that the role of the e-commerce company is to facilitate the transaction of buying and selling through their online portal, and all responsibilities, guarantees, warrantees and after sale services falls under the domain of the merchant/Seller.

Contract 3. Between the merchant/seller and the buyer/purchaser of the actual contract of sale of the goods displaced on the online marketplace platform.

E-commerce companies offer their online marketplace services to the buyers/purchasers through various modes including issuing of coupons and vouchers and through various websites accessible through the platform. As per the legal principles, the contract is entered into between the merchant and the buyer. The role of the e-commerce companies in general business practices is confined to providing services so as to enable the merchant to list catalogues, prices, etc. It is further to be noted that since the actual control to list down and display information of the product solely rests on the merchant, e-commerce companies in their terms and conditions categorically clarify that the product being displayed is informational in nature and discretion is given to the customer to use their own wisdom for the same since e-commerce companies has no control over it. The safety valve which e-commerce company have is that they enter into a separate marketplace agreements with the merchant/seller wherein the merchant/seller is put into contractual obligation to be true and correct about the information of the product which is being displayed by them at their online marketplace platform.

As evincible in Figure 10.3, the procedural matrix which is involved in the completion of the transaction gets transpired thus:

1. The terminus a quo gets initiated by an order placed by the buyer/purchaser, using the online marketplace platform of the e-commerce company. The order then gets marked to the merchant/

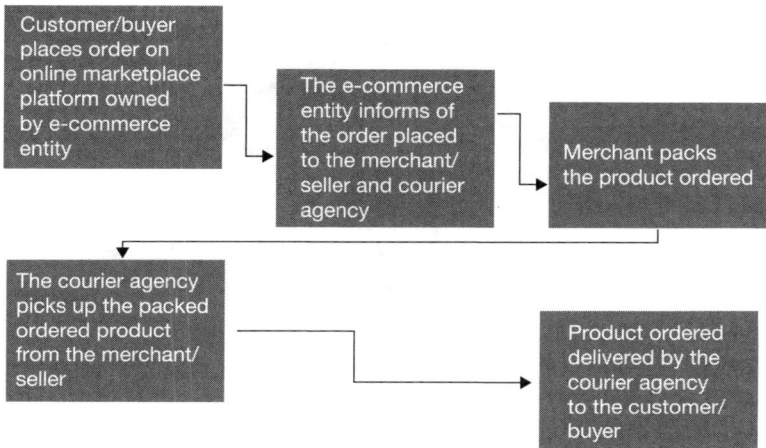

Figure 10.3 *E-Commerce Process at a Glance*

seller who had displayed the product. The merchant/seller being an independent third party seller is bound by an online marketplace agreement as entered with the e-commerce entity.

2. Once the order is placed, the ordered product is picked up from the designated merchant/seller by a third-party logistics service provider and is brought on to the logistic service provider facility. Further, the role of the e-commerce entity is only of a facilitator of marketplace platform and the transactions therein including that of payment solutions to merchant and to buyer/purchaser, and it does not have any control over the transactions between the purchaser, seller, logistic service provider and the courier agency.

3. Throughout the entire cycle of the processing of the order, until the delivery of the product, e-commerce entity has no control at all over the existence of the product, packaging of the product, delivery of the product. Neither at any point of time, it attained any type of ownership, right, title or interest in the ordered product nor had any control/possession of the product. The ownership of the product lies with the merchant/seller until the delivery of the product. The possession of the product changes hands from

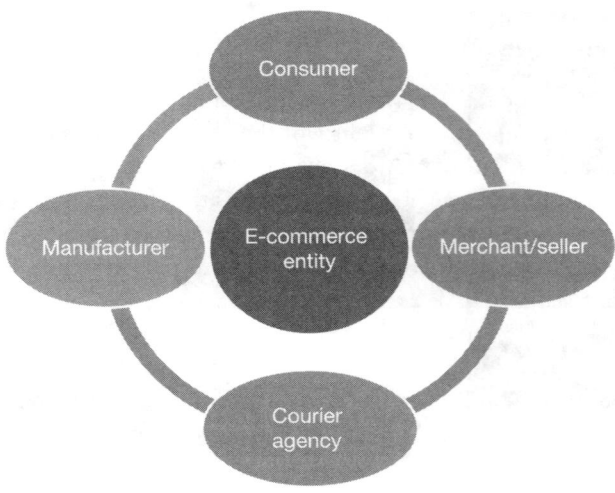

Figure 10.4 *System Participants*

the merchant to the service provider, then to the courier agency and finally to the purchaser (see Figure 10.4).

At the helm of the entire transaction is the e-commerce entity. However, the e-commerce entity in the entire process is not the owner of the product displayed at their marketplace platform with the ownership solely resting in the merchant/seller. Also, the e-commerce entity is neither the warrantor nor the guarantor of the product/services being offered. The grievances with respect to the warranty, quality, after sale services, etc., falls squarely within the contractual obligation of the merchant/seller as they are the owner of the product displayed to be sold.

In order to ensure compliance of the regulatory laws with respect to the MRPs, retail prices, sale prices, etc., the e-commerce enters into marketplace agreement with the merchant/sellers wherein the obligation with respect to laws is reposed upon them. The model of business is such that the role of an e-commerce entity is nothing more from providing an online portal through which the seller/merchant gets an opportunity to expand their business and access buyers/ customers which otherwise they would not be able to have.

However, the essence of the model business as it now exists is that the merchant/seller have to let go of their freedom in negotiation for better access and more profits since the e-commerce entities by virtue to their large consumer base are able to attract the merchant/seller with a possibility of supply of never exhausting consumer base. And for having access of the consumer base of e-commerce entities, the merchant/seller is made contractually obligated to take all the possible liability either regulatory or otherwise. The supply of the product ordered, correct delivery on time, defect-free product, warranties, guarantees, post-sale services, etc., are made the obligation of the merchant/seller, manufacturer and the courier service agencies.

10.6. E-Payment System in E-Commerce in India

Abrazhevich (2004) states that an e-commerce business model it is not only confined to the placement of orders and delivery of the same, rather it also offers different modes of payments to the buyers/ customers. Payments are accepted and remitted in electronic form hence is known as electronic payments or e-payments.

The merchant selling products on the e-commerce platform receives money through the platform itself. The mode of payment offered by these entities includes e-payment system along with cash on delivery (COD). As per Kaur (2012), traditionally the mode of payment as existed was either through cash or cheque. However, with the introduction of Internet, different modes of payments other than that of the traditional mode also started to come into foray. One of the modes of accepting payment in online sales is through e-payments. There is an unequal usage of e-payments around the world. One of the basic reasons is the difference of regulatory framework prevailing in the economies. Izhar et al. (2011) stated that it can be noted that more advanced the economy, more are there options of e-payment, and less developed the economy lesser options are available in terms of e-payment systems.

Bidgoli (2002) stated that e-payment system is generally secure and not so complex. The regular users of e-payment systems find it more convenient to transact using Internet than in cash or cheque, since it involves less time and is more efficient than traditional means of payments.

10.7. Legal Issues in E-Commerce

With the advanced and increased use of online media, online business is becoming a fast-emerging trend. Every five in eight companies are operating online, conducting e-commerce business. But being functional online doesn't mean you can escape legal matters.

There are various legal issues associated with e-commerce businesses as well. And if these issues are not taken care of in time, they can lead to serious problems for your business.

Described below are some of the common legal issues an e-commerce business faces.

10.7.1. Contracts

The following are some issues that can arise in case of e-contracting:

1. *Online identity.* Online transactions often occur between parties who have no pre-existing relationship, which may raise concerns of the person's identity with respect to issues of the person's capacity, authority and legitimacy to enter the contract. Digital signature is one of the methods used to determine the identity of the person. The regulatory framework with respect to digital signatures is governed by the provisions of the IT Act.
2. *Security.* Companies that keep sensitive information on their websites must ensure that they have adequate security measures to safeguard their websites from any unauthorized intrusion. A company could face security threats externally as well as internally. Externally, the company could face problems from hackers, viruses and so on. Internally, the company must ensure security against its

technical staff and employees. Security can be maintained by using various security tools such as encryption, firewalls, access codes/passwords, virus scans and biometrics.

3. *Authentication.* It is needless to state here that Internet has dispensed with the need of physical presence at the time of entering into a contract. However, that does not mean that the requirement of authenticating the identity of the person signing the agreement is dispensed with (Bidgoli, 2002). There are various technologies for authenticating the documents, electronic records and identity of the persons which have evolved over a period of time. It is very rare that the transactions that take place over the Internet is conducted between two known persons; hence, it is very important to authenticate the details and information about the other party. Most of the times, e-payment is secured if initiated under a secure environment and unless some unauthorized person misuses the credit and debit card credentials of the remitter (Kamath, 2017). The IT Act, 2000 contain specific provisions that govern and regulate e-signatures and issuance of electronic signature certificate. As per the IT Act, 2000, an electronic signature will be deemed to be secured in the following cases:

   a. The signatory was in complete control of the signature creation data at the time when the signature was affixed and

   b. The data related with creation of signature was kept and affixed in specific manner as prescribed by the Act or rules.

10.7.2. Identity Theft and Impersonation

As per the Information and Privacy Commissioner of Ontario (2014), identity theft involves acquiring key pieces of someone's identifying information in order to impersonate them and commit various crimes in that person's name. A case of true 'identity theft' is the one where the thief misappropriates information relating to the identity of a person—information such as name, address, telephone number, date of birth, mother's maiden name, driver's license number, or health card number—then masquerades as the victim, effectively taking over their identity. In terms of the IT Act, 2000, the offence of identity theft would be committed if the unique identity of a person, namely, electronic signature and password, is misused, fraudulently and dishonestly. The punishment that has been prescribed by the Act for identity theft is a fine up to ₹1 lakh or imprisonment up to 3 years or both. The punishment for impersonation is also same as of identity theft. The Act states that any person who by means of any communication device or computer resource cheats by impersonation shall be liable with imprisonment up to 3 years or a fine up to ₹1 lakh or both. The Indian Penal Code provides for cheating by impersonation as well and provides a punishment of imprisonment up to 3 years and/or fine.

10.7.3. E-Commerce Vis-à-Vis Privacy

As e-commerce entity cannot function in the absence of electronic transactions, similarly an electronic transaction cannot be conducted without the collection of any private information which includes but is not limited to personal details such as name, address phone number, email id, etc., and financial information such as debit/credit card credentials, bank account details, etc. Along with the stated primary information, the e-commerce entities also collect some secondary information such as preferences, choices in the area of business of such e-commerce entity, for example, cab service providers have the knowledge of the places that we frequently visit, shopping sites gain the knowledge with respect to the things we like, etc. Collection of these kind of personal information also places some responsibility upon the e-commerce entities to maintain secrecy of the data of the users. The user of the information majorly has two concerns with respect to the information that is shared by them to e-commerce companies:

1. Non-consensual access to the information
2. Misuse of information shared

The IT Act deals with the concept of violation of privacy in a limited sense; it provides that the privacy of a person is deemed to be violated where images of their private body areas are captured, published or transmitted without their consent in circumstances where they would have had a reasonable expectation of privacy. The act also prescribes a punishment of imprisonment of up to 3 years and/or fine of up to ₹2 lakhs for the violation of privacy (Wittmann & Vancouver, 2007).

10.7.4. Data Protection

With the pronouncement of the landmark judgement of Puttuswamy vs. Union of India also known as the 'Right to Privacy Judgement', and with the exposure of data leak by Facebook, the issue of data protection has never been at the forefront as in the present context. With the judgement on 'AADHAAR' still pending in the Supreme Court, it would be interesting to see how the scenario is going to change in the coming years with respect to the matter of data protection and privacy. However, India has in the year 2011 notified rules under Section 43A of the IT Act titled 'Reasonable practices and procedures and sensitive personal data or information Rules, 2011' which provides a framework for the protection of data in India ('Data Protection Rules').

10.8. Conclusion

The emergence of e-commerce business model has unleashed the repressed personalized consumer demand possible by offering various lucrative offers in order to establish their consumer base. A direct communications transmission between manufacturers and consumers helps in improving the strategy of an opportunity to reflect to the market. Governments and international organizations are at vigil to tackle this menace by the tools of policy and provisions so as to fight and prevent the consumer/buyers who are ordinary citizens and to develop the cybercrime-free e-commerce. The obligation for a united fight against the cyberattacks is not only of the governments of the day and the international organizations but also of the customers who are obliged to be aware and cooperate in the prevention of cybercrimes. Cybercrimes can be regulated and defeated by mutual cooperation, coordination among the organizations and Internet users. Governments should provide the safety and technical support to prevent the cybercrimes. Internet users should also take precaution of not falling into the trap and be the victim of these electronic frauds. The responsibility is mutual and together only the same can be fought. In India, there is no 'universally acceptable' global cyber law standards. However, in the present digital age, the same is of necessity to tackle cyber issues. With the government policies shifting to promote digital technologies and transaction under the ages of its official 'Digital India' campaign, it becomes far more imperative to put in place a sound and reliable policy to cater to the threats that are posed through Internet. However, there does exists a legal framework in the field of cyber world in India such as IT Act 2000 and subsequent amendments that were made in it; the true nature and extent of the same and its effectiveness is yet to be tested.

Challenges and issues of e-businesses is one of the vital areas of research. With increasing popularity of World Wide Web and the regular emergence of new and modern technologies intended for the web, the quantum of research that requires attention is extraordinary. A sound understanding and knowledge of web-based interface is fundamental for designing any working and effectual websites.

Advancements in Internet-focused technology have made e-commerce an operational truth now. The whole gamut of e-commerce entity rests upon two fold points: First, the establishment of consumer base by offering lucrative offers and convenient shopping experience and second, security and trust with respect to the information shared by the customer/buyer in the form of a sound and effective data protection policy.

E-commerce has unleashed a revolution. It paves the path in which future shopping will be done. Thus, it would be appropriate to quote William Gibson: 'The future is here. It's just not widely distributed yet'. The chain of ever upcoming and new wireless communication technologies like 3G and 4G are an evidence of e-business/economy; the Internet economy will continue to nurture vigorously. These modern technologies act as a catalyst in the growth of e-business, and Internet users would purchase more products and buy more regularly online, which will reap benefit to both fresh and reputable companies.

References

Abrazhevich, D. (2004). *Electronic payment systems: A user-centered perspective and interaction design* (Doctoral thesis). Eindhoven University of Technology, Netherlands.

Bidgoli, H (2002). *Electronic commerce: Principles and practice.* Academic Press.

Dewanjee, R., & Vyas, R. (2016). Cyber crime: Critical view. *International Journal of Science and Research, 5*(1) 2319–7064. https://www.ijsr.net/archive/v5i1/NOV152579.pdf

Fianyi, D. Israel. (2015). Curbing cyber-crime and enhancing e-commerce security with digital forensics. *International Journal of Computer Science Issues, 12*(6) 78–85. https://arxiv.org/ftp/arxiv/papers/1610/1610.08369.pdf

Information and Privacy Commissioner. (2014). *Identity theft: A crime of opportunity.* Ontario, Canada. https://www.ipc.on.ca/wp-content/uploads/Resources/id-theft-e.pdf

Izhar, A., Khan, A., Khiyal, M., Javed, W., & Baig, S. (2011). Designing and implementation of electronic payment gateway for developing countries. *Journal of Theoretical and Applied Information Technology, 26*, 84–90. doi:10.13140/2.1.2270.7847

Kalia, P., Arora, R. & Law, P. (2017), Information Technology Act in India: E-commerce value chain analysis. *NTUT Journal of Intellectual Property Law and Management, 5*(2), 55–97.

Kamantauskas, P. (2014). Formation of click-wrap and browse-wrap contracts. doi:10.7220/2029-4239.12.1.3. https://www.semanticscholar.org/paper/Formation-of-click-wrap-and-browse-wrap-contracts-Kamantauskas/590358875b31462aa238356286aa5228e6f42b7a

Kamath, N. (2017). *Law relating to computers internet & e-commerce (6th ed.).* New Delhi: Universal Law Publication Co.

Kaur, M. (2012). *E-commerce.* New Delhi: Kalyani Publication.

Kumar, V. (2017). An study of e-commerce and its legal frame work: With special reference to India. *International Journal of Law, 3*(3), 89–94. http://www.lawjournals.org/download/124/3-3-29-194.pdf

Nemat, R. (2011). Taking a look at different types of e-commerce. *World Applied Programming, 1*(2) 100–104. http://citeseerx.ist.psu.edu/viewdoc/download?doi=10.1.1.684.6401&rep=rep1&type=pdf

Smith, K. (2008). An analysis of e-commerce: E-risk, global trade, and cybercrime. *SSRN Electronic Journal.* 10.2139/ssrn.1315423

Unni, V. K. (2002). *Trade marks & emerging concepts of cyber property rights (3rd ed.).* Kolkata: Eastern Law House.

Wittmann, J. E., & Vancouver, B. C. (2007). Electronic contracts. Negotiation and Drafting Major Business Agreements, Proceedings of the Conference Federated Press. Toronto, Canada. http://docplayer.net/12955999-Electronic-contracts-jeffery-e-wittmann-vancouver-bc-negotiation-and-drafting-major-business-agreements-conference-federated-press-october-2007.html

CHAPTER 11

Regulating Network Effect and Market Power

Khushbu Kumari

11.1. Introduction

The term 'network effect' was initially coined to understand the growth of telephone network in the early 1970s. But in the digital age, it has gained much more momentum and significance. It has become one of the best parameters to analyse the digital markets economically (Balto, 1999). The positive network effect can be understood as, 'a product displays positive network effects when more usage of the product by any user increases the product's value for other users (and sometimes all users)' (Jorgenson, 2015). Similarly, there can be negative network effect as well. The negative network is not an issue of interest in the following study. In general, there are two types of positive network effects, that is, direct network effect and indirect network effect (Katz & Shapiro, 1985). Direct network effect is when the value of a product or service is directly proportional to the number of users, meaning, the more the number of the user, the higher the value. For example, WhatsApp network. WhatsApp is a messaging app that allows sharing of images, documents, location details, etc. Suppose that WhatsApp has 100 subscribers to its network and it is not possible for the users of WhatsApp network to communicate with subscribers of competing networks. If a new consumer subscribes to the WhatsApp system, the 100 original subscribers can now make contact with an additional person, without having incurred any additional cost themselves. For this reason, the benefit to those subscribers is sometimes described as a network externality.

Whereas indirect network effect arises where higher usage rates for one product or service increases the attractiveness of that network for another group (Bundeskartellamt, B6-35/17). Thus, for instance, game developers like Farmville create applications for Facebook users because of the massive popularity of this particular social network, and Facebook users profit from the rich offerings of the games. Likewise, the more people sell their spare items using OLX, the more buyers are attracted to the platform, and the more sellers will list their products.

It is significant to understand the meaning of online platform to understand the phenomenon of network effect. If we start from the beginning, the earliest civilizations had the barter system used to fulfil each other needs by swapping the products they required with the product that they had in excess. This practice was replaced by the market system with the advent of currency. The marketplace has sellers who need to sell things and buyers who need to buy things in exchange for currency. Then the term 'platform' came in, which was simply a marketplace where distinct users came together to exchange goods, services, information, etc. It brings both the seller and the buyer ta a single place and ultimately enhances the economy. The offline platform has existed since the end of barter system, for example, in the rural area, a village market and, in an urban area, a mall or a shopping complex. The online platforms only came in the mid-20th century but have grown exponentially since then. The online platforms can be two-sided or multi-sided, depending on the number of distinct user groups. One of the core features of the two-sided market is that 'the demands on two sides are independent'. Some businesses that operate in the e-commerce sector such as online search engines, booking sites or social networking websites may often function as two-sided platforms, which offer their services and also as intermediaries to a different group of clients (e.g., consumers, buyers, advertisers, suppliers). The search engines are a gateway to Internet content (Stucke & Ezrachi, 2016). Their function is to map out the information available on the Internet. Generally, the search engines do not charge a fee for providing information.

The network effect plays a crucial role in the growth of e-commerce compared to traditional brick and mortar market (Stapp & Hagemann, 2018). The shifting of choice of a buyer in e-commerce costs nearly nothing in terms of monetary value and takes few nano-seconds to switch from one website to another. Whereas in traditional brick and mortar market, it costs a lot more money and time. Hence, the network effect acts as a catalyst in driving the fate of a platform in e-commerce. Therefore, to usefully harness the result of network effect, the players of e-commerce can adopt practices such as lower the prices for the product or service to attract more users, or lower the costs for a particular type of user to attract more users of another kind, making it more favourable to both the kinds of users (Sammut-Bonnici, 2010)

The alleged aftermath of network effect and potential predatory pricing practices of players of e-commerce drew the attention of competition authorities. It is being argued that network effect acting along with another economies of scale have the potential of creating tendencies towards market concentrations around the big players of e-commerce. Also, the stronger network effect can result in lock-in (Marten, 2016). Therefore, the antitrust authorities took on the matter of adjudicating network effect.

The next part attempts to establish a relation between the network effect and Competition Law. The third part analyses the case laws dealing with network effect in the search engine cases. The fourth part deals with the diametrical ideology that the network effect alone does not imply dominance in the dynamic technologically run market.

11.2. Network Effect and Competition Policy

Network effect is an effective tool for growth in the online platform market (Currier, 2017). The online platforms are generally multi-sided or two-sided. For example, search engines like Google, wherein the user looking for information makes for one side and the advertisers looking to put the advertisements on Google make the other side. Similarly, in the example of social networking websites like Facebook, there are the user logging in to the website to socialize and there are advertisers looking to put the advertisements on the website. The economic analysis is that the greater the number of users on one site, the better are the chances of the advertisements to be seen ergo increasing the value of the website (Currier, 2017). Therefore, network effect is thought to potentially be the source of market power because bigger firms would have stronger network effect as they will have more users, making it difficult for the smaller firms to compete in the market (Bose & Parsheera, 2016). This argument was central to the pleadings in the United States vs Microsoft Corp. The case was brought up before the antitrust authority for tying up Internet explorer with the operating system. Microsoft had a leading position in the market of operating systems. Therefore, it was alleged that by tying Internet Explorer to Windows OS (its popular product), Microsoft has reduced the incentives for consumers to opt for other browsers. Hence, the presence of network effect was the driving factor behind such strategy of Microsoft. The European Commission specifically pointed out the importance of network effect and the barrier to entry derived from it. The Commission held that 'the nature of the barriers to entry in the client PC operating system market serves to reinforce the conclusion that Microsoft holds a dominant position in this market. These barriers to entry derive from the *network effects* in the market' (Case COMP/C–3/37.792 Microsoft).

The Commission, while determining the dominant position, relied on the network effect and held,

> It has been established in this Decision that Microsoft holds a dominant position in the client PC operating system market with a market share that is currently well above 90%. The client PC

operating system market, as well as the two other markets relevant to this case are characterised by strong direct and/or indirect network effects. (Case COMP/C–3/37.792 Microsoft)

The fear is that due to network effect, the first movers in the market might win even with an inferior product or despite the barriers of entry and hence would be raised without bound. Maurice E. Stucke and Ariel Ezrachi (2016) have argued that in case of search engines, there can be decrease in the quality of service however small it may be without the affecting one's dominance position due to network effect. Therefore, they have directed their solution towards quality competition as, in the digital economy, consumers are increasingly offered free goods and services in return of their private data (Stucke & Ezrachi, 2016). The antitrust concerns have been raised against Google in the search engine cases before the EU Commission and the Competition Commission of India (CCI). The next section deals with both the investigations in detail.

11.3. Antitrust Investigations Against Google

Google started as an Internet search engine, which remains as its front-runner product. A search engine is defined as a service that searches the Internet for specific items that correspond to the terms or keywords specified by the user (Encyclopedia[1]). So, Google's business primarily remains to provide information based on the user's query. It provides for three types of search results: generic search results, specialized search results and, in addition to these, online search advertisements. So, when a user enters a query, Google's programmes essentially run two sets of algorithms: generic search algorithm and specialized search algorithms (European Commission, 2017a, 8). The generic search algorithms function to rank pages containing any possible information. Whereas the specialized search algorithms 'are specifically optimized for identifying relevant results for a particular type of information' (European Commission, 2017a,

---

[1] https://www.encyclopedia.com/science-and-technology/computers-and-electrical-engineering/computers-and-computing/search-engine

8). Both these, generic search result and specialized search result, are shown together on Google's general search result pages. Google's comparison shopping service is one of the specialized search services. This specialized service helps the users to compare products from merchants in response to their queries (European Commission, 2017a, 11).

11.3.1. Google Search (Shopping) Case before the EU Commission

Apart from the general services provided by Google as mentioned above, general search results page also returns online search advertisements that are drawn from Google's AdWords. AdWords is Google's auction-based online search advertising platform (European Commission, 2017a, 9). The AdWords results are available to the advertisers for purchase. There are two aspects to the AdWords. First, it matches the keywords used as query by the users with the keywords on which the advertisers have associated their advertisements. Second, it ranks the relevant search advertisements within the pool based on the 'Ad Rank' (European Commission, 2017a, 9). The ranking is based on two factors: one, the maximum price allocated to each click by the advertisers and second, the quality rating of the search advertisement also known as 'quality score'. In general, Google has two consumers—users and advertisers—and is called a two-sided platform. However, Google mostly depends on advertisers for revenue generation (Surblytė, 2015)

Google entered the market of comparison shopping services in Europe in 2004 with a product named 'Froogle' (Humphries, 2017). It was re-named 'Google Product Search' in 2008 and again in 2013 as 'Google Shopping'. The purpose of this product is to allow the users to compare products and prices online and find the deals from online retailers (European Commission, 2017b)

The proceedings against Google first opened in November 2010 against the various complaints filed in relation to various of its practices (European Commission, 2010). The Commission had to investigate the following questions:

1. Whether Google abused its dominant market position by promoting its own comparison shopping service over the competing entities?
2. Whether Google used a strategy to demote the existing market players of comparison shopping service?

The first step of the Commission was to delineate the relevant market and then establish dominance and then, based on the acts of Google, decide if there was abuse of dominant position. The Commission took 'general search services' and 'comparison shopping services' as the two relevant product markets. The Commission concluded that the 'general search services' make a distinct product market based on the following factors:

1. The general search services constitute an economic activity. Although no monetary consideration is paid by the user in return of such service, consideration is paid in the form of providing data with each query. Second, due to the two-sided platform nature of such service, the number of user groups reflects into increase of value of the number of users in the other group.
2. *Limited demand side substitutability.* The web can be explored by alternative methods such as content sites, specialized search services, social media, etc. Therefore, there is limited demand substitutability between general search service and other online services (European Commission, 2017a, 30).
3. *Limited supply side substitutability.* The general search service requires resources of various kinds such as developing of algorithms, indexing of the data, deep pockets to invest on such innovation and time. These also act as barriers to entry for the newcomers. Therefore, there is limited supply side substitutability between general search service and other online services.

The 'comparison shopping services' was considered to be the other relevant market because it is a specialized search service and is not substitutable with any other online service such as online retailers, offline comparison shopping services, online search advertising services, etc. The relevant geographic market for general search services and comparison shopping services was concluded to be national in scope.

The second step of the investigation is to determine the dominance of Google in the given relevant market. Article 102 of Treaty on the Functioning of the European Union, defines dominant position as 'a position of economic strength enjoyed by an undertaking which enables it to prevent effective competition being maintained on the relevant market by affording it the power to behave to an appreciable extent independently of its competitors, its customers and ultimately of its consumers'.

The Commission concluded that the dominance of Google in the national market for general search services is based on the following factors:

1. *Market share.* The Commission has used the market share by volume as a proxy because of the very fact that the general search service is available free of cost to the users and also precise and verifiable value for calculation of revenue per search was difficult to be obtained. Therefore, the Commission relied on other factors such number of site visits, number of pages views, etc., to calculate the market share. The Commission, based on the information available, reached to the conclusion that Google enjoyed strong position across the European Economic Area (EEA) since 2008 except for Czech Republic (European Commission, 2017a, 58–62).
2. *Barriers to entry and expansion.* The Commission established that Google is dominant in the given general search services because of the existence of various barriers to entry and expansion. The very first requirement for a general search service is significant investment in terms of time and resources because the investments are humongous in nature. For example, Microsoft has been investing a significant amount in R&D since it launched its general search engine 'Bing' (European Commission, 2017a, 62). Second, the primary costs like investment in equipment and personnel are very high. Finally 'obtaining the large quantity of data necessary to develop an effective [general] search engine (e.g., the information upon which relevancy algorithms can be built and improved)

would be a significant barrier to entry' (European Commission, 2017a, 62).

Above mentioned are the barriers during the initial stage but further, to compete viably, general search service requires certain volume of queries to improve the relevance of the results for the query. Therefore, greater the number of queries, the faster it can work to determine the pattern of user behaviour and can improve its search accordingly. Another important aspect is that the existing general search services keep investing to make the product better whereas matching that level of investment is difficult for a new entrant.

Lastly, the nature of two-sided platform is regulated by positive feedback on both sides of the general search services and online search advertising service, and this creates an additional barrier to entry (European Commission, 2017a, 64).

The effects of barriers to entry and expansion have been clear given the facts and circumstance in the general search services market. Since 2007, Bing has been the only significant entrant to the market. It was upgraded in 2009 and its share since then has never exceeded from 10 per cent of the EEA. Since, 2007, many general search services exited the market and remaining have abandoned their general search technology in the favour of third-party technology. For instance, Yahoo abandoned its general search technology to Bing and now completely relies on it to empower its portal; Ask.com abandoned its general search technology and relies on Google to empower its portal.

There have been other entrants to the market, but none of them have been able to acquire a significant market share. For example, DuckDuckGo is a US-based general search service which entered the general search services market in 2010 and has been able to acquire only 0.8 per cent of the total market in December 2014. It also relies on the third parties to power its traffic (European Commission, 2017a, 66).

3. *The infrequency of user multihoming and the existence of brand effects.* Multihoming is a behaviour of users to change from on general search service to another. But the Commission has found that even with the technical ability of the users to switch between different

general search services, the actual switches are very less in number (European Commission, 2017a, 67). Also, the Commission concluded that because of strong brand name of Google, the users rely and trust on the relevance of search results of general search service of Google (European Commission, 2017a, 69).

4. *Lack of countervailing buyer power.* The Commission concluded that the countervailing buyer power is insignificant because each user only represents a tiny fraction of the volume of total search in a given national market of general search services (European Commission, 2017a, 70).

Therefore, based on the market share, barriers to entry, infrequency of multihoming, brand strength and lack of countervailing buyer power, the Commission concluded that Google enjoys dominance in general search services market nationally.

Once the dominance was established, the next step in the investigation process was determining the abuse of dominance by Google in the relevant market based on its acts. Article 102 of Treaty on the Functioning of the European Union and Article 54 of the EEA Agreement specify that the dominant entities are entrusted with special responsibility of maintaining competition in the market and not distort the same through any of their actions either directly or indirectly (Whish & Bailey, 2012). The Commission has always advocated that the dominant undertakings have 'a special responsibility not to allow its conduct impair genuine undistorted competition on the common market'.[2]

It concluded that Google relied on its dominant position of search engines market in general search to influence its comparison shopping services than playing fair. Based on the evidence collected during the investigation, it was established that Google is dominant in general search engine market.[3]

---

[2] Case 322/81, NV Nederlandsche Banden Industrie Michelin vs. Commission, EU:C:1983:313, paragraph 57; Case C-209/10, Post Danmark, EU:C:2012:172, paragraph 23; Case C-457/10 P, AstraZeneca v Commission, EU:C:2012:770, paragraph 134; Case T-286/09, Intel v Commission, EU:T:2014:547, paragraph 205.

[3] Intel vs Commission, EU:T:2014:547, paragraph 205.

The Commission concluded that the Google's conducts result into abuse of dominant position because of the following reasons:

1. *The position and display of competing comparison shopping services in Google's general search result pages.* Google favours its own comparison shopping services over the competing comparison shopping services when it comes to positioning and display of the same. The competing comparison shopping services can only appear as generic search results and are prone to ranking of their web pages in the generic search results and hence can be demoted based on the algorithms like PageRank.[4] Whereas, the comparison shopping services of Google are displayed rich and differently than the competing comparison shopping services and are also not subject to ranking based on the algorithm.[5]

2. *The importance of user traffic for comparison shopping services.* 'Traffic is the most important "asset" of a [specialized] search engine; it increases the relevance of [specialized] search services for a variety of reasons'.[6] The traffic is considered the most essential element for the comparison shopping services to be able to sustain in the market. The traffic increases the relevance and attractiveness for the merchants willing to sell their product or offer their services through the comparison shopping services. It increases revenue generation and also the credibility of comparison shopping services. It attracts the potential partners and other Internet users. It also strengthens the position of comparison shopping services to negotiate with the merchants as they would only want to put up their product at a place with significant traffic.

The revenue generated from traffic further helps invest and improve the usefulness of the services provided.[7] The traffic helps in machine learning effects and hence improves the relevance of the results of comparison shopping services. The Commission discovered during the investigation that 'comparison shopping ser-

---

[4] Ibid., para 344, 345, p. 77, 78.
[5] Ibid., para 378, p. 103.
[6] Ibid., para 444, p. 120.
[7] Ibid., para 446, p. 121.

vices run a popularity algorithm (the most clicked, most searched products and offers are showed in the higher ranks of our results pages) which performs better and better with increasing amounts of queries and traffic.[8] It further helps the comparison shopping services to suggest search terms that may be of interest for users based on the volume of traffic received by them. Lastly, traffic allows generating original user reviews.[9]

3. *The traffic diverted by Google from generic search result to its comparison shopping services cannot be effectively replaced by the other sources available to competing comparison shopping services.* The Commission concluded that the Google's generic search traffic diverted to the comparison shopping services of Google amounts to a large proportion of traffic and the same amount of traffic cannot be availed by the competing comparison shopping services by any other means.[10]

4. *Objective justification and efficiency claims.* The Commission concludes that Google has failed to justify its conduct either as objectively necessary or as beneficial to the consumers (European Commission, 2017a, 197).

A dominant search engine would attract maximum advertisers, which means the number of advertisers attracted by a search engine is directly proportional to its popularity. This sets in snowball effect and will result into the generation of more revenue which can be used to attract more consumers and also the data collected by the search engine can be used to enhance the result further.

The Commission established that Google has given a prominent position to its comparison shopping service by displaying it especially at the top or the right-hand side of the search result. Google kept its comparison shopping service free from the generic algorithm and treated it distinctively from other comparison shopping services. Since rest of all the other comparison shopping services were subjected to a generic algorithm, this led to the demotion of rivals.

---

[8] Ibid., para 447(2), p. 122.
[9] Ibid., para 450, p. 123.
[10] Ibid., para 539, p. 162.

The Commission made it clear that it neither had any issue with Google treating its comparison shopping service distinctively nor it had any problem with it keeping its rival under generic algorithm. But it is only objected to the fact that Google used its dominant position in search engine market to promote its comparison shopping service which resulted in the demotion of its rivals in the search results. So, the stand of the Commission is clear that one cannot abuse its dominant position to distort the competition.

A similar investigation was initiated against Google by the Federal Trade Commission (FTC) in the USA. The facts were similar as allegations were made against Google for using its dominant position as a search engine for its own advantage in the other businesses (Wyatt, 2013). The FTC ended up freeing Google of any charges but, soon after, the findings of some of the members of FTC were leaked which condemned the actions of Google under the Sherman Antitrust Act (Mullins, Winkler, & Kendall, 2015).

11.3.2. The CCI Order Against Google

In a similar case in 2012, Bharat Matrimony (now called as matrimony. com) and CUTS (Consumer Union & Trust Society) filed a complaint against Google Inc. to the CCI for abuse of dominance. On 8 February 2018, the CCI after investigation penalized Google Inc. on account of search bias and preferential treatment of its vertical services and use of restrictive clauses in the syndicating agreements.[11]

The central question before the CCI as put forth by Google Inc. vide its argument was whether providing of free search services form the basis of non-applicability of Section 4 of Competition Law which deals with abuse of dominance. Google contended that their services are free, and they don't charge any kind of monetary consideration from the users for the enjoyment of their services. Therefore, in the absence of consideration, there is no sale or purchase of goods or services and hence the provisions of the Competition Act are not applicable on Google services.

[11] Bharat Matrimony vs Google India, Case No. 07 & 30 of 2012.

The Commission opined that in an era of increasing digitalization, data is the new oil fuelling economies. The value of a platform is ascertained by the number of viewers it can rope in. The platform with maximum number of viewers attracts advertisers as they would want to reach the bigger audience. Also, the data generated from each view can further be turned into any number of revenues generating artificial intelligence (AI) based innovation. Hence, Google's revenue model is based on such data exploitations. The CCI once for all settled the question that direct monetary compensations alone cannot form the basis for applicability of provisions of Competition Law, especially in digital economy.

The CCI delineated online general search services and online search advertisement services as two different relevant product markets after a detailed analysis of all the factors under Section 19(7) of the Competition Act, 2002 (Roy & Kumar, 2008) and has established that these two markets are not a substitute but complementary. The relevant geographic market was considered to be India because the supply of online web search service depends on local specification requirements, language difference and consumer preferences, etc., which is unique and distinct in India. Also, the supply is subjected to the legislative framework of the country. Hence, the relevant geographic market is delineated as India.

Both the Director General (DG) and the Commission found Google to be dominant in both online general web search services and online advertisement search services after intently considering the factors, such as market share, Google's critical position due to its vertical integration, lesser probability of users switching to other competing search engines based on the logic that the high technology services demand continuous innovation and owing to the size, only Google would be able to keep up. The Commission also considered factors such as resource, economic power, commercial advantages, entry barrier, etc., to establish dominance. A wider scope has been taken by the Commission than merely relying on market share owing to the technological aspect of the case.[12]

---

[12] Ibid.

The Commission emphasized on the role of network effect and laid that

> [I]n multi-sided digital platforms, the network effects are more pronounced. New users tend to choose platforms or networks that already have a large user base which can ultimately even lead to a dominance by a firm in the market. No doubt, network effects can also facilitate introduction of innovative products, yet it cannot be disputed that network effects can raise switching costs for users and barriers to entry for potential competitors. As a consequence, market entries become less likely and users switch less frequently to other suppliers, which has a market power enhancing effect.[13]

The Commission also held that 'network effects can be regarded as significant above a given sign-up rate, when a critical mass is attained. Beyond that point, more and more customers will be interested, since the benefits of the service increase with the number of subscribers'.[14]

However, the Commission made it clear,

> [S]uch effects may not necessarily lead to dominance of a single company, they entail potential anti-competitive risks because they may facilitate formation of a dominant position and curb market contestability, since the most appealing company for new customers is the one that already has the largest customer base.[15]

Attending to the nature of digital space, the Commission held that to correctly asses the conduct of a dominant enterprise, it is significant to consider the 'fastmoving innovation, the novel products and services at issue, and the nature and extent of network effects that might exist'.[16]

Once the dominance was established, the Commission found three specific conducts to be in the violation of the Competition Law out of the several findings suggested by the DG in its investigation report.

---

[13] Ibid., para 199.
[14] Ibid., para 198.
[15] Ibid., para 200.
[16] Ibid., para 201.

. It can be seen in the both the cases that the antitrust authorities have specifically considered the nature of multi-sided platforms by considering the scope and extent of the network effect. It can be observed that a substantial reliance has been placed on network effect while determining the dominance.

11.4. Network Effect and Entrenchment: Not a Linear Equation

There is another aspect of the debate on the role of network effect in creating dominance in the market. The argument is that in the times of digital platforms, wherein the user is looking for a more individual and personalized experience, network effect may not imply entrenchment. Cathrine Tucker (2018) has taken the example of Google Plus and Google Buzz to establish that network effect in digital platform cannot alone explain the establishment of dominance. Google Plus was an attempt of Google to enter the market of social networking. Google already had a huge database of user information from its existing services such as Gmail and YouTube. But yet Google Plus failed to make a cut in the market due to the fact that the service did not provide anything more than the existing social networking platforms. Theoretically, Google's access to the huge database should have been a powerful tool, as it provided the users with an already established environment to establish social network. Instead, the same was unwelcomed by the users on account of violation of personal information.

Schumpeter (2003, 81–90) rightly argues that 'in technologically dynamic markets, however, such entrenchment may be temporary, because innovation may alter the field altogether'.[17] Argenton and Prüfer (2011) in support of this argument have suggested a model explaining the success of Google's search engine over that of Yahoo's and Microsoft's. They propose the higher quality of technology of Google to be the reason for establishing dominance. But there are

---

[17] It was also mentioned in United States v. Microsoft Corp D.C. Cir. 2001–12. https://www.justice.gov/atr/case-document/file/504276/download

limitations to the model as it examines the early days of the search engine market. Nevertheless, there has been emphasis on the incremental innovation over network externalities (Argenton & Prüfer, 2011). Concurrently, Bork and Sidak (2012) while examining whether the network externalities act as a barrier entry in case of search engines have considered scale not to be a barrier to entry (Bork & Sidak, 2012).

11.5. Conclusion and Implication

Network effect as a tool is widely used by the online platforms in their business strategies for growth. But there are situations when the technical advancement has superseded the network effect. For example, theoretically, Google search engine should have never surpassed the Microsoft search engine (Internet Explorer) and Facebook should have never surpassed Orkut (existing social media platform) because of the network effect. The shift in digital platforms are catered by number of factors, depending upon the need of the user. The shift to personalized and individualized preferences has left little to be decided on the basis of numbers of users or firms' size. Therefore, the antitrust authorities while assessing dominance and implication of network effect in the process should maintain balance (Bork & Sidak, 2012). In the changing dynamics of the market, the antitrust authorities need to observe and not interfere with the forces of market until the network effect leads to gross violations of the tenets of the Competition Law.

Reference

Argenton, C., & Prüfer, J. (2011). Search engine competition with network externalities. *Journal of Competition Law and Economics*, *8*(1), 73–105. http://ssrn.com/abstract=1808624

Balto, D. A. (1999). Emerging antitrust issues in electronic commerce. *Journal of Public Policy & Marketing*, *19*(2), 277–286. http://www.ftc.gov/public-statements/1999/11/emerging-antitrust-issues-electronic-commerce

Bork, R. H., & Sidak, J. G. (2012) What does the Chicago School teach about internet search and the antitrust treatment of Google? *Journal of Competition Law & Economics*, *8*(4), 663–700

Bose, A., & Parsheera, S. (2016). Network effects in India's online businesses: A competition law analysis. https://www.cresse.info/uploadfiles/2017_pa14_pa2.pdf

Currier J. (2017). 70% of value in tech is driven by network effects. https://medium.com/@nfx/70-of-value-in-tech-is-driven-by-network-effects-8c4788528e35

European Commission. (2010). Antitrust: Commission probes allegations of antitrust violations by Google. European Commission Press Release. http://europa.eu/rapid/press-release_IP-10-1624_en.htm?locale=en

European Commission. (2017a). *Case AT. 39740: Google Search (Shopping)*. Antitrust Procedure Council Regulation (EC) 1/2003. https://ec.europa.eu/competition/antitrust/cases/dec_docs/39740/39740_14996_3.pdf

European Commission. (2017b) Antitrust: Commission fines Google €2.42 billion for abusing dominance as search engine by giving illegal advantage to own comparison-shopping service. European Commission Press Release. http://europa.eu/rapid/press-release_IP-17-1784_en.htm

Humphries M., (2017). Froogle released in Europe. *Geek.com.* https://www.geek.com/consumer/froogle-released-in-europe-557196

Jorgenson, E. (2015). The power of network effects: Why they make such valuable companies, and how to harness them. *Evergreen.* https://medium.com/evergreen-business-weekly/the-power-of-network-effects-why-they-make-such-valuable-companies-and-how-to-harness-them-5d3fbc3659f8

Katz, M. L., & Shapiro, C. (1985). Network externalities, competition and compatibility'. *American Economic Review, 75*(3), 424–440.

Marten, B. (2016). An economic policy perspective on online platforms. Working Paper 5, Institute for Prospective Technological Studies Digital Economy. https://chapters.ssrn.com/sol3/chapters.cfm?abstract_id=2783656

Mullins, B., Winkler, R., & Kendall, B. (2015). Inside the U.S. antitrust probe of Google. *The Wall Street Journal,* 19 March. https://www.wsj.com/articles/inside-the-u-s-antitrust-probe-of-google-1426793274

Roy, A., & Kumar, J. (2008). *Competition law in India.* Eastern Law Book.

Sammut-Bonnici, T. (2010). Network strategy in digital economy. MPRA Chapter No. 50620. https://mpra.ub.uni-muenchen.de/50620/1/MPRA_chapter_50620.pdf

Schumpeter, J. (2003). *Capitalism, socialism and democracy.* Routledge.

Stapp, A., & Hagemann, R. (2018). Hearings on competition and consumer protection in the 21st century. Comments submitted to the Federal Trade Commission by Niskanen Center. https://www.ftc.gov/system/files/documents/public_comments/2018/08/ftc-2018-0050-d-0027-155052.pdf

Stucke, M. E., & Ezrachi, A. (2016). When competition fails to optimize quality: A look at search engines. Yale JL & Tech, *18*, 70. https://heinonline.org/HOL/Page?handle=hein.journals/yjolt18&div=4&g_sent=1&casa_token=&collection=journals

Surblytė, G., ed. (2015). *Competition on the Internet.* Springer Berlin Heidelberg.

Tucker, C. (2018). Network effects and market power: What have we learned in the last decade? *Antitrust, Spring*. http://sites.bu.edu/tpri/files/2018/07/tucker-network-effects-antitrust2018.pdf

Whish, R., & Bailey, D. (2012). *Competition law* (7th edition). Oxford University Press.

Wyatt, E. (2013). A victory for Google as F.T.C. takes no formal steps. *The New York Times*, 3 January. http://www.nytimes.com/2013/01/04/technology/google-agrees-to-changes-in-search-ending-us-antitrust-inquiry.html

CHAPTER 12

E-Commerce and Blockchain Intertwined

Concept and the Law

Purva Mishra and Astha Dubey

12.1. Introduction

We are in the era of a global market; buying and selling stuff comfortably sitting on the sofa is what people want today. The busy schedules have worsened their lives, and this easy mode to reach out to the things they need is what they savour the most. This online transaction between the parties has now become the face of marketing techniques known as the electronic commerce or e-commerce. Presently, all the commercial transactions are done through this platform. One of the advantages of being electronically involved in commercial activities is that the transfer of money can be easily done without cash in hand. The present scenario allows them to take the help of a third party, that is, banks, to instantly buy items online by paying online.

With the growth of technology, the traditional concept of money exchange is eroding. Financial technology has advanced towards the ease of the customer following the customer-oriented view of marketing. Even in the financial technological system, an intermediary is required for all the online transactions to pass through it. Often the system requires that there must not be any such third party so that no information is passed to a third person. This can be done if the customer is directly able to conduct the transaction with a system where they get to keep the secret information with themselves without the help of any third party. Blockchain technology does this exact thing by helping people make online transactions by simply investing in crypto currencies and buying and selling stuff through the same.

The most important feature of blockchain technology is that it is free from any regulatory authority. The dimension of e-commerce is not free from such control and thus all the transactions made online are being tracked and a record is maintained from their original domain. Also, this recording can easily be tampered and so there is no security as to privacy of this data is concerned. The Blockchain technology is free from such hassles since the complexity of entering the chain has almost made it impossible to break into the system. All these advantages of this technology have deviated people away from the conventional path of using credit cards to go shopping; instead, they opt for the newest way of using crypto currencies and fetching the benefits of scientific and commercial development.

This chapter would uncover the development of blockchain technology and the benefits it has been providing ever since. It would see how blockchains are formed using complex calculations and crypto currencies and how using this new technology can be beneficial to the public at large. Apart from crypto currencies, this chapter also tries to present the importance and relevance of blockchain technology in smart contracts and how it could work in the banks.

12.1.1. Fintech or Financial Technology

Fintech, a portmanteau of 'financial technology', is used to describe new tech that seeks to improve and automate the delivery and use of financial services (Fortney, n.d.). It helps companies as well as the consumers to manage their finances and work towards the advancement of technology related to the finance sector. It helps make it easy for the customers to build their portfolio by making investment in the businesses and corporate sector which would ultimately work in the direction of progress of the services provided. Fintech has expanded to incorporate any technological innovation in, and automation of, the financial sector, including advances in financial literacy, advice and education as well as streamlining of wealth management, loaning and borrowing, retail banking, fundraising, cash transfers/payments, investment management and more. Financial technology has been used to automate insurance, trading and risk management (Aldridge & Krawciw, 2017). The invention of mobile phone and computer has already increased the pace of these services to be helpful for the consumers where they have been using the technology to get all kinds of financial services, from bank money transfer to online transactions via net banking and smart cards like credit/debit cards. Fintech has been increasingly disrupting the traditional systems of banking, finance, corporate sector, etc., in the time ahead. It may overtake most of the work from these traditional sources, and, in this way, even consumers would shift from the conventional way of financial services to the modern and progressive road.

This can be understood in the way that globally, fintech users have moved from early adopters in 2015 to early majority in 2017, with 33 per cent of the surveyed population indicating they are regular users of fintech services. This trend indicates how much it has grown and become acceptable among consumers (EY, 2017).

Global investment in financial technology inflated quite a pair of, 200 per cent from $930 million in 2008 to quite $22 billion in 2015 (Accenture, 2016). This increasing number portrays that people are inclined towards using the technology meant for them. People have now acknowledged that they are smart enough to use such a technology and avail its benefits. In the initial days, due to governmental regulations—no push by the government—and very less number of bank accounts in the poor countries, which almost hold more than half the population of the world, this technology could not get a boom (Basu, 2017.). This is the sole reason why the investment figures portrayed above is very low. But, with new developments in science and commerce, the new blockchain technology has helped the consumers find a new path and so the trends of investing in fintech have been changing. The ways in which this new-found technology has been effective is many-fold and thus consumers are shifting to this new use of modernity.

Blockchain technology is one of the latest improvements done which has come to the aid of the customers to choose from the many options available online without any control or regulation from an authority and also completing the transaction in an efficient way. The security of data along with sufficient anonymity provided in the completion of such transactions with the help of blockchain technology is the most favoured feature, leading to the psychological shift of people towards this changing trend. The goal of blockchain is to allow digital information to be recorded and distributed, but not edited (Kagan, 2019). These features have made it a new choice for the consumers as well as for those who are new to this showbiz.

12.2. Blockchain Technology

Blockchain technology is not new to the world, yet it is counted as one. The outlines of this technology came up in 1991 when a need to develop some technology to continue online transactions without providing all the information to some third party was felt. Two researchers, Stuart Haber and W. Scott Stornetta implemented a system where the documents, once uploaded, cannot be tampered with. This breakthrough was unfounded until its first application in 2009 with the introduction of Bitcoin in the financial market. The Bitcoin protocol is built on blockchain. In a research paper introducing the digital currency, Bitcoin's pseudonymous creator Satoshi Nakamoto referred to it as 'a new electronic cash system that's fully peer-to-peer, with no trusted third party' (Fortney, n.d.).

Blockchain technology is not just useful in the area of e-commerce but also in other aspects. It can be used to store data about property exchanges, stops in a supply chain and even votes for a candidate. Apart from this, blockchain technology has many other uses too. For example, Stampery is a company which can stamp email or any files using blockchain. It simplifies certifying of emails by just emailing them to an email specifically created for each customer (Crosby et al., 2016). Since it is cost effective, many companies are using the technology for daily use. Also talking about the music industry, there has been a rise in the demand of transparency in the royalty payments by artists and songwriters. This is where the blockchain can play a role by maintaining a comprehensive, accurately distributed database of music rights and ownership information in a public ledger.

The process of blockchain is a bit complex and may take some time to enter the minds of many, but this complexity has made the whole system and process difficult to tamper with. This unique feature that the process is very difficult to hack is the most promising and catchy attribute of the blockchain technology.

The process of the use of the blockchain technology can be explained in the following way. The way a buyer opts to buy clothes from a retail shop, the same can be done with the help of crypto currencies such as Bitcoin. So, if it is assumed that the buyer is willing to spend his Bitcoin on the clothes from an online portal, here is where the blockchain technology comes into play. The buyer clicks buy on the online site and pays in Bitcoin. As soon as this happens, the computers connected at Bitcoin try to solve a complex mathematical problem which is known as 'hash'. As soon as the 'hash' is solved, the transaction is completed and publicly recorded, which again is an enormous amount of work.

Proof of work (PoW) is the consensus strategy used in the Bitcoin network to publicly record any transaction. When a node wants to publish a block of transactions, it has to be proved that the node is not likely to attack the network. Generally, it means computer calculations. In the PoW, each node of the network calculates a hash value of the block header. The consensus requires that the calculated hash value must be equal to or smaller than a certain given value. When one node reaches the target value, it would broadcast the block to other nodes and all other nodes must mutually confirm the correctness of the hash value. If the block is validated, other miners would append this new block to their own blockchains (Zheng et al., 2017) and then this record is shown to every other network at Bitcoin. The perk of this transaction is that the recording publicized cannot be removed or changed by one individual. Once used Bitcoin cannot be used again by anyone else thus avoiding the double spending possibility of a crypto currency. Since the transaction is sent to every network at Bitcoin, there is no one server where all the information is stored. If there would have been one, an expert hacker would have easily tampered with the records and so the Bitcoins could have been used twice since some of the recordings could have been erased and there would have been no record of such transactions. But this has been cured by the multiple copies of every transactions and only in exceptional cases, where more than half of the network has been hacked by the imposters, can this be betrayed.

There is one more security benefit attached to using the blockchain technology. When a buyer uses credit/debit cards to ensure payment, s/he has to provide some details printed on the card. This information is provided to a third party that can meddle with this information. Each user owns a pair of private key and public key. It was aforementioned that the transaction is publicly recorded but the data is not. The 'public key' is for entering into transaction with the other party which can be seen by the party contracting with the buyer but the 'private key' is the key to the Bitcoin wallet which has to be kept in secret. The private key that shall be kept in confidentiality is used to sign the transactions. The digital signed transactions through public key are broadcasted throughout the whole network. One who gets to know about this 'private key' can have access to the wallet and can transact on their behalf. Only 'public key' is recorded at the Bitcoin network and not the 'private key'. This ensures the required privacy of the consumers of this technology. The other party only gets to verify the transaction with the help of public key. And this transaction gets notified and saved in the network.

There are significant challenges and roadblocks in the application of this technology in the international forum. Some of these are as follows:

1. *Cost.* The technology required for the whole process is quite costly. The computers to process the complex mathematical problems must be energy efficient and of high quality. When it comes to blockchains that do not use crypto currency, the processors will need to be paid or otherwise incentivized to validate transactions. All of this makes the whole technology costly.

2. *Privacy.* The 51 per cent quota for the hackers to cross can be very rare but the possibility cannot be ruled out. This can be understood when a new crypto currency is introduced and only a handful people have been using it. The hackers can easily tamper with the data and this can be very painful for a consumer. Thus, privacy breach can be a huge uproar in the use of this technology. This can also happen to a fully proclaimed crypto currency since the imposters can have a hand in that particular area too.

   Privacy can also be understood in other words. Each person gets a private key. The private key becomes the highest vulnerability of a blockchain system whether it is stored on a piece of paper, screen, disk, in local memory or in the cloud. Users tend to use digital wallets which needs the private key. After a transaction is complete, the private key never gets public but remains with the owner alone.

3. *Susceptibility.* Newer crypto currencies and blockchain networks are susceptible to 51 per cent attacks, as mentioned above. This can create a framework in the mind of the consumers that the technology may not be a full proof plan to be executed and so they might back off from the use of this technology which may hamper the advancements of such technologies.

4. *Inefficiency.* Solving the complex mathematical problem through computers is a very time-taking process, and it is speculated that a lot can be done in that time period. This has been a problem which needs to be corrected by the framers of the technology. This may attract more consumers of the same technology.

But then again blockchain is being accepted at the international forum due to its many advantages. The selling point of the blockchain technology for businesses in the market is pretty good. Some of these advantages are as follows:

1. *Decentralization.* Blockchain does not store any of its information in a central location. Instead, the blockchain is derived and unfolds across a network of computers. When a new transaction is made, the network is updated, and the block is added so that every network connected can see it. The most important part of this is that since there is no regulating authority, there is no one server for the same and this is the reason why privacy is rarely breached.

2. *Accuracy.* Transactions on the blockchain network are approved by a network of thousands or millions of computers. This removes almost all human involvement in the verification process, resulting in less human error and a more accurate record of information. Even if there is some error in one of the networks, the whole system would not suffer since at least 51 per cent of the network must be destroyed for that purpose.

3. *Cost.* In a transaction, there is always a third party involved that needs to be paid over and above the actual transactions. The blockchain technology eliminates the presence of this third party and so the cost is saved. Also, in Bitcoin, the fees to be paid in the transaction to the third party are saved which makes it cost-efficient.

4. *Privacy.* Although users can access details of transactions, they cannot access identifying information about the users making those transactions. It is a common misperception that blockchain networks are anonymous, when in fact they are only confidential.

5. *Security.* Once a transaction is recorded, its authenticity must be verified by the blockchain network. Numerous computers on the blockchain rush to verify that the small print of the acquisition area unit is correct. After a computer has validated the transaction, it is added to the blockchain in the form of a block. Thus, security is ensured.

6. *Transparency.* Even though personal information on blockchain is kept private, the technology itself is almost always open source. Keeping data on the blockchain open source makes tampering with data much more difficult.

Thus, blockchain technology has proved its worth in the domain of e-commerce. Today, many have accepted its prominence and have agreed that it can be a very useful tool for the future generations. In recent times, blockchain has played an increasingly significant role in various spheres of our lives, and e-commerce is not an exception. Blockchain projects related to logistics of goods, different payment methods on the Internet and decentralized marketplaces are appearing in great numbers in the markets. These have some benefits over the present ancient businesses model, namely, trans-boundaries, trust-free basis, decentralization, low costs, group action speed, etc. (Elementh Foundation, 2017).

The next section will discuss about smart contracts, banks and crypto currency and how they have been around in the arena of e-commerce influencing the financial services across the globe. The effect of blockchain technology on these areas will also be debated in the following section.

12.2.1. Cryptocurrency

In the era of e-commerce, cash and checks have taken a back seat. To make the most out of the e-commerce business, sellers are opting for electronic payment methods for their customers. Presently, there are essentially three types of electronic payments: card payments, bank transfer payments and e-wallet payments. From paper money, credit cards to digital wallets, the mode of monetary exchange is continuously evolving, and there is no doubt that the next definitive step is adopting cryptocurrency. In order to understand the desire to develop cryptocurrencies, an analysis of the present scene of e-commerce transaction is essential.

Before cryptocurrencies, there were many other types of digital currencies including virtual currencies and money issued by central bank accounted for in a computer database (including digital-base money). The problem with some digital currencies like those created by an organization and transacted on a platform for example, loyalty points created by companies or digital coins created by Internet-based platforms, is that they do not hold any legal value and cannot be exchanged for actual monetary value as they could be transacted only inside the restricted platform.

Second, a distinct feature of electronic data is that it can be copied any number of times at minimal cost. This feature is highly unacceptable in case of financial transactions. Therefore, if cash data files are copied and the duplicates used as currency, they cannot be opted as a secure payment instrument. This particular problem is termed as the 'double spending problem'. In order to prevent the 'double spending problem', basic electronic payment systems are based on a central authority. The authority verifies the legitimacy of the payments and keeps the present scenario of ownership on check. The authority controls the creation, transaction, bookkeeping and verification of the digital currencies. Being the manager of the accounts of the users, for example, in banks, trust needs to be maintained so that the account holders do not fear that the central authority would run away with their money, that is, account should be maintained properly in any situation. A major threat to centralized systems is their vulnerability to hacker attacks, technical failures and malicious governments that can easily interfere and confiscate funds (Crosby et al., 2015).

The situation points to the need for a decentralized digital currency so that it can be transacted on various platforms and money supply can be controlled by various sources. Also, in order to prevent double spending and build up a trustworthy transparent system, a trusted ledger without central authority is needed. As e-commerce is growing at a tremendous pace, the obsolete global financial system represents the biggest barrier to its expansion (Stephens, 2018). And there is a booming need for a currency easily accessible and secure, having the above-mentioned characteristics.

The answer to the same can be found in cryptocurrencies. It is a term used to refer to a digital currency that is used for performing digital transactions and uses cryptography to ensure the security of the transactions. With the emergence of Bitcoin by Satoshi Nakamoto in 2008, who called it a peer-to-peer electronic cash system (Nakamoto, 2018), many new cryptocurrencies have found their way into the field. More than 1,000 altcoins, that is, alternative versions of Bitcoins, and crypto tokens have been created, with at least 919 trading actively on unregulated or registered exchanges

(Lee, Guo, & Wang, 2018). Cryptocurrencies use different timestamping schemes to ensure the validity of transactions added to the blockchain ledger without the requirement for a trusted third party. One of the first timestamping scheme invented was the proof-of-work scheme and the most widely used proof-of-work schemes are based on SHA-256 and scrypt (Steadman, 2013). Other than Bitcoin, there are various other cryptocurrencies, that is, altcoins or alternate coins such as Litecoin, Ethereum, Ripple NEO, etc.

Blockchain's distributed the ledger technology, and decentralized authority of cryptocurrency serves as a public financial transaction database. Literally, cryptocurrencies are entries about currencies in decentralized consensus databases. The term 'crypto' is used because the consensus-keeping process is secured by strong cryptography. They are irreversible transactions as one cannot undo the process and also pseudonymous as they are received on addresses. Most importantly, these are fast, global and secure. And also, the supply of cryptocurrencies is limited as there is a set final limit; in case of Bitcoins, it is 21 million, and they are expected to reach their final number by the year 2140 (Volastro, 2014).

Moreover, adopting cryptocurrencies early on, retailers like Overstock.com—which became the first major retailer to accept Bitcoin as payment in the year 2014 (Wertz, 2017)—will definitely have the first mover advantage. Such major retailers will help normalizing the idea of crypto transactions and increase the acceptance and demand for the currency which will definitely have profitable market in the future. Further, the transaction fees in case of cryptocurrencies are significantly lower and the settlement is instantaneous which gives them an edge over the bank transactions. Also, being hack proof and having no central authority gives the provision of check and balance in the hands of the user. But a major problem here can be from the investor's perspective, that is, taking on an additional currency with the inherent risks of fluctuating value, as a fundamental value of the currency is hard to comprehend but still people invest. An analysis of this can be done by studying about initial coin offerings (ICOs) where investors invest via cryptocurrencies.

In the stock market when a business opens up, they want people to buy stock. Buying stock in a business basically means buying a piece of the business. When they do that, it is called Initial public offering (IPO). It is so called because it is the first time they are available in the stock market or it is the first time the people are available to buy their stocks.

In cryptocurrency there are ICOs. This is when a developer creates cryptocurrency, there are benefits of buying it early like if the cryptocurrency skyrockets, then that certain individual is going to benefit a lot. So, in ICO just like IPO, the developer creates the cryptocurrency. It is before the launching of the currency, the developer offers ICO for raising funds. So, a company looking to create a new coin, app or service launches an ICO. The investors buy in a hope that it will do very well in the future and they would generate fortune through it. The company holding the ICO moves further in its goals, launches the product or starts its digital currency using the funds of the investors.

The reason that gives hope to the investors is that the ICOs over the past several years have produced tremendous returns. However, it has also led people astray. Because they are largely unregulated, ICOs have become a hub of frauds and scam artists, looking to prey on people.

Here, the solution can be analysing the investor's thought process. It is needed to be properly channelized and evaluated and this can be done via media and news as positive information may lead to more investments and proper genuine information. It can be seen that just like stock markets cryptocurrency has got its own ever-growing market where investors invest in order to earn profit just like in case of stock markets. And just like no business is without risk the crypto market is no different than stock market. Now, having gone through the investors' point of view, another angle to be observed is the legality of cryptocurrencies.

12.2.1.1. Legality of Cryptocurrencies

According to the Library of Congress, an 'absolute ban' on cryptocurrencies applies in eight countries: Algeria, Bolivia, Egypt, Iraq, Morocco, Nepal, Pakistan and the United Arab Emirates (LoC, 2019). With 'implicit ban' in another 15 countries, Japan is believed to be the hub for cryptocurrency trading in Asia. The government has a specific Payment Services Act-based framework which allows cryptocurrency trading and exchanges.[1] On 8 March 2018, the European Commission presented an action plan regarding advancing in technology-enabled innovation in financial services (fintech), such as blockchain, artificial intelligence and cloud services (LoC, 2019). In the USA, only Bitcoin has got a legal status and is a taxable commodity. In Holland, there is a special region, called Bitcoin City where all bitcoin transactions including retail purchases, trading and business are completely legal. On the other hand, the Reserve Bank of India (RBI) does not support the sale or purchase of cryptocurrency and the government also does not provide any recognition to virtual currency or related transaction. According to a notification by RBI in April 2018, it said that it had repeatedly 'cautioned users, holders, and traders of virtual currencies, including bitcoins, regarding various risks associated in dealing with such virtual currencies' (RBI, 2018). And in pursuance of those warnings, it had barred all entities which are regulated by the RBI from either dealing in or providing services to those dealing in such currencies (RBI, 2018). But this circular has been held unconstitutional by the Supreme Court in Internet and Mobile Association of India v. RBI case. Therefore, dealing in virtual currencies is now legal in India.

Not illegalizing cryptocurrencies doesn't always mean that the government of the country supports or promotes virtual currencies in any way. Though the legality is still a question mark in various countries, the future for cryptocurrency cannot be doubted as it is the foreseeable future of digital transactions.

12.2.2. Smart Contracts

A smart contract is a computer protocol, essentially self-executing contracts with terms of the agreement to enforce the negotiation or performance of a contract. Nick Szabo, a legal scholar, as well as cryptographer, in the year 1994, realized that the decentralized ledger could be used for smart contracts, blockchain contracts or digital

---

[1] Payment and Services Act 2009. www.japaneselawtranslation.go.jp/law/det ail/?id=3078&vm=02&re=02

contracts to help you exchange currency, property, shares or anything of value in a transparent, dispute-free way while avoiding the services of an intermediary. Smart contracts not only define the terms of the contract but also automatically administer them.

Smart contracts can take place as the option for even small social interactions in day-to-day life. For example, the common vending machines used on a daily basis is a type of smart contract which performs a particular set of functions upon inserting a coin. Further, they can find their way into various other fields like the government. Even though it is believed that voting systems cannot be rigged, smart contracts can be used in order to make the procedure fool proof as the votes cast would then require decoding and the task of hacking is impossible. Personal health records could be maintained on blockchain. Also, supervising drugs, regulating compliance, testing results and managing healthcare supplies too can make use of smart contracts.

Overall, the most important benefit of smart contracts is autonomy, that is, the absence of a middle man which leads to less costs of contracts and also reduces the time spent behind the process as usually a lawyer or a notary is needed to be hired and paid even for a rent contract. Also, as everything is on record and the contract also enforces obligations the chances of litigation are substantially low. This could seem to imply that smart contracts could be a threat to the lawyers but what can actually happen is that it may change the way lawyers work inside the firms as contract can be generated by terms only on legal basis and for this legal advice is definitely necessary.

12.2.2.1. Legality of Smart Contracts

Smart contracts are expected to increase efficiency in financial services, healthcare and so on. The Chamber of Digital Commerce, Washington, DC tried to make the position of smart contracts in terms of legality clear (Stanley, 2018). Accordingly, a smart contract to be legally binding must necessarily fulfil the three elements of a traditional contract. An offer must be made, acceptance must be granted to the terms and that some form of value must be transferred at a current or future time as according to the terms of contract, which doesn't seem to be a problem when it comes to a smart contract. Also, even though smart contracts eliminate the use of lawyers, the developers may need a lawyer for coding proper legal contracts.

Self-help remedies have been elucidated as 'legally permissible conduct that individuals undertaken in absence of obligation imposed by law and without the assistance of an official in efforts to prevent or remedy a civil wrong' (Brandon et al., 1984). Smart contracts act as self-help remedies as they can execute the contract on their own at the completion of contract. Also, in case of penalty, when one party fails to oblige the terms of contract, the smart contract can execute penalties as specified in terms of the contract. To explain precisely, smart contracts, like any other contracts, put obligation of fulfilment on both the parties to the contract. When a client tries to buy something online, it takes a form of contract. As soon as a product is selected to be bought by the client, the money from his wallet is not transferred to the retailer, instead when the product is shipped to the client, the money is automatically transferred to the retailer. Thus, the contract self-executes its clauses as soon as the conditions are fulfilled by both the parties and that the transaction is completed with the help of blockchain technology.

Therefore, smart contracts being self-executing is a type of self-help remedy because resolution via court is not necessary. Thus, question on its legality can be futile.

Moreover, if the terms of the contract are clear and as there is no chance of tampering information, smart contracts can be the way towards solving most problems without going into court trials. Like in cases of gift contracts, there can be no room for doubts as to whether the gift was actually promised or not. Therefore, leading to significant reduction in cases where problem of the case usually has roots in facts of the case. Smart contracts though have not been totally legalized yet, can be seen in our day-to-day life where we do give commands to machines and a digital contract is initiated and enforced. Therefore, their existence cannot be neglected.

Moreover, being based on blockchain which acts only as a platform of creating a secure, shared record of a transaction between two parties, smart contracts can be processed at various blockchains like Bitcoin, but have a limited processing ability when it comes to documents. Ethereum is the most advanced for coding and processing smart contracts.

Therefore, the abovementioned characteristics of smart contract when it comes to e-commerce can be highly advantageous in doing fast, secure and easy transactions as well as will be hassle free.

12.2.3. Banks and Blockchains

Blockchain can be utilized by banks as the technology that might help reduce fraud within the financial sector, where 45 per cent of financial intermediaries such as stock exchanges and money transfer services are usually target of financial crimes. Further, millions are spent in keeping up with KYC, that is, know your customer behind verifying and identifying the authenticity of the users. Blockchain would help avoiding repetition of the KYC process by enabling the organization to access the verification details of a client by another organization. Also, loan procedures, payments and so on will become easier and the transaction costs will significantly reduce for the user as well as banks will have to spend lesser behind the managing task. Therefore, on one hand as it helps the users and developers, on the other hand it can solve a major problem of the missing regulator in blockchain. Banks can exercise as regulators and use blockchain system in order to manage the data which can be accessed by individuals at any time.

12.3. Conclusion

E-commerce refers to commercial transactions conducted electronically on the internet. And blockchain nonetheless paves the way towards a more efficient, cost effective and secure financial transaction. Blockchain has shown its potential for transforming old-school industry with its key characteristics: decentralization, persistency, anonymity and auditability (Zheng et al., 2017). Blockchain-facilitated cryptocurrencies because of lack of a regulatory authority cannot be expected to replace the fiat money completely but can be a secure alternative just like credit cards and e-wallets. Also, with everything going digital and cryptocurrencies gaining popularity, smart contracts can be the need and necessity. As need for contracts at a digital level for social interactions too would need to be fast, secure and hassle free. Banks too in order to reduce frauds and provide a secure trustworthy finance service can use blockchain. Though the legality of blockchains-enabled transaction facilitators is still a big question, but with time it will definitely find its way into the e-world sooner or later in order to evolve. Blockchain possesses an immense potential in empowering the nationals of the developing countries if widely adopted by e-governance applications for identity management, asset ownership transfer of precious commodities such as gold, silver and diamond, healthcare and other commercial uses as well as in financial inclusion. Blockchain-enabled financial technologies being the next definitive technique in the order to further simplify financial transaction cannot be ignored given the future possibilities of almost everything going online. In order to clear the air regarding cases of transnational crimes and provide legal remedies and dispute resolution techniques for the same, a global legal framework needs to be established. Although the discretion of legalizing blockchain-enabled financial technologies is on individual nations, a common consensus needs to be reached at a global level for basic rules and regulations.

However, this is solely dependent on national political decisions (Miraz & Ali, 2018). Therefore, blockchain will not only revolutionize the e-commerce world but will also help major other sectors such as healthcare, automobile and even the government in one way or the other.

Reference

Accenture. (2016). Global fintech investment growth continues in 2016. https://newsroom.accenture.com/news/global-fintech-investment-growth-continues-in-2016-driven-by-europe-and-asia-accenture-study-finds.htm

Aldridge, I., & Krawciw, S. (2017). *Real-time Risk: What investors should know about fintech, high-frequency trading and flash crashes.* John Wiley & Sons.

Basu, I. (2017). FINTECH: Why Fintech is failing to fly. http://www.fundsglobalmena.com/spring-2017/fintech-why-fintech-is-failing-to-fly

Brandon, D. I., Cooper, M. L., Greshin, J. H., & Harris, A.L. (1984). Self-help: Extrajudicial rights, privileges and remedies in contemporary american society. *Vanderbilt Law Review, 37*, 845–850. https://heinonline.org/HOL/Page?collection=journals&handle=hein.journals/vanlr37&id=860&men_tab=srchresults

Crosby, M., Nachiappan, Pattanayak, P., Verma, S., Kalyanaraman, V. (2015). Blockchain technology beyond Bitcoin. Sutardja Centre for Entrepreneurship & Technology Technical Report. https://scet.berkeley.edu/wp-content/uploads/BlockchainPaper.pdf

Crosby, M., Pattanayak, P., Verma, S., & Kalyanaraman, V. (2016). Blockchain technology: Beyond bitcoin. *Applied Innovation, 2*(6–10), 71.

Elementh Foundation, (2017). Blockchain and e-commerce. https://github.com/ElementhFoundation/Documentation/blob/master/ElementhWhitepaperEN.md#blockchain-and-e-commerce

EY. (2017), *Fintech Adoption Index, 2017.* https://www.ey.com/Publication/vwLUAssets/ey-fintech-adoption-index-2017/$FILE/ey-fintech-adoption-index-2017.pdf

Fortney, L. (n.d.). Blockchain Explained. *Investopedia.* https://www.investopedia.com/terms/b/blockchain.asp

Kagan, J. (2019), Fintech. *Investopedia,* 25 Jun. https://www.investopedia.com/terms/b/fintech.asp

Lee, D. K. C., Guo, L., & Wang, Y. (2018). Cryptocurrency: A new investment opportunity. *Journal of Alternative Investments, 20,* 16–40. doi:10.3905/jai.2018.20.3.016

LoC. (2019). Regulation of cryptocurrency around the world. https://www.loc.gov/law/help/cryptocurrency/world-survey.php

Miraz, M. H., & Ali, M. Applications of blockchain technology beyond cryptocurrency. *Annals of Emerging Technologies in Computing (AETiC), 2*(1), 2018.

Nakamoto, S. (2018) Bitcoin: A peer-to-peer electronic cash system. https://bitcoin.org/bitcoin.pd

RBI. (2018). Prohibition on dealing in virtual currencies (VCs). https://www.rbi.org.in/Scripts/NotificationUser.aspx?Id=11243

Stanley, A. (2018). Can code really be law? New report clarifies smart contract misconceptions. *Forbes,* September 2017. https://www.forbes.com/sites/astanley/2018/09/27/can-code-really-be-law-new-report-clarifies-smart-contract-misconceptions/#2bbd023634e2

Steadman, I. (2013). Warry of Bitcoin? A guide to some other cryptocurrencies. *Ars Technica,* 5 November. https://arstechnica.com/information-technology/2013/05/wary-of-bitcoin-a-guide-to-some-other-cryptocurrencies/

Stephens, R. (2018, December 4). The future of cryptocurrency: Why e-commerce is the answer. https://medium.com/swlh/the-future-of-cryptocurrency-why-e-commerce-is-the-answer–822e62ba12f5

Volastro, A. (2014). CNBC explains: How to mine bitcoins on your own. *CNBC*, 23 January. https://www.cnbc.com/2014/01/23/cnbc-explains-how-to-mine-bitcoins-on-your-own.html

Wertz, J. (2017). How crypto can work for e-commerce businesses. *Forbes*, 29 November. https://www.forbes.com/sites/jiawertz/2017/11/29/crypto

Zheng, Z., Xle, S., Dai, H. N. Chen, X., & Wang, H. (2017). An Overview of Blockchain Technology: Architecture, Consensus, and Future Trends. Conference proceedings of IEEE 6th International Congress on Big Data, Honolulu, USA. https://ieeexplore.ieee.org/document/8029379

CHAPTER 13

Conclusion

Pralok Gupta

E-commerce has been growing at an exponential rate not only in India but also in many other countries. This exponential growth could be attributed to increasing Internet penetration at low costs and availability of affordable smartphones that allow the owner to make online transactions without requiring a computer and a home Internet connection. Although such penetration is more in developed countries, developing countries are also showing an increasing trend and, in some cases, are even among the first to adopt the new technologies. The rapid emergence of this sector across geographies has raised questions whether and how to regulate this sector.

Regulating e-commerce activities is a challenging job for any government. Both developed and developing countries are experimenting with regulating various aspects of e-commerce in their respective jurisdiction. Given the fact that e-commerce is entering all walks of life in one way or another, the governments cannot ignore regulating this sector. However, while regulating this sector, the governments need to ensure right regulatory balance that neither obstructs the growth of e-commerce firms nor harms the consumers and, at the same time, contribute to the coffers of the government.

The governments in various countries including India are contemplating about regulating different aspects and players involved in e-commerce transactions. However, due to significant technology interface and fast-changing nature of these technologies, regulating e-commerce is complex and different as compared to the traditional commerce. In traditional commerce, there is a physical presence of sellers, and the transactions between buyer and seller take place in the real world, whereas in e-commerce, the sellers and buyers meet in a virtual space making it difficult to impose regulations on such transactions.

The literature on e-commerce regulations suggests that such regulations are not easy to implement, and they have their own costs and benefits. Finck (2017) examined digital data-driven platforms and their impact on contemporary regulatory paradigms and argued that lawmakers in various countries are trying to determine how to regulate digital platforms. Two interrelated questions that regulators face in this context are: Who should regulate platforms and how these should be regulated? Stowel and Vergote (2016) worked on the regulatory environment for platforms, online intermediaries, data and cloud computing and the collaborative economy. According to them, digital platforms, such as Facebook, Google, Amazon, Alibaba, Uber, TaskRabbit, Airbnb or Kickstarter, etc., are playing an increasing role in the economy; however, they are also involved in a number of legal disputes, especially when they operate at the margin of existing laws (for example, labour law in the case of Uber, data protection law in the case of Google and Facebook).

According to Cohent and Sundararajan (2017), a growing fraction of the world's economy involves in digitally enabled peer-to-peer exchange, and the regulatory barriers on such exchanges may slow the growth of employment in an economy. However, since the interests of digital, third-party platforms are not always perfectly aligned with the broader interests of society, some involvement from the government is required.

India is also witnessing this regulatory dilemma where some stakeholders are welcoming regulations on e-commerce companies whereas others consider these as obstacle to the future growth of this sector. The aura of investment running into billions of dollars in Indian e-commerce space and employment opportunities created through such investments is so powerful that any idea of regulating this sector is discarded at the outset by many who are of the opinion that the growth of this rising sector should not be curtailed by government through regulations. In general, regulations are perceived as against industry by market players, and it is being argued that market forces are the best judge to determine the equilibrium and hence there should be no government intervention. However, market forces do not always produce optimum results; rather, there are market failures too. This is particularly true for the monopoly or oligopoly markets. The e-commerce market in India is no different. Therefore, some government intervention is required for regulating e-commerce in the country for the benefit of all. This will help addressing both domestic considerations and international play in the e-commerce sphere.

On the domestic front, the lack of regulations for different segments of e-commerce is resulting into unfair and unethical practices by various players. Huge growth and investment prospects in e-commerce should not be an excuse to allow or to continue with such practices. For instance, data breaches and transfer of personal information to the third party by various e-commerce players is rampant. The licensing agreement between the user and the service provider is difficult to handle by an average user and worded in such a way that users inadvertently give their consent. Many times, information is collected and shared in spite of the users categorically denying the permission to collect such information. A recent research at the Princeton found that Google tracks users' location even if the user explicitly tells it not to do so (*Business Today*, 2018). Thus, privacy of individuals is often compromised in an unregulated digital environment. Fortunately, the Supreme Court of India has said that the right to privacy is a fundamental right and the Justice Srikrishna Committee on the data protection also recommended that the citizen's rights have to be protected.

Similarly, significant capital dumping is happening in the Indian e-commerce space by those having money powers, and huge losses are being incurred by offering deep discounts to expand the market reach and customer base. Although the consumers get benefitted by such discounts, they are fatal to the new entrants who are of tiny size as compared to the tech giants offering these discounts. The sellers listed on online platforms are compelled to offer massive discounts failing which they are either delisted from the platforms or are discriminated. Therefore, regulatory intervention is required to put a check on capital dumping and such unfair practices.

As far as international dimensions of e-commerce are concerned, e-commerce has become one of the important discussion points at various multilateral body meetings, such as the WTO and the G20. There are efforts by some countries to frame multilateral rules for e-commerce although many others are opposing such initiatives. India, so far, is opposed to multilateral rules governing e-commerce and considers that given the nascent nature of this sector in most of the countries and their domestic priorities and sensitivities, the existing policy space should not be curtailed by framing multilateral rules.

The discussion on regulating e-commerce in India and other countries is often polarized wherein some are in the favour of regulating it and others are not. Instead of whether to regulate or not to regulate, the discussion should be on how to regulate. Developed countries, where e-commerce is in a relatively mature stage, have experimented with various regulatory approaches for regulating e-commerce entities. These include state regulation, self-regulation by the industry and co-regulation by the industry and the government together. Neither of the two extreme approaches—state regulation and self-regulation by industry—may prove beneficial for e-commerce. The state regulation approach may be constrained by the lack of necessary technical expertise with the state to regulate the sector. On the other hand, self-regulation by the industry may lack transparency, and industry players may tend to act in their own interests without considering the interests of other stakeholders. Co-regulation approach that involves all stakeholders, including consumers, may serve as an appropriate approach in this sphere as it gives the opportunity to include the feedback of industry and other stakeholders while designing and implementing any future regulation for e-commerce.

References

Business Today. (2018). Google tracks your movements, even when you explicitly tell it not to. 13 August. https://www.businesstoday.in/current/world/google-tracks-your-movements-even-when-you-explicitly-tell-it-not-to/story/281268.html

Cohent, M., & Sundararajan, A. (2017). Self-regulation and innovation in the peer-to-peer sharing economy. *University of Chicago Law Review, 82*(1), 116–133.

Finck, M. (2017). Digital co-regulation: Designing a supranational legal framework for the platform economy. (LSE Law, Society and Economy Working Papers, 15/2017). London School of Economics and Political Science, Department of Law, London, UK.

Stowel, A., & Vergote, W. (2016). Digital platforms: To regulate or not to regulate? Message to regulators: Fix the economics first, then focus on the right regulation. http://ec.europa.eu/information_society/newsroom/image/document/2016-7/uclouvain_et_universit_saint_louis_14044.pdf

About the Editor and Contributors

Editor

Dr Pralok Gupta is currently working as Associate Professor (Services and Investment) at the Centre for WTO Studies, Indian Institute of Foreign Trade, New Delhi, since May 2012. Earlier, he has served in the Uttar Pradesh State Government and Industrial Finance Corporation of India. Dr Gupta has a PhD in Economics and Social Sciences from the Indian Institute of Management (IIM), Bangalore and has also been a visiting and full-time faculty to various institutions in India, including Indo-German Chamber of Commerce.

He has been actively engaged in policymaking by the Ministry of Commerce and the Ministry of Finance on various trade and macro-economic issues. He has done extensive quantitative and qualitative analysis of trade and investment flows in various sectors for India and other countries. He has been a member of the India's negotiating team for services for Regional Comprehensive Economic Partnership (RCEP) agreement and the India–EFTA agreement. He has also been an expert member of the core team for drafting 'Trade Facilitation in Services' proposal, submitted by India at the WTO. He has been involved in negotiating 'e-commerce' and 'trade in services' chapters in RCEP negotiations and headed sub-group on payment systems set-up by the Government of India for formulating Draft E-commerce Policy. He has also been actively involved in FTA negotiations and discussions of India with other countries such as New Zealand, Israel and Latin American countries.

Apart from these engagements, based on his expertise, he has been appointed as member of the 'Task Force on Services Sector Exports' and member (Sectoral Expert) of the 'Inter Ministerial Sub-Group on Data in Trade in Services' by the Ministry of Commerce; Member of the 'Technical Group on Data in Trade in Services' under the Chairmanship of the Director General of Commercial Intelligence and Statistics, Kolkata; Member of the 'FICCI National Council on Services' by Federation of Indian Chambers of Commerce and Industry (FICCI) and Honorary Patron on the Advisory Board of Centre for Advanced Trade Research of the Trade Promotion Council of India.

He has been actively engaged in providing training on various trade issues to the delegates and diplomats from developing and least developed countries (LDCs). He has also been involved in providing specialized training to high-level delegation from various LDCs, including Afghanistan, Ethiopia, Mongolia and Myanmar, and has developed specialized courses and case studies for such specialized training programs for the LDCs. He has conducted training on New Approaches for Services Trade Negotiations for Cambodia, Laos, Myanmar and Vietnam (CLMV) countries in collaboration with ASEAN Secretariat and Indian Mission to ASEAN.

He has also been associated with various consultancy and research projects for corporate bodies, the government and international and multilateral institutions, such as the Organisation for Economic Cooperation and Development (OECD), the British High Commission, UKIERI, European University Institute, South African Institute of International Affairs, National Council for Applied Economic Research (NCAER), Indian Council for Research on International Economic Relations (ICRIER), etc. He has presented his research work at various international conferences, including the Royal Economic Society, London; the World Bank, Washington DC; Cambridge University, UK; UN-ESCAP, Bangkok; Venice International University, Venice; etc. He has been actively engaged in publishing books, book chapters and journal articles at national and international levels. His articles on contemporary economic issues are regularly published in highly circulated business dailies, such as *The Economic Times*, *The Financial Express*, *LiveMint*, *Business Standard*, etc.

Contributors

Himani Aggarwal is a student at the University of Oxford, pursuing MPhil in evidence-based social intervention and policy evaluation. She is also working as a consultant for Immunisation Systematic Review with International Initiative for Impact Evaluation. In the past, she has worked on trade and e-commerce projects with Directorate General of Foreign Trade (DGFT), Ministry of Commerce and Industry, Government of India and Responsible Futures project with sustainability department of the University of Bristol. Himani holds a bachelor's in economics from the University of Delhi and a master's in economics with specialization in economic policy from the University of Bristol. During her studies, she has been an active social worker with organizations such as Students4Students and Rotaract, where she managed multiple educational and health-support projects for at-risk population at leading positions.

Pritam Banerjee brings several years of experience in the areas of logistics operations, trade facilitation and trade policy. He is currently Consultant with the Asian Development Bank (ADB) as a Logistics Sector Specialist. Prior to his work with the ADB, Dr Pritam was the Senior Director for Public Policy with the Deutsche Post DHL Group, responsible for South Asia. He also served as a consultant for major clients of Deutsche Post DHL Group, finding solutions to regulatory and policy problems related to their supply chains. He previously served as the Head of Trade Policy, Confederation of Indian Industry's (CII) Trade Policy Division and with the World Bank in Washington, DC, where his work focused on trade facilitation and trade in services. He is a member of the National Trade Facilitation Steering Committee and was most recently a special invitee to the Committee on Ease of Doing Business Reforms, constituted under the Ministry of Commerce as a part of Prime Minister Modi's initiative on reforms. He serves as an executive member of the Federation of Indian Chambers of Commerce and Industry (FICCI) Logistics Task Force, and he led FICCI's interaction on Goods and Services Tax (GST). He also serves as a guest faculty at the Indian Institute of Foreign Trade

(IIFT), Foreign Services Institute (FSI) and National Academy of Customs, Indirect Taxes, and Narcotics (NACIN). He has a PhD in public policy from the Schar School of Policy and Government, George Mason University and master's degree in economics from Jawaharlal Nehru University. He has extensively published on issues related to international trade, regional integration, regulatory reforms, logistics and connectivity, and trade facilitation.

Rahul Nath Choudhury is a Visiting Research Fellow at the Institute of South Asian Studies, National University of Singapore. His primary research interest includes foreign direct investments, e-commerce, international trade and trade integration. Rahul has diverse experience of working in both the public and the private sectors in the academia and in the industry in various capacities.

Sourav Das hails from Chittagong, Bangladesh. He is pursuing master's in business administration (International Business) from the Centre for Management Studies, Jamia Millia Islamia (a central university). He, since his graduation days, had keen interest in the field of research and have also accomplished many such assignments back then.

Astha Dubey is a third-year law student at Hidayatullah National Law University, Atal Nagar, Chhattisgarh. She is pursuing her graduation in BA LLB (Hons.).

Akanksha Garg is working as an Assistant Professor under commerce domain in Delhi College of Arts and Commerce, Delhi University, for past 3 years. She also has 3 years of banking experience. She has published a number of research papers on e-commerce and Fintech and presented her work in various conferences.

Sayal Gupta is a Mechanical Engineer and is currently pursuing master's in business administration (International Business) from the Centre for Management Studies, Jamia Millia Islamia. He is currently preparing his theses on the topic of data protection and privacy in a globalized world. He wants to pursue his Doctorate in the field of international digital trade, covering all policy and legal aspects of the same.

Vaishali Gupta is Assistant Professor at the School of Computer Science and Engineering, Galgotias University, NCR, Delhi. She is pursuing her PhD in machine learning from Indira Gandhi Delhi Technical University for Women, Delhi. Her research interests include artificial intelligence, big data analytics and e-commerce.

Zaki Hussain is currently a PhD scholar at the Department of Economics, Jamia Millia Islamia, New Delhi. Previously, he had worked at the Centre for WTO Studies, IIFT, New Delhi.

Pravin Jadhav teaches economics at the Institute of Infrastructure, Technology, Research and Management (IIT-RAM), Ahmedabad, Gujarat. Prior to joining IIT-RAM, Dr Pravin was teaching at the University of Petroleum and Energy Studies (UPES), Dehradun. He was awarded PhD by IIFT, New Delhi.

Samridhi Jain is a Research Assistant at ICRIER, New Delhi, where she covers projects on disaster financing and reinsurance for the Ministry of Finance. She holds a bachelor's from Ambedkar University, Delhi, and master's degree in economics from the University of Mumbai. Samridhi is an ardent researcher, working on different areas of economic policies. She has more than two years of experience, touching upon subjects such as insurance, reinsurance, climate change, agriculture and ecommerce. During her previous job in DGFT, Ministry of Commerce, she was closely associated with the government's policy for export of agricultural products, mining, fertilizers, etc. Aside from being a researcher, she has also worked with various NGO's spreading the thought of 'education for all'.

Komal Kapoor is an Assistant Professor of Law at Delhi Metropolitan Education, Noida, affiliated to Guru Gobind Singh Indraprastha University (GGSIPU), Delhi. She obtained her Bachelor's degree in Law from the Vivekananda Institute of Professional Studies, GGSIPU in 2013. She also obtained post-graduate diploma in Intellectual

Property Rights from the Indian Society of International Law, New Delhi. She completed her Master's of Law in Business Laws from National Law University, Delhi, in the year 2016. She is currently pursuing doctorate of philosophy from Rayat Bahra University, Mohali. Her area of specialization includes Intellectual Property Rights and Cyber Laws.

Khushbu Kumari joined Centre for Innovation Intellectual Property and Competition (CIIPC) at National Law University, New Delhi, as a Research Fellow in April 2018 and has been working on the project titled 'IP in Agribiotech in India'. She has previously worked at the Centre for WTO Studies, IIFT, as a Research Fellow, in the field of services in international trade law especially with regard to FTAs and RTAs. She has also taught at Kalinga University, Raipur from August 2016 to February 2017. She has joined a project called 'Mission Creep' at Victoria University of Wellington, New Zealand, for her PhD course since February 2020. Her other areas of interest include the cross-jurisdictional studies in competition law, e-commerce and its implication on market, market structures of e-commerce, and the developing theories on e-commerce.

Purva Mishra is a third-year law student at Hidayatullah National Law University, Atal Nagar, Chhattisgarh. She is pursuing her graduation in BA LLB (Hons.).

Sunayana Sasmal is a Research Fellow (Legal) at the Centre for WTO Studies, IIFT, New Delhi. She holds a BA LLB with specialization in international trade and investment law from National Law University, Jodhpur. She has earlier worked with CUTS International and law firms focusing on economic law issues. Her primary interests include trade and investment law and policy, intellectual property laws, human rights and the balance between regulatory powers of the State and international economic laws. She aims to continue writing and researching on issues that plague the developing countries and on how to provide suitable negotiating voices at the table.

Shreyansh Singh is a Research Fellow (Legal) at the Centre for WTO Studies, IIFT. He conducts research to assist India's trade negotiations, both at the WTO and other forums. His main fields of research include trade in services and intellectual property law. He has presented his research at various forums, including the United Nations Conference on Trade and Development (UNCTAD), Singapore Management University (SMU), ADB, etc.

Parkhi Vats is currently working as a Research Assistant at the International Cotton Advisory Committee, Washington D.C. She has previously worked at the WTO Secretariat, Geneva as an intern and at the Centre for WTO Studies, IIFT, New Delhi as a Research Fellow.

Index